BROTHERS
IN
BLOOD

Other Books by Clark Howard

NOVELS

The Arm
A Movement Toward Eden
The Doomsday Squad
The Killings
Mark the Sparrow
The Hunters
The Wardens

NONFICTION

Six Against the Rock
Zebra
American Saturday

BROTHERS
IN
BLOOD

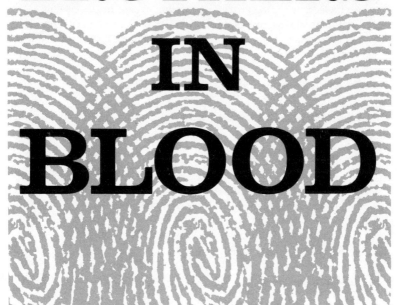

CLARK HOWARD

St. Martin's/Marek

New York

Design by Kingsley Parker

Library of Congress Cataloging in Publication Data

Howard, Clark.
    Brothers in blood.

    "A St. Martin's/Marek book."
    1. Murder—Georgia. 2. Crime and criminals—
Georgia—Biography.   I. Title.
HV6533.G4H68   1983   364.1′523′0922 [B]   82-16894
ISBN 0-312-10610-6

First Edition
10 9 8 7 6 5 4 3 2 1

In most works of nonfiction dealing with crime and criminals, it is sometimes necessary to change names and alter identities in order to protect certain persons. *Brothers in Blood* is no exception.

The convicted murderers in this story, and the accessory to their crimes who testified against them, touched many lives over the years as they grew from childhood to adolescence to young manhood.

To avoid any possible embarrassment to the many individuals who were involved with them in one relationship or another—whether as case worker, foster parent, corrections official, girlfriend, crime partner, prison friend, or otherwise—the author has changed names, concealed identities, and created composite characters based upon more than one real person. Thus, while all the events described in this book actually took place, words or deeds attributed to any one character do not necessarily correspond to the statements or actions of any particular individual.

Once again to
Alex Jackinson,
my friend first,
and then my agent.

Contents

1

CARL ISSACS

1

Billy, the youngest of the four, started crying shortly after they left Seminole County. He buried his face in his hands and shook his head back and forth. "Jesus Christ, what've we done?" he muttered into his palms. "What've we done? What've we done?"

Carl, who was driving, glanced in the rearview mirror at his younger brother and frowned. Wayne, their half brother, older than both of them, turned in the seat next to Carl and stared coldly at Billy. Glancing at Wayne, Carl noticed that his eyes were like bullets: two black dots, fixed, unyielding, threatening.

"What in the name of Christ have we done?" Billy muttered again.

"Shut up, Billy," said Carl.

"Jesus, back there—we—"

"I said shut up!" Carl's voice had an edge this time.

Wayne faced forward again, looking out the windshield with the same flat gaze he had turned on Billy. Grunting softly to himself, he said "*We,* huh? As I recall, you didn't do nothing but watch."

"He did more than watch," Carl said.

Wayne glanced at Carl but did not argue the point. Instead he turned the other way and reached into the back seat. He put his hand on the knee of the fourth person in the car: George, a black man with a soft, shy grin, wearing thick eyeglasses.

"How you doing?" Wayne asked.

George shrugged. "Okay, I guess."

Their eyes met and held. A warmth, an understanding, passed between them. Wayne squeezed George's knee and winked without smiling. Then he faced forward again.

Carl, eyes on the road, resumed concentrating on the one 3

thought uppermost in his mind: getting the hell out of Georgia. It should not take long. Seminole County was in the farthest southwest corner of the state. Its southern boundary was the Florida state line; part of its western boundary was the Alabama line. It was toward Alabama that they were now heading. They crossed the Chattahoochie River into that state less than thirty minutes after leaving the woods where they had abandoned their last stolen car in favor of this one: the 1970 Chevrolet Impala that had belonged to the woman.

Carl closed his eyes tightly and shook his head. No, goddamn it, he didn't want to think about the woman. Anything but the woman.

"You okay?" Wayne asked, looking curiously at him.

"I'm fine."

"Want me to drive?"

"No, I'm fine."

Carl pressed the car forward, along the bypass around Dothan, Alabama, and on out Route 84 east. They had crossed into the Central time zone, from Eastern time in Georgia, so they had gained an hour; even so, it was beginning to get dark. Route 84 changed from four lanes to two. Carl turned on the headlights. They passed through Clayhatchee and Enterprise, Elba and Danley. Carl had forgotten to check the odometer when they left the woods in Seminole County, so he did not know how far they had come overall; but he had remembered to check it as they were bypassing Dothan, so he knew they were about fifty miles from Dothan.

In Danley he decided to get off the main highway, turning onto a state route, 141, and heading north. It was on that road, toward eight o'clock, that Billy started sobbing again in the back seat.

"I want to go home," Billy cried. "I want to get as far away as I can. I want to go home and see my mamma."

"Your *mamma*!" Wayne spat the word out. "What in hell did your *mamma* ever do for you, boy?"

"I don't care! I want to go home! I want to go where I don't have to think about today!"

"Only one place you can do that, boy," Wayne told him flatly. "Hell." Billy began to sob louder. "Shit," said Wayne. He nudged Carl's arm. "Pull over to the side of the road, will you? I got to take a piss."

Carl slowed down and guided the car onto the shoulder. He felt Wayne nudge his arm again.

4

"Come on," Wayne said quietly.

Carl and Wayne got out and stepped across a narrow culvert. They walked a few yards into a field.

"Has Billy still got a gun?" Wayne asked, unzipping his trousers.

"No. I took it away from him in the trailer and haven't given it back to him. It's in the trunk."

"That's good," Wayne said calmly, "because I think we're gonna have to kill him."

Carl's mouth dropped open. "Kill him? He's your brother, man."

Wayne shook his head. "He's *your* brother. He's only my half brother."

"Hell, that don't make no difference, Wayne. Quit talking bullshit."

"I ain't talking bullshit. The kid's coming apart. He's losing it, man."

"Look," Carl said, "let's find a town and put him on a bus to Baltimore."

"You crazy?" Wayne asked irritably. "Put him on a *bus*? Why, shit, he'd tell everybody on there what happened before it even left the depot. No, man, we got to do him."

"Jesus Christ, Wayne, he's only fifteen—"

"I don't give a shit." Wayne finished and zipped back up. "Look, Carl, we can't turn him loose the way he is. He ain't responsible. And I can't take having him with us, with all that crying and moaning, and that shit about what happened. He's getting on my nerves and he's giving me a bad headache."

"I don't care if he is," Carl said firmly. "We're not killing him."

Wayne glared at Carl. They were standing in residual light from the car's headlights, and even though there was darkness all around them, they could see each other clearly. Wayne was twenty-six, and Carl not quite twenty. But Carl was the imaginative one, the creative one—his mind was always at least a split second ahead of Wayne's. Carl always *seemed* to be leading, even when he wasn't. Wayne was a little slow, and he knew it. Most of the time, because it was so much easier, he acquiesced: to Carl's decisions, Carl's wishes, Carl's plans. He could see it was going to be that way now. The same old shit.

"We're not killing him," Carl said again.

Wayne sighed quietly and looked away into the darkness of the field. "Shit," he said softly.

They stood there without speaking for a minute or two. It was May but the night air was cool and damp. Carl shook a cigarette out of his pack and offered it to Wayne. Without looking at Carl, Wayne accepted it. Carl took one for himself and lighted both of them with a single match.

"Say, babe, are you hungry?" Carl asked.

"Yeah, some," said Wayne.

"Let's find someplace to eat. We can decide about Billy then."

"All right."

Returning to the car, they started driving again. Up the road a few miles they came to an interstate highway, Route 331, and turned north. Fifteen miles farther along, another state road, Route 10, bisected it and Carl changed directions again, heading west.

"Do you know where the hell you're going?" Wayne asked without rancor.

"Hell, no."

They came to Greenville and drove once around the town without seeing anyplace to eat. "Let's try the next one down the line," Carl said. They drove thirty miles farther, to Oakhill. There they found a Dairy Queen.

Without asking either of them what they wanted, Carl and Wayne went inside and got takeout orders for Billy and George. When Wayne handed the black man his bag of food, he said, "Cheeseburger and fries, George. And a shake." George smiled and accepted the food without comment. Billy took his bag from Carl the same way.

Carl and Wayne got their own food and sat at an outside table to eat. It was not as cold there as it had been out in the open field. The burgers and fries and hot coffee tasted good and warmed them up inside.

"Well, what now?" Wayne asked around a mouthful of food.

"You mean about Billy? Or about us?"

"Both," said Wayne.

"Far's Billy's concerned," Carl said, "I think we ought to take him home. Least take him as far as Baltimore. We owe him that, Wayne. We got him to come with us; we got him into all this; now we ought to take him home."

Wayne stared over at the car for a moment. He could see his friend George eating his food in the same slow and easy manner in which George did everything. There was nothing that 6 George did fast or urgently. *Nothing.*

"What about us?" Wayne asked, looking back at Carl.

"I say we make a run for Canada," Carl proposed. "It's the only way we got any chance at all of escape. Another country, you know? 'Cause our asses are dead in the good old U.S. now."

"Yeah, we fucked ourselves good back there in Georgia, all right," Wayne agreed.

Carl leaned forward and lowered his voice. "What about your nigger? What about George?"

Wayne's bullet eyes flashed suspicion. "What about him?"

"You and me, we'd move a lot faster if there was just the two of us. Wouldn't attract nearly as much attention either."

"I'm keeping George with me," Wayne said. It was an unequivocal statement, leaving no room for argument.

Carl shrugged. "Sure. Okay." At that moment he made up his mind to split from Wayne and George when they got to Canada. He would find somebody else to partner-up with. It wouldn't be any trouble for him. Carl was personable, likable, easy to be with; he had always managed to find someone, male or female, to throw in with him. It would be no different in Canada.

"Just one thing," Wayne said when they had finished eating. "You got to do something about Billy. That crying shit. I can't take that, man. It gives me a headache. I'll go along with taking him back home, but you got to make him stop that crying and carrying on."

Wayne got back in the car and Carl summoned Billy out to the table. He had a talk with him and told him they were going to take him home. He made Billy promise to stop crying and stop talking about what they had done.

"What we done is over," Carl told him. "Can't nobody undo any of it. We stepped over a line, all of us, and now we got to keep going. There can't be no stopping, no turning back, not even no looking back. You understand?"

Billy nodded glumly. "Is Wayne pissed at me?"

"You bet your ass he is. But he'll get over it. Long as you quit the crying."

"I'll quit," Billy promised.

"Good," Carl said, putting his arm around Billy's shoulders. "Come on, let's hit the road."

They stayed on Route 10 through Rosebud, Pine Hill, and Dixon's Mills, then Carl turned onto Interstate 43 and headed north on a parallel with the Mississippi state line, fifty miles 7 away. Twenty-five miles up the interstate, Carl decided to take another state road and turned onto Route 28, heading west again. At ten-thirty he checked the odometer and estimated that they had put about 250 miles behind them since leaving Georgia. They were almost all the way across Alabama. The next road sign they came to read: LIVINGSTON 2. Carl slowed the car's speed to forty. The first dirt road they came to, he turned in, drove a short distance from the highway, and stopped.

"Let's get some shuteye," he said.

"Good idea," said Wayne. "Billy, you change places with me and get up here in front."

Wayne got into the back seat and curled up with his head in George's lap. Carl and Billy stretched out as best they could in front and smoked a cigarette together. For a few minutes there was occasional quiet talk, confined either to the back seat or to the front seat, but after a while, toward eleven o'clock, the three young men and the boy fell silent and began to doze. Carl was the last one to drift off. He smoked a final cigarette alone, flipped the butt out, and for a few moments stared through the open window at the starry sky overhead.

This is a long, long way from Hartford County, Maryland, he thought.

2

The farm the family rented was near Jarrettsville, Maryland, a dozen miles south of the Pennsylvania line. It was one of those tight, miserly little spreads that gave its tenant just enough to get him and his family through to the next year, so it could give him just enough again for the year after that, and the next, and the next. A one-step ladder, no place to go, barely breaking even. The kind of existence that in the city was called a hard-knock life.

Archie, the father, made ends meet by taking the two older boys, Roy and Wayne, and hiring the three of them on as helpers at a nearby dairy farm. Roy was twelve and Wayne was fourteen—plenty old enough to help out, Archie said. The boys agreed. They enjoyed working with Archie, even Wayne, who was not really Archie's son but was from the "other" family to which Carl heard occasional allusions. It was all rather confusing to his eight-year-old mind.

All Carl really knew was that there were lots of siblings around. There was Ruth, who was twenty; Lois, seventeen; Ann, fifteen; and Wayne, fourteen. There was also an older brother, Jimmy, who was twenty-two, but he had gone off on his own and did not live with them. The five of them, Carl knew, were from his mother's first or "other" family; their last name was Coleman, different from his, which was Issacs. Their father was a man named Carson Coleman; and that was all he was, a name, because hardly any of the kids remembered ever seeing him.

Carl's own family was fathered by Archie Issacs, his dad, and consisted of Roy, who was twelve; Hazel, ten; Carl himself, eight; Robert, six; Billy, four; George, two; and Wanda, whom his mother had just brought home from the hospital, and whom she swore to anyone who would listen that this, her twelfth child, was absolutely, positively, and definitely the last one. Carl himself hoped so. It was nice to have brothers and sisters, but, Jesus Christ, with that many around you weren't even a name—you were just a number in the sequence of it all, like he was number eight, between Hazel, number seven, and Robert, number nine. And as far as any individual attention went, forget it. A slap across the temple or a twisted ear was all the individual attention he ever remembered receiving. Except from his granddad.

His mother's father used to come visit them on Saturdays and for some reason the old guy seemed to like Carl best of all the kids. Carl guessed it was because he was at what Granddad called a "good playing age." George was too little to be any fun; Robert was kind of a crybaby; Roy was too old; and the rest of the kids were girls. But Carl, at eight, was perfect.

"Hey, you, boy, come on, let's wrestle," Granddad would challenge, and the two of them would go at it on the grass or in the hay or even on the living room floor. "Ah, you're a good strong boy, Carl," Granddad would say as Carl, all gawky arms and legs, would be all over him, flailing and twisting and squirming while accomplishing nothing but loss of breath. When he got too hot and excited, Granddad would easily flip him down and pin him and hold him place until he calmed down and was ready to quit. Then the two of them would sit on the front porch together and talk until it was time for Granddad to go somewhere with Archie or Betty, his mother. But before he left, Granddad always gave him a chore to do; usually it was to sweep the front porch. "Let me find that porch nice and clean when we get back, Carl," he would say, "and there might be a surprise for you if I do."

Granddad never failed to find the porch clean. Carl took broom and dustpan and went after it with a vengeance. He swept corners, cracks, and crevices. Not a leaf, twig, or grain of sand or dirt escaped his attack. When Granddad returned, his favorite grandson had done his best to please him, and Carl was rewarded with a candy bar or other suitable, usually edible, compensation. His granddad was special. Because he made Carl feel special.

The times Carl remembered on the Hartford farm were mostly good times. There had to have been bad times also, but at eight he either overlooked or did not remember them. About the only bad thing he would later remember was Jarrettsville Elementary School. Carl didn't like school at all; his free time was spent making up excuses not to go, or pretending to be sick in order to be allowed to stay home. But usually he failed to get away with it. It was Ruth, the eldest girl, who was in charge of seeing that the younger kids went to school. Carl's mother had always leaned heavily on Ruth. For as far back as he could remember, Carl had always heard, "Ruth, do this," or "Ruth, do that." Betty usually had a waitress job—between babies, anyway—and because of that a great deal of the home-making responsibility fell to Ruth, and eventually to Lois and Ann. They didn't like it much, although Ruth appeared to mind it less than the others. Ruth seemed to genuinely care for the younger kids, and looked after them with a touch more interest and concern than the other older girls.

It was not a bad life there on the farm—no worse, really, than the life of any rural family with a house full of kids, depending on the vagaries of nature for income. Perhaps if everything had remained the same, if there had not been any upheaval in his mother Betty's second union, if all of them had just remained there in Hartford County and the younger kids had grown up on the farm, many things might have been different. But nothing remains the same in life, and Carl learned that at an early age. First they moved, to another tenant farm in the same county, a place owned by a man named Reeves. Carl did not like it as much as he had the Jarrettsville place, and he had to transfer from Jarrettsville Elementary to Hartford Hill Elementary, which he also did not like. Not that he had cared that much for the former school, but at least it had been familiar and he had known what he could get away with. Now he had to learn third-grade basics all over again: who the toughest kid in class was, just how much the teacher would tolerate, what the truant officer looked like. A whole new set of rules, new guidelines. The first of many to come.

There were other changes, too—subtle, unobtrusive changes, compounding slowly. Ruth got married, to a man named Russell whom Archie did not like. Of course, it wasn't any of Archie's business; Ruth wasn't an Issacs, she was a Coleman, from Betty's "other" family. But that didn't stop Archie from arguing about it; he was still the head of the family. A good solid head, too; Archie *liked* being a husband and a father. Especially a father. On Sundays it was Archie who dressed up all the little kids and took them off to church; Archie who played with them, listened to their endless problems about school, about the other kids, about games that didn't go right; Archie who examined their scratches and scrapes at bedtime 11 and made uncanny predictions about the rate of healing: if Archie said a cut would be well by Saturday, it *would* be.

But Archie was still a man, an old-fashioned man, accustomed to giving orders. Perhaps he learned from Betty how easy it was to say, "Ruth, do this," and "Ruth, do that," when he wanted something done. But Ruth was a young married woman now and took fewer orders. Betty, for some reason Carl did not fully grasp, was not at home as much as she once had been, and that too gave Archie cause for complaint. And a more legitimate reason to depend on Ruth, who he knew had strong feelings for the younger children. Then when Betty *was* home, she berated Archie for calling on Ruth for help, when Ruth wasn't even his real daughter. Archie accused Betty of staying out so much because she did not like her own kids—and to Carl's amazement, Betty did not deny it.

The foundation of Betty's "second" family began to deteriorate. Archie grew bitter: it showed in his face. He stopped calling on Ruth for help; in fact, stopped having anything at all to do with Ruth and her husband Russell. Of course, that also displeased Betty. Archie, as the old saying went, felt damned if he did, damned if he didn't. He insisted that Betty stay home more, that she come directly home from her waitress job and not go out to bars with her friends from work. Betty agreed to whatever Archie asked—then continued doing just as she pleased. She was a hardheaded woman, and no man was about to tell her how to live. She hadn't taken it from Carson Coleman, she sure wasn't going to take it from Archie Issacs.

One night at the supper table, it ended. It was a night when Betty was home. There were four boys at the table: Carl, Robert, Billy, and little George; and one girl, Hazel. The older girls, Lois and Ann, both Colemans, were out somewhere; the older boys, Wayne Coleman and Roy Issacs, were also gone. The baby, Wanda, was asleep in her crib.

It was the same old argument, started as usual by Archie: Betty wasn't at home enough; Betty drank too much; Betty didn't give a damn about her kids; Betty had let Ruth go and marry that fellow Russell and now she wasn't even around to help with the kids anymore. Archie was damned tired of it. Why didn't he leave if he was so tired of it? Betty asked. By God, he just might do that. Do it then, Betty didn't care. Don't tempt me, I just might. Do it then—*All right!*

Archie rose from the table, went into their bedroom, dragged a battered old suitcase from under the bed, and threw all his

12

clothes in it. He didn't have much; no one in the family did. Hard-knock lives don't produce much in the way of material possessions. But what he did have he packed, quickly, determinedly. As he walked back through the kitchen he did not even stop to kiss his kids; he just said one "goodbye" to all present and left. Carl thought he saw tears in his dad's eyes as he passed by him. Some of the kids began to cry—sudden uncertainty is a terrifying thing to children. But Betty reassured them.

"Stop that crying now! Hell, he'll be back!"

But she was wrong.

Archie Issacs, like Carson Coleman before him, never came back.

3

When Carl awoke from sleeping cramped in the stolen car out-side Livingston, Alabama, he looked over his shoulder and saw that George, the black man, was awake and looking at him through the thick eyeglasses he wore.

"What time is it?" Carl asked.

"I don't know," George said quietly, so as not to wake Wayne. "I don't have no watch."

Carl stared coldly at him. Lying, he thought. Just like a nigger. "Don't bullshit me, man," he said tonelessly. "You've got that woman's watch. I saw you take it off her arm. Now what the fuck time is it?"

George smiled shyly and fished a lady's Timex wristwatch out of his shirt pocket. "Little after five," he said.

Carl nodded curtly. He picked up a pistol from the floor-board and stuck it under his belt. Suddenly realizing that the air in the car was close and stale from their four bodies, he rolled down his window. Then he went a step farther and opened his door and got out of the car. Like the night had been, the morning air was cool, crisp, and thin. Small coag-ulants of fog clung here and there in patches of briars and bushes, and across a barbed-wire fence Carl saw an early-grazing cow. Turning up his shirt collar against the chill, Carl lighted a cigarette and inhaled the sour sleep taste from his mouth. He ran a hand through his long, light brown hair, which felt greasy and dirty because he had not washed it since Saturday night and now it was Tuesday morning. He hated sleeping in goddamned cars; he always felt so grubby after.

Pulling his shirt out to cover the gun in his waistband, Carl walked a short distance down the dirt road to the highway. Standing at the side of the pavement, he looked up and down both ways. Everything was quiet. Tossing his cigarette butt into the culvert, he shook out another one. You're smoking too much, asshole, he told himself, but he lighted it anyway. Probably have lung cancer by the time I'm twenty. It suddenly occurred to him that it wouldn't be long before he *was* twenty. His birthday would be August ninth, and it was now May something; he wasn't sure of the exact date. It was somewhere around the middle of the month. He and Wayne and George had escaped from the prison farm in Maryland on May fifth; that seemed like about ten days ago, so now it must be the fifteenth or thereabouts. Less than three months until he would be twenty.

Carl sighed. Still in his teens and he felt like a goddamned old man. He'd never felt like a kid, *never,* at least, not that he could remember. Momentarily his mind raced back over the years: the foster homes, the reform schools, the beatings, the sick loneliness, the stark terror of not *having* anybody.

Grunting, he took a last long drag on the cigarette and flipped it away. "Time sure flies when you're having fun," he said aloud, hiding his own pathos even from himself.

Carl walked back to the car and got behind the wheel just as Wayne woke up.

"Jesus Christ, I'm freezing!" Wayne said. "Who opened the fucking window?"

"He did," George said, bobbing his chin at Carl.

"Roll up the fucking window, will you, bro?" Wayne shivered and pressed himself closer to George.

Carl rolled up the window and started the engine. He thought about turning on the heater but Billy was slumped forward asleep in the passenger seat and the blower would have hit him directly in the face. As Carl started to put the car in gear, he realized that the back window was fogged up and he could not see. Opening the glove compartment, he found a rag. He tossed it into the back seat onto George's lap.

"Get out and wipe off the windows," he said.

"Why me?" George asked. It was not a challenge, rather almost a plea, a whine.

Carl stared at him in the rearview mirror. He did not answer.

"Why me, huh?" George asked again. He glanced at Wayne and saw that his white friend was too busy trying to warm up to give him any help.

Carl continued to stare. Presently George got out and wiped off the windows.

15

Carl backed the car onto the highway and turned toward Livingston. Before they had gone a mile they got a flat in the right front tire. "Shit," said Carl, guiding the car onto the shoulder. He and Wayne and George got out and looked at the tire. It had picked up a flatheaded cement nail.

"Get the jack out of the trunk, George," said Wayne.

"Never mind, I'll do it," Carl told him, reaching back in the car for the keys. Letting the nigger wipe off the windows was one thing; changing a tire was something else. As he got the keys, Carl nudged the still-sleeping Billy. "Wake up, Billy, come on. Get out of the car. I got to jack it up."

Carl got out the spare and the jack, set the parking brake, and raised the front of the car. Before he got the first lug nut off, Billy knelt beside him urgently.

"Carl! There's a cop car pulling off the road behind us!"

Carl's mouth went dry. He drew the pistol from under his shirt, released the safety, and replaced it. "Work on the tire," he told Billy. "Wayne!" he hissed."You and George sit down on the bank." Rising, he saw a patrol car parked behind their car. A deputy with a potbelly and chewing-tobacco stains on one corner of his mouth got out and strolled over to them.

" 'Morning, Officer," Carl said with a smile.

"Looks like you boys havin' a problem," the officer observed by way of making conversation.

"Just a flat," said Carl.

The officer glanced at the car's plates. "Where 'bouts in Georgia y'all from?"

"Donalsonville. Down in Seminole County, just across the Alabama line."

"You don't sound like no Georgia boy," the deputy observed.

"Been in the Army for a spell," said Carl. "All that movin' around and bein' with different folks makes a feller talk different."

"Yeah, that's so, I reckon. Where you boys headed?"

"Over to Columbus, Mississippi. Taking my brother back to the Air Force base over there."

"Who's the nigger?" the deputy asked, lowering his voice.

"Oh, him," Carl lowered his own voice. "He's in the Air Force at Columbus too. He was hitchhiking and my brother recognized him. We figured we ought to give him a ride; charitable thing to do."

"I s'pose," the deputy allowed. He took a last look around.

16

"Well, long as there's no problem, I'll get back to my patrol. Watch your speed now, hear?"

"We sure will, Officer." Carl waved as the police car went off down the highway.

For a long, sick moment none of the four said anything. Wayne and George just looked at each other with open mouths but no words. Billy sat on the ground and leaned his face into the crook of one arm. Carl stared down at the ground and tried to spit but couldn't. The Sumter County deputy was the first law enforcement officer they had come into contact with since leaving Georgia. Being that close to authority drove home to all of them for the first time the enormity of what lay behind them.

"Jesus!" Wayne said finally. He was a naturally emaciated-looking man, gaunt, often stooped, with unusually recessed eyes. Now pale, his face frozen by the presence of the officer, he looked almost dead.

Carl quickly finished changing the tire and herded them all back into the car. They headed toward Livingston again.

"We've got to get another car," Carl said, as much to himself as to the others. "The thing in Georgia is twelve hours behind us. They could find out about it any time. When they do, they'll go to looking for this car."

Driving into town, they found that Livingston had a small state college, Livingston University, and near the campus was a shopping mall. It was still too early for anything except a coffee shop to be open, but Carl knew that in an hour or so the small parking lot would begin to fill up with cars. He parked the stolen Chevrolet in a place close enough to the stores that he was sure other cars would park on both sides of it.

"You guys wait in the car," he said easily, trying to keep his voice as casual as possible; he knew Wayne resented it when he sounded like he was giving orders. After all, Wayne *was* the older brother, or older half brother, to be exact. He did have the most experience, had served the most prison time, had been around the most. And it did look a little odd to have a brother younger by six years do the thinking and figuring and leading. But Carl did just that. Which was lucky for Billy, Carl thought. If Carl *hadn't* been able to lead, Billy would be lying dead in an Alabama field somewhere.

"Where you going?" Wayne asked, in order to project himself into the plan Carl had already made.

17

"Get us another car," Carl said.

"Don't you want somebody for backup while you're doing the hot-wiring?" Wayne asked.

"Shit, I won't have to do no hot-wiring," Carl replied confidently. "In a nice little Alabama college town like this one, probably half the people that got cars leave their keys in them."

Carl was right. He walked away, in the direction of a residential area located adjacent to the mall. In less than fifteen minutes he returned, driving a nearly new 1973 Chevrolet Caprice, green with a black vinyl top, that he had found with the keys in the ignition.

"Get the stuff out of the trunk, boys, and let's go," he said, smiling from behind the wheel.

"This here's the third straight Chevrolet you've stole, Carl," Wayne said dryly. "Getting in a rut, ain't you?"

"I'm just a General Motors man, I guess," Carl replied with a smile.

The two half brothers laughed in harmony, for the first time in a long time. They were still laughing when the four of them drove off the parking lot in the new car and headed east, toward Mississippi.

4

When Carl came home from school one day, no one was there. He was ten years old. Hazel, who was with him, was twelve. Robert was eight; Billy was six and in first grade.

Archie had been gone for quite some time and Betty was working as a waitress in Belair, Maryland. Betty was nearly always there when they got home. When she wasn't, she saw to it that someone else was: usually one of the older girls, Ann or Lois. But this time there was no one. And Betty did not come back.

Carl was the oldest boy there so he decided it was up to him to cope. He told Hazel to stay and mind the younger boys, and he trudged up to the landlord's house and asked Mrs. Reeves if he could use her telephone. He called several numbers that Betty kept on a card in her bedroom, numbers of places she worked from time to time. She was not at any of the numbers. Finally, at the bottom of the card, was Ruth's telephone number, at the house she had moved to with her husband Russell. Carl called Ruth, and Ruth came at once and got all of them.

Ruth already had Wanda, the baby, and George, the toddler, and now she had four others as well. Ruth was twenty-two. She and Russell were young marrieds, still on the bottom rung of life's ladder, trying to get a start. It's difficult for young marrieds when they have a kid or two of their own; but with six between the ages of one and ten, it goes beyond difficult to impossible. And Ruth was a Coleman, from the "other" family, not even obligated to this Issacs brood. But Ruth loved the kids; she was determined to do the best she could for them.

For two desperate months, she tried. She had the older children transferred to a school near where she lived. She went to the farm and collected all their clothes: a meager supply, most of them worn, torn, buttonless, unwashed, unironed. She set about mending them, making them look as decent as possible, 19 making them do. She revised her food budget to stretch Russell's ordinary salary to extraordinary lengths. At meals she ate less than she wanted so there would be more for the kids. Steadfastly she refused to try and find their mother; if Betty could abandon them like that, then let her. Ruth would care for them—somehow.

But it was a losing proposition. There were some things, like totally worn-out shoes, that could not be mended; clothes that were too threadbare to hold a patch; dollars that simply would not stretch any farther. Ruth, however, would not give up. "Things'll get better," she told the older children, as she kissed them and sent them off to school. "Things'll work out. You'll see."

One of the teachers telephoned the Maryland state welfare authorities. "We've got four children named Issacs down here that someone should come look at. They're wearing clothes that are practically rags, shoes with cardboard for soles; it's terrible. Some of the other children are making horrible fun of them. I'm afraid one of the boys—Carl is his name—is going to do something violent if someone doesn't stop it. He's a very high-strung boy; he's been in fights at school before. Right now he looks as if he's about to blow up."

Two social workers, a man and a woman, came to the school. Hazel, Carl, Robert, and Billy were brought into the principal's office. Bill was too young to realize what was going on, and Robert knew only that this was something different from the regular school routine, like a fire drill. Only Hazel and Carl sensed that something drastic was about to happen to them.

"Who takes care of you children at home?" one of the welfare workers asked Carl. She seemed to know that he was the strong one, even though Hazel was obviously older.

"Our big sister," Carl answered.

"Where's your mother?"

"We don't know."

"I see. Well, where's your father?"

"He run off," Carl said. It was the first time he had ever thought that, much less said it out loud. *He run off.* But that was, he now realized, exactly what Archie had done. Run off. Left his kids. Left Carl's mother. Left Carl. The son-of-a-bitch, Carl thought in his ten-year-old mind. He didn't even know what a son-of-a-bitch was; he just knew it was bad.

"We're going to take you children with us," the welfare worker said. "We'll get in touch with your sister later."

20

The man and woman took them, all piled together in the back seat of a car, to a building they had never seen before, and sat them on a bench in a hallway outside some offices with closed doors. Carl thought briefly of running away, but he did not want to leave the others. He might have taken Robert with him; Robert was eight and could have kept up. But it was out of the question to think of taking Billy; he was simply too little. And of course he could not take Hazel; she was a girl, and girls didn't run away. So Carl remained on the bench and waited.

People came and went in the hall. Some of them glanced at the four youngsters sitting there, but no one appeared overly curious about them; they were used to seeing waifs alone on the hard bench waiting to have their lives restructured by the state of Maryland. For the most part, the four children did not look at the people as they passed. Afraid, the four of them kept their eyes downcast; they saw only shoes coming and going.

At one point, after they had been there for what seemed like a very long time, a door opened and one of the welfare workers who had brought them there, the woman, paused in the doorway looking back, and said, "I know, but there are *four* of them. And apparently two more with the sister. That's not going to be easy. I've already made a dozen telephone calls with no success."

"You'll just have to keep trying," said an authoritative voice inside the room. "Make a dozen more calls. You'll connect."

The woman pulled the door closed behind her, looked at the four youngsters briefly and shook her head, then went into another office and shut the door.

After a while, Hazel began to sniffle, trying to hold back tears. Carl put an arm around her and patted her shoulder, as he recalled seeing grown-ups do. "There, there, Hazel," he said quietly. "There, there, now." Like "son-of-a-bitch," he had no idea what, if anything, "there, there," meant; it just seemed to fit the situation.

Another hour passed. And another. Billy leaned against Robert and went to sleep. The others began to get hungry. And Carl began to get angry. They got no right to make us sit here so long like this, he thought. We ain't done nothing to be punished like this. Ruth's gonna be plenty sore when she finds out what they've done to us. Jesus, my ass is sore from this bench! This is worser than having to sit on that high stool in the corner in class. Lots worser.

Now Carl stopped looking at feet and began looking up at faces. It was hard to be angry at people's feet; much easier to get mad at a face, a look, an expression. He drilled his young eyes into people as they passed. Some of them, seeing his unyielding stare, frowned, as if they had never seen such cold, inflexible hatred in one so young.

It was after dark before the social worker came back out of the office. A coworker, passing in the hall, said, "Getting in some overtime, I see."

"Not by choice," the woman replied.

She was met in the hall by two other welfare workers, a man and another woman.

"All right, kids, we've found places for you to stay. Hazel, you go with this nice lady," she handed the woman a file folder, "and Robert and Billy—come on, Billy, wake up now—you two go with this nice man. Carl, you come with me."

Before Carl could fully grasp what was happening, Hazel went walking off with the other woman and Robert and Billy were holding the hands of the man and being led away. Carl suddenly felt very alone, very frightened. At that moment, tears would have come very easily—if he had let them.

"Come on, Carl, let's go."

The woman took him out to a parking lot and let him get into the front seat of a car with her. They drove off.

"Do you know where Glencoe is?" the woman asked.

"No," Carl answered.

"Try 'no, ma'am,' Carl," she said.

Carl swallowed down a dry throat. "No, ma'am," he obeyed.

"Glencoe's a little community up north of Cockeysville. Do you know where Cockeysville is?"

"No, ma'am."

"Oh, well. It doesn't matter. You're going to like it there. You'll be living with a family named Denmark. Edward and Jennifer Denmark. They have a son named Jacky who's about two years younger than you. You'll like it with them."

"Yes, ma'am." Carl stared straight ahead into the darkness beyond the headlight beams. "Uh, ma'am, can I ask a question?"

"Of course."

"When can I see my sister Ruth again?"

"That's something that will have to be worked out later."

Carl waited, thinking she would say more on the subject, thinking she might say *when* it would be worked out, or *how*.

22

But that equivocal answer was all he got. He wondered where Hazel was, and Robert and Billy. Probably in other cars with the other people, being told they were going to like it where they were going too. *You're going to like it.* Somehow he wasn't too sure. She said it like someone would say, *Now this isn't going to hurt.* When it always did.

The Denmark home was a small white frame-and-stucco house set back on a neatly trimmed lawn with flower beds and shrubbery so precisely cut that they looked almost artificial. The whole place seemed to be manicured, an advertisement for the all-American middle-class housing tract. "See, isn't this nice?" the welfare woman said, as she pulled into the drive. "You're going to like it here just fine."

She parked and got out of the car. Carl remained seated, eyes fixed on the garage door at the end of the drive, jawbones clenched.

"Come on, Carl."

He got out and followed her to the front porch, feeling utterly dispossessed, having nothing but the threadbare clothes on his back, shoes with flopping soles and worn-down heels on his feet; having no one that he could say was *his,* on *his* side, for *him.* He had never felt so totally alone in his entire life.

A woman came out on the porch to meet them. She was not a lot taller than Carl, but she seemed more powerful than her ordinary stature would suggest.

The welfare woman put her arm around Carl and urged him forward.

"Carl, this is Jennifer Denmark, your new mom."

5

After they left Livingston, Alabama, in the newly stolen car, Carl kept the radio playing continually to try and pick up a report from Georgia. The others in the car knew without being told why the radio was playing; every time the music stopped they all fell quiet and listened to the newscaster. Carl found a news broadcast on the hour on one station, and on the half hour on another, and they listened to both of them from eight o'clock throughout the rest of the morning. They heard nothing about Georgia.

"They ain't found out yet," Wayne said, after hearing the twelve o'clock news.

"They've found out," Carl said confidently. "Something like that don't stay hid long."

Since leaving Livingston, they had zigzagged back and forth across the Alabama-Mississippi border, heading north. Carl changed routes frequently, going on and off interstate highways at random. From Livingston he took a state highway, Route 28, to another state highway, Route 17, to still another, Route 30. In Scooba, Mississippi, they made a stop to buy gas, beer, and some junk food. Then they headed north on Interstate 45 to Columbus, and from there got on Route 12, which took them back into Alabama to Vernon. Carl was watching the odometer better this time; he had driven 125 miles by the time they got to Vernon.

"We gonna have to get rid of this car pretty soon if we do much driving in Alabama," Wayne said. "It'll be on a hot sheet."

"Not this shift it won't," Carl replied logically. "It'll be reported stolen on the eight-to-four shift; it won't be on no hot sheet until the four-to-midnight cops come on duty. We're good until late this afternoon. By then we'll be well out of
24 'Bama."

Wayne said nothing further. Carl was right again.

They took Route 17 north out of Vernon and drove 35 miles to Weston. There they picked up another interstate, 43, and were still on it twenty-five miles farther north when it became a four-lane highway. Carl felt so good driving a near-new car, the newest he had ever been in, and the traffic was moving along in such a nice, comfortable flow, that he decided to hell with the back roads for a while, he was going to stay on the main highway.

"If I see a state police car," he said to Wayne, looking at him in the rearview mirror, "have your boy back there get down out of sight. A highway patrolman probably wouldn't think nothing about seeing three white boys in an Alabama car; but three white boys and one black might make him suspicious."

"Right," said Wayne. Carl saw him turn and wink at George. "Hear that, Georgie? We might have to hide you."

"I been hid before," George said with his slow, lazy smile. Wayne laughed.

Around noon they crossed into Tennessee. Billy, riding up front with Carl, had been extremely quiet all morning, which Carl knew suited Wayne all right, but it got on Carl's nerves a little. He tried to get Billy to relax.

"Come on, Billy, lighten up a little," he said. "It ain't the end of the world, you know."

"Not for you, maybe," Billy replied sullenly.

"Not for nobody," Carl insisted. "We'll land on our feet; wait and see."

"Why, hell, yes," Wayne said from the back seat. He reached forward and patted Billy on the shoulder. "You gonna be all right, kid."

Billy nodded but did not respond to Wayne's words of encouragement. Wayne was his half brother but Billy hardly knew him. He had not seen him in years prior to ten days ago when Carl brought him around and introduced him. Wayne was almost as much a stranger to Billy as that nigger George sitting back there with him. And Billy had been curious about George when they left Baltimore a week earlier. "How come Wayne's dragging that four-eyed nigger along?" he asked Carl in private. Carl had grinned lewdly.

"Don't you know? Really?"

Billy had shrugged, embarrassed. "Well, I wasn't sure. I mean, I didn't like to think anything like that about my own brother, even if I don't know him so good."   25

"Wayne's spent a lot of time locked up," Carl explained. "When a man's locked up a lot, when he can't get to no women, he has to make do the best he can. George is how Wayne makes do. See?"

"Yeah, but he's out now. He don't have to make do. Why does he have to drag him along now, with us?"

"Maybe he's just used to it that way. Or maybe he's in love with the fucking guy. Hell, I don't know, Billy. Ask him, why don't you?"

Billy had not asked Wayne, of course, nor had he bothered Carl about it again. He had just accepted that George was going to be with them as long as Wayne was with them.

Shortly after they crossed into Tennessee, they were hungry and thirsty again. They stopped in Winchester for gas and to buy more junk food and beer. Then they pressed on in a north-easterly direction. Carl had no map, but knew if they kept going roughly toward Kentucky and West Virginia, that they had to reach Maryland. Carl was the only one doing any driving; Wayne did not like to drive, Billy was not that good a driver, and George did not know how to drive at all. Not that Carl would have trusted George at the wheel anyway; not only was he half blind, but Carl did not trust niggers to do anything intelligent.

In Tennessee, the little towns went past like an unwinding reel of film: Sewanee, Jasper, Sweetwater, Bucktown, Pine Top, Claxton. From low rolling ridges of plowed fields and growing crops, they gradually came into the foothills of the Great Smoky Mountains that spilled over into Tennessee from North Carolina. Farther north they passed through the Swan Forest and Wildlife Management preserve, an area that looked much as it must have a thousand years earlier; its trees and bogs and flora a fecund, moss-covered sanctuary from civilization.

"It's sure pretty," Billy said quietly, to no one in particular.

"Give me the city any day," Wayne said. "When I take a step, I like to feel concrete under my feet. Ain't that the best thing, Georgie?" he asked, patting George's thigh.

"Sure, tha's best," George replied lazily.

Billy made no further comments on the passing landscape.

For the first half of the afternoon, as he had done all morning, Carl kept the radio on and they listened to the news roundups twice an hour. Still there was no report from Georgia. No word at all.

26

"Goddamn!" Wayne said. "Surely to Christ they've found out by now. I mean, Jesus, how long's it been, Carl?"

" 'Bout twenty hours," Carl said.

"Hell, that's plenty of time, ain't it?"

"Plenty plus some. There ain't no way they don't know."

"Why ain't it on the news then?" Billy asked quietly from beside Carl.

"I don't know." Carl pushed the dashboard lighter in, waited until it popped out, and lighted a cigarette. "It could be a fucking trick."

"What kind of trick?" Wayne demanded.

Again Carl said, "I don't know." He thought about it for a minute. "Maybe they don't want us to know they're looking for us yet."

"Why?" asked Wayne.

"Hell, Wayne, I don't know!" Carl replied with an edge. "I can't answer everything." He wrenched the radio off and exhaled a deep drag of the cigarette. Sometimes being the goddamned leader wasn't all it was fucking cracked up to be.

From Tennessee they passed into Kentucky. Carl was beginning to get tired; he had driven more than four hundred miles. But despite the cramp in his right calf, he wanted to go at least a hundred miles more. The reel of highway kept unwinding in front of the car, and in Kentucky the names of the little towns became more colorful: Mountain Ash, Julip, Black Snake, Mary Alice, Sunshine. Then there was Harlan, a coal-mining town just north of the Cumberland Mountains. Carl remembered reading somewhere that there had once been a sign outside that town that read: DON'T GET CAUGHT IN HARLAN AFTER SUNDOWN, NIGGER. He hoped the sign was still there.If it was, he was going to read it aloud for George's benefit and then laugh like hell. He knew it would probably piss Wayne off but he didn't give a shit. Served him right for dragging a nigger fuck-boy around with him in the first place.

When they got to Harlan, however, Carl saw no such sign anywhere. It had probably been there a long time ago, he decided, a little disappointed. Maybe back during the war, before he was born. This was 1973, he reminded himself. White folks weren't allowed to put up signs about their "black brothers" anymore. People couldn't even call them "colored" anymore. Now they were "blacks." And they had "rights." What a lot of shit.

From Harlan they kept on to Oven Fork, Ermine, Ashcamp, 27

Beaver Bottom, Chloe. They passed Fishtrap Lake and Carl made a mental note of the name. Then they pulled into Pikeville and Carl decided he had driven enough. Nearly six hundred miles since stealing the car back in Livingston. He drove around until he found a motel, a Holiday Inn.

"How many nights?" the clerk asked.

"Just one," Carl said. "We come up to do a day's fishing out at Fishtrap."

"How many in the room?"

"Three," said Carl. They would sneak the nigger in.

"I can give you a room with two double beds on the second floor."

"Fine."

Carl paid for the room in advance. They took their few belongings out of the trunk and went upstairs. The first thing Carl did when they got into the room was turn on the television.

And the first news story they watched told of what had been discovered earlier that day in Seminole County, Georgia.

All four of them sat on the beds and watched transfixed as the newscast showed a videotape of a cleared space at the edge of a field, where a neat, flower-bedded mobile home was set on a permanent foundation. There was a crowd of people in the little clearing, and a number of uniformed policemen keeping them back from the trailer. There was a square-faced man in his forties, his expression etched with grief. There were ambulances, stretchers, bodies being removed.

The two white men and the boy did not say anything when the newscast was over; but the black man, George, looked down at the floor and shook his head emotionally.

"God, God, God," he moaned in a trembling voice, "you white boys done got me in big trouble now!"

6

"You're late," Jennifer Denmark said the second Carl walked in the door. "You know your dad likes for you to have everything ready to go when he gets home."

"Sorry," Carl half mumbled. Jacky, the Denmarks' real son, was at the kitchen table eating a slice of chocolate cake.

"Sorry, what?" Mrs. Denmark said pointedly.

"Sorry, Mom." The word almost stuck in his throat every time he used it. She wasn't his mom, not his *real* mom, yet she insisted he call her that. And not just occasionally, either—all the time. Yes, Mom. No, Mom. Thank you, Mom. I'm sorry, Mom. Please, Mom. Mom, Mom, Mom, from the time he woke up in the morning until the time he went to bed at night. Sometimes when he forgot, she merely reminded him as she just had. Other times, if he was in range, she pinched him or twisted his ear or pulled his hair. Quick, jerky little punishments that she seemed to do almost with relish. Carl hated her for it.

"You'd better hurry and change. Then go on out to the garage and get everything ready," she said.

"Can't I have something to eat first, Mom?" he asked, watching Jacky devour the chocolate cake.

"You don't have time. Dad'll be home any time. Go on now, do as I said."

Carl's shoulders dropped an inch. "Yes, Mom."

In the basement, where a corner was fixed up for him with a bed and bureau, he took off his school clothes and put on his work clothes. Then he went out to the garage and began getting things ready for Edward Denmark, Jennifer's husband. Edward worked for the department of public parks as a maintenance man; he also had a part-time business of his own, mowing and edging lawns in Glencoe's upper-class neighborhoods. He used an unmarked parks department pickup truck in his private business. Carl loaded the truck for him every day, and went with him to help mow and edge.

In the garage, Carl rolled out the mower and attached a canvas grass catcher to it. He put the edger beside it, and checked both to make sure they had full tanks of gasoline. Once he had forgotten to do that and Edward had run out of fuel in the middle of mowing a lawn. Edward had been very upset about it, but he had not laid a hand on Carl; he merely lectured him and told him not to do it again. Edward Denmark was like that: unruffled, quiet, an almost introspective man who rarely raised his voice. Just as Carl was required to call Jennifer "Mom," so was he expected to call Edward "Dad." But Carl didn't mind that. He liked Mr. Denmark; and anyway, he no longer had a real father of his own. On the day he had forgotten to check the fuel tank, he asked Mr. Denmark not to tell his wife about it, and Mr. Denmark did not. Carl knew that if Jennifer had known about it, she most certainly would have punished him for it.

When Carl had the mower and edger ready, and was getting out the broom, rake, and trash bags, Mr. Denmark came home and backed the truck up to the open garage door. "Load her up, Carl," he said, getting out. "I'm going to grab a quick bite."

Carl almost asked if he could come in and have something to eat too, but he checked himself. Mrs. Denmark had already told him he didn't have time to eat anything; proving her wrong would be something he would just have to pay for later. So he simply loaded the truck and sat in the cab to wait.

Jacky, the Denmarks' real son, never helped Mr. Denmark. He was, according to Mrs. Denmark, too young. But Carl, who had lived with the Denmarks three years, had been Jacky's age when they made *him* start helping—something that he had never quite understood. Except that Jacky somehow got away with a lot of things. He did not, for instance, have to address his mother as "Mom" every time he opened his mouth. And he did not have to clean his plate every night; whenever Jacky didn't like something, he was always "allergic" to it. Carl had to eat every scrap on his plate or be punished for it. Carl was not permitted in the living room; Jacky was. Jacky had his own bedroom; Carl had a corner of the basement. Jacky wore clothes from a department store; Carl's came from a discount house. Jacky's word was always accepted, Carl's always suspect.

Mr. Denmark came out of the house carrying a plastic cup of coffee. He put it in a holder on the dashboard and they drove toward their first customer. They usually did two yards a day, mowing, edging, raking, and bagging. Each lawn took about an hour. Mr. Denmark did good work; when he finished a yard, it looked just like own: manicured. He was a slow, painstakingly neat worker who never hurried through a job, always taking enough time to do it right, to do it well. Carl enjoyed working with him; he looked up to him and admired him. Even after he had worked with him for about a year and found out that he was a petty thief.

Edward Denmark had access to the garages of nearly every customer he had. It was necessary, he explained to them initially, so that he could put the bagged grass inside in case it rained. Often the residents of a house were not at home when he and Carl did their work. It was usually on those occasions, Carl noticed, that Denmark unobtrusively prowled around the garage to see what he could take that wouldn't be missed. It was seldom anything big or anything valuable: a bag of barbecue charcoal from a garage that had several in stock; a screwdriver or other small hand tool from a toolbox or tool rack; two or three logs of firewood from a stacked cord; a can of paint, a good bristle paintbrush; even a Christmas ornament or two from a storage box.

Carl was stunned. Mr. Denmark was so casual about it. Thinking Carl was paying no attention to him, he would just take the article he wanted and put it under a tarpaulin in the bed of the truck. Later Carl would see it around the Denmark garage or in the house. Carl never mentioned it to anyone, and never let on to Mr. Denmark that he was aware of it. But it troubled him for months. There was no reason for Mr. Denmark to steal; he had a good job, earned good money, and the things he stole were so inexpensive that he could have bought them many times over. Why then, Carl wondered, did the man steal?

He never figured it out. But for the rest of his life he looked upon stealing simply as something people did. *All people.*

After Carl had been with the Denmarks for about two years, a murder-suicide incident occurred a few houses down the street from them. A divorced woman who lived alone in her home was involved with a married man who visited her two or three times a week. The woman had mentioned to a close neighbor that the man wanted to marry her but there was no way he could get out of his present marriage. She had given him an ultimatum: either leave his wife or stop his affair with her. Thinking there was no way out, the man had come to her house one night with a gun, killed her, then taken his own life.

For a long time the house was posted by the police department as the scene of a crime, and no one could go near it. Later, after the case was closed, the dead woman's estate settled, and the property put up for sale, housewives in the neighborhood still made their children stay away from it. Jennifer Denmark made it very clear to her son Jacky that he was not to play around the house at any time, and was never, under any circumstances, to set foot on the property. She told Carl essentially the same thing, although not as strongly; with his work schedule helping Mr. Denmark, Carl had precious little time to play anywhere.

Then one night Mrs. Denmark changed her mind and decided that Carl *could* go near the murder house. In fact, she decided to take him there herself.

"Put on your sweater, Carl," she told him one night just before bedtime. "I want you to take a walk with me."

Carl was puzzled. He looked at Mr. Denmark for guidance or explanation; but Mr. Denmark kept his eyes fixed on his newspaper, studiously avoiding Carl's silent plea.

Mrs. Denmark and Carl walked down the street. The neighborhood was dark and quiet, only a few houses with lights still on in the front rooms.

"You know, Carl," Mrs. Denmark said, "you've been getting very careless lately in your conduct. You come in late from school; a few times so late you didn't have Dad's equipment ready to load. Quite often you fail to show me the proper respect by calling me 'Mom' as you're supposed to—"

"I don't feel right calling you 'Mom,'" Carl finally blurted out. He had wanted to say it for three years.

"Please don't interrupt when I'm speaking, Carl. That's a perfect example of what I'm talking about: your attitude. There is absolutely no reason for you not to feel right about calling me 'Mom.' I'm more of a mother to you than anyone's ever been."

"I've got a real mom," Carl said stubbornly.

"Oh? Well, tell me, Carl, what has your *real* mom ever done for you? Does she feed you? Clothe you? Give you a home?"

Carl did not reply. There was only one answer to those questions, as Mrs. Denmark well knew, and Carl would be damned before he would give her the satisfaction of verbalizing it. But apparently she did not expect him to.

"No, Carl, your *real* mom gives you none of those things. Your *real* mom has never given you *anything.*" She took him by the arm, stopping him, turning him to face her. "Listen to me, young man, you had better resign yourself to the fact that your *real* mom is no damn good. *No damn good!*"

Still holding his arm in one of her strong hands, she easily guided him up the driveway of the murder house. Carl felt himself begin to shiver. She pushed him ahead of her into the darker darkness of the front porch.

"You know what happened in this house, don't you, Carl?"

"Y-y-yes, Mom—" he replied through quivering lips.

"What happened in this house was caused by people just like your mother, Carl. People who were no good. The woman was no good because she was letting a man who wasn't her husband go to bed with her. And the man was no good because he was going to bed with a woman who wasn't his wife. No-good people, Carl. And they ended up murdered. They came to a bad end. Do you want to come to a bad end, Carl?"

He tried to answer but the words would not sound. Mrs. Denmark shook him irritably.

"Answer me! Do you?"

"N-n-no, Mom—"

"Then you had better change your attitude!" she hissed. "Because if you don't, you're going to end up bad, and something terrible will happen to you, just like it did to them!" She shook him back and forth by the arm, making him flop like an old rag doll. "Do you understand me? Do you? Do you?"

"Y-y-yes, M-m-mom—!"

"All right then!"

Mrs. Denmark dragged him back home, sniveling, crying, trembling all the way, his nose running mucus down over his mouth, the muscle of his left arm aching from the viselike grip of her fingers. At the house, she opened the basement door and started him down the stairs. The door was slammed after him and he was left alone in the basement. Fearfully he went to the corner where he slept and got undressed. He dreaded turning out the light and going to bed, because he was certain that he was going to have bad dreams about the murder house.

He did.

When Carl was thirteen, the Denmarks signed him up for the Boy Scouts. They did not ask him whether he had any   33 interest in participating in the scouting program; they simply told him that it would be good for him and that he would like it. It was one of the few times in Carl's life that the assurance "you'll like it" turned out to be true. He did like the Scouts. And to give credit where it is due, the Denmarks treated him as if he were their own when it came to outfitting him. They took him to an authorized Boy Scout clothing department and bought him a full uniform with all the accessories. Of course, Jacky came along and was similarly uniformed; he was joining the same troop as Carl. But that fact did not detract from Carl's appreciation of his equal treatment—if anything, it underscored it. For the first time since being left with the Denmarks, he was getting exactly the same things that Jacky was getting: purchased in the same store, costing the same price. Carl felt something that day that he had never felt before: he felt that he was as good as Jacky.

It was ironic that scouting, the thing that Carl liked most about his three years with the Denmarks, was to be the thing that caused him the most trouble with them. Most of his infractions in the past had been minor ones: not cleaning his plate, being late, an untidy sleeping area; or the nebulous transgression of "poor attitude." Nothing ever very serious.

But a bit of mischief that occurred outside the Denmark house would cause the biggest breach of all in his relationship with them.

The mischief was a kind not uncommon among young Boy Scouts camping out in the woods for a weekend. They cleared the ground for their camp, unbundled their equipment, and pitched their tents. There were four to a tent and they all worked together to get it up properly and sturdily, centerpole steadily in place, the four tent ropes drawn tautly to stakes driven into the ground. The scoutmaster would come around later to check their work and grade them; putting up the tent correctly was not only for their living comfort, but also aided their progress toward merit badges. Even so, even considering the double importance of the work, they were not dissuaded from mischief. It was commonplace for four boys to go to sleep at night in a shipshape, perfectly pitched tent, only to wake up the next morning with the four corners fallen in on them, the result of cut tent ropes or pulled tent stakes.

That was the mischief Carl and his three tent partners got into. After getting their own tent squared away, they sneaked down the line to another tent and, each taking a corner,

34

cut the tent ropes and ran like hell while it caved in on its occupants.

Carl and his tentmates were back in their own tent, rolling on the ground with laughter, when the scoutmaster entered, followed by Jacky Denmark.

"Are these the boys you saw do it, Jacky?" the scoutmaster asked.

"Yes, sir. Him—" he pointed at Carl "—and those other three."

The scoutmaster could have put them on restriction and assigned them extra clean-up duty around camp; or he could have made them knot the cut ropes together and repitch the tent; or he could have applied one of any number of other punishments. But the troop had been especially difficult of late—the youngsters were becoming more and more rowdy all the time—and the scoutmaster was feeling the pressure of dealing with them. So he decided to make examples of Carl and his tent partners.

"You're all suspended from further scouting activity," he told them. They knew what the word "suspended" meant; kids in school were being suspended all the time. Usually they showed up the following day with one of their parents in tow, and the problem they had created would be resolved. But on rare occasions the student did *not* show up, the next day or ever, and was never seen around school again. So being "suspended," while not necessarily fatal, was still something to be dreaded. And doubly so the way the scoutmaster explained it.

"You will not be permitted to participate in any future meetings or trips; your Boy Scouts of America identification will be taken away from you; and you will no longer be allowed to wear any part of the Scout uniform. At some later date, we will hold a hearing on what you've done and decide whether the suspension will be permanent or whether you will be reinstated. In the meantime, you're all out of the Scouts."

Carl and the other three were ostracized for the rest of the camping trip, and made to sit in the far back of the chartered bus on their way home on Sunday night. After disembarking the bus at Scout headquarters, when Carl and Jacky were walking home together, Carl said, "You shouldn't have told on us like that, Jacky."

"You guys did it," Jacky replied self-righteously, as if that fact alone justified his informing.

"It was just a joke," Carl defended. "Didn't hurt nobody. 35

Anyway, you better not tell Mom or Dad that I got suspended."

"I will so tell," Jacky said. "They got a right to know you're no good. 'Sides, they'd find out anyway."

"Maybe, maybe not. If I can get back in the troop, there won't be no need for them to know."

"Oh, ha!" Jacky said scornfully. "They aren't gonna let you back in the troop. You're no good, Carl."

"Quit saying I'm no good!" Carl snapped.

"Well, you're not no good," Jacky went blithely on. "Mom said you weren't. She's said it lots of times. You're no good and your real mom is no good."

They were in front of the Denmark house now. Carl took Jacky by the shoulders and stopped him. "Listen, Jacky, please don't tell on me. They bought me this nice uniform and everything—"

"I'm telling," Jacky said flatly.

Carl's jaw clenched. A low-pitched, almost churning sound emitted from low in his throat, like an old engine trying to start. A look of panic-stricken desperation came over his face: his eyes widened, lips tightened, teeth gnashed together. The sound from his throat became louder, more piercing, like that of a forest creature that knows it is trapped. Carl shook his head back and forth and raised both hands, closed into fists, to his ears.

Then he lashed out.

He hit Jacky in the mouth with his right fist, in the nose with his left, the eye with his right, the ear, the cheek, the mouth again, the eye again—

Jacky began to scream. The Denmarks' porch light turned on. Mrs. Denmark came rushing out. She ran across the lawn toward them, Mr. Denmark following just a little faster than his usual slow pace. When Mrs. Denmark reached them, she closed her fist and smashed Carl in the face. The weight behind the punch dropped Carl to his knees. She hit him again with her fist, and again, just as he had been doing to Jacky. He tried to crawl away from her but she kept up with him, raining heavy-fisted blows down on his head. Finally he cowered into as small a target as he could make himself, and just let her pound him. He had no idea how long she kept hitting him; it seemed like an hour. Then suddenly she stopped and when he looked up she had her arm around Jacky and was walking him to the house. Mr. Denmark was following along behind them.

36

They all went into the house, and a second later the porch light went off.

Carl sat on the lawn in the dark for a while, sobbing and using his sleeves to wipe away his tears and the blood from his nose. When he felt he could, he stood up and straightened out his clothes and brushed himself off. He started to walk away from the house, and as he did the porch light came on again.

"Carl!"

It was Mr. Denmark, probably sent by his wife to get him. Carl ignored him and walked onto the adjacent lawn.

"Carl, come on back!" Mr. Denmark called. Still Carl kept going, hurrying now. Then he heard another voice—hers.

"Carl! You get back here this minute!"

Carl started running.

7

"See if it's daylight yet," Carl said to Billy, nudging him out of bed. Billy, in his underwear, crossed the motel room and parted the drapes an inch. Outside, a thinning fog was hanging over Pikeville, Kentucky, but the grudging nighttime was giving way to daybreak.

"Just about," Billy said. "It's foggy, though."

"Good." Carl sat up on the side of the bed. "Wake them up," he said, nodding toward the other bed in which Wayne and George slept.

"Do it yourself," Billy replied, looking toward his half brother and the black man with revulsion. "I ain't going near them." He went into the bathroom and closed the door.

Carl walked around the other bed and slapped Wayne smartly on his exposed bare shoulder. "Let's go, Wayne. Time to hit the road, man." Stepping over to the TV, Carl turned on the set, then started getting dressed. As he put on his shoes, Billy came out of the bathroom and also started dressing. Slowly a picture came into focus on the TV screen: it was a Department of Corrections mug shot of Wayne with a Maryland State Prison number hanging around his neck. "Come on, Wayne, roll out of there," Carl said, shaking him this time.

"Yeah, get up, Wayne, you're famous this morning," Billy said half to himself. "We're all famous now."

Carl came over to Billy. "I want you to keep your mouth shut today, you hear? I got Wayne to agree to take you back home, and that's what we're doing. Now don't say nothing to piss him off, understand?" Billy started to turn away in disgust; Carl grabbed his arm and pulled him back. "Understand?"

"Yeah, I understand," Billy said, jerking his arm away.

38   All four of them saw their pictures on the TV screen as they

dressed: Wayne's and George's from Maryland State Prison, Carl's and Billy's from the Baltimore Police Department. They listened soberly to the newscaster's crisp words: ". . . authorities throughout Georgia and adjoining states pressing a relentless search today for the four men. The Federal Bureau of Investigation entered the manhunt late Tuesday afternoon. . . ."

Billy shook his head glumly. "The FBI. They'll catch us for sure."

"Bullshit," said Wayne. "The FBI ain't no better than any other cops."

"They always are on TV shows," George offered seriously.

"Fuck TV," said Wayne.

Billy turned away from them and went to look out the window. "Fog's lifting a little," he told Carl.

"Good," Carl said, clapping his hands together. "Okay, let's get our asses in gear and split!"

Carl went to the sink and rinsed his face with cold water. Having toweled dry, he stared at himself in the mirror. The news hadn't mentioned the woman, he thought. What the hell was happening with the woman? Then he shut his eyes tightly and shook his head.

Don't think about the woman, he ordered himself.

Fifteen minutes later they were on the road again, Carl, as usual, driving. One route out of Pikeville led to West Virginia, the other to Virginia, both state lines some thirty miles away. Carl had to pause a moment deciding which road to take. West Virginia, he knew, bordered on Maryland up around Hagerstown; he knew where that was because an older Issacs brother, Roy, was serving time in the state penitentiary there. But Carl did not want to go to that part of Maryland; he wanted to come into the state closer to Baltimore, so they could drop Billy off in Parkville as quickly as possible and then make their dash for Canada. The best route to do that, it seemed to him, was through Virginia.

He got on Interstate 460, deciding to take that into Virginia, then cut north on the first back road that looked like it had possibilities of going anywhere.

There was also another problem he had to deal with. "How much money you got left?" he asked Wayne.

"Less than a dollar. 'Bout eighty cents."

Billy, he knew, had no money, and Wayne always carried for George as well as himself. Carl had three dollars and some change.

"We got to hit someplace," Carl said. "I'd like to have enough money so we won't have to do no more jobs until after we get rid of Billy."

Wayne grunted softly; Carl glanced at him, realizing he had used a poor choice of words in saying "get rid of Billy." Carl quickly continued talking about the problem at hand. "I think we ought to hit two or three little country stores and get as much as we can before we cross into Maryland."

"We ain't gonna make no money robbing country stores," Wayne said. "What we ought to do is find a town and rob us a fucking bank. The fucking FBI's after us already anyhow."

"They might be after us," Carl reasoned, "but they don't know where we are. If we rob a bank we'll be telling them. No, it's best to do a few little places that involve nobody but local cops."

"Whatever you say," Wayne sighed quietly. It never did any good to suggest anything to Carl: he usually had his mind made up when a discussion started.

About fifteen miles from Virginia, at the town of Grundy, Carl turned off the interstate highway and took a state road, Route 83, heading east. He was surprised to learn that the road was taking them toward the West Virginia state line. "Shit," he said to himself; he must have got his directions mixed up. He did not say anything to the others; it would just make them nervous if he let on that he was not sure in which direction they were traveling. Next time they stopped for gas, he had to remember to get a road map.

Nine miles up Route 83, they passed through the hamlet of Stacy and kept going. About four miles farther, they came to a crossroads where there was a country store. Only one vehicle, a pickup truck, was parked outside.

"This looks good for a start," Carl said. "Ought to be good for a few hundred." He pulled alongside the store and turned the car around so that it was pointed toward the road. He left the engine running. "Let's go."

As Wayne got out, he looked in at Billy, who had been riding in the front seat with Carl. "Let's go, you," he said.

"I'm not going," Billy said stubbornly, staring straight
40 ahead.

"The hell you ain't." Wayne started to open the passenger door.

"Let him stay," said Carl. "Shit, it's just a country store: a two-man job. Come on, Wayne. Billy, keep that motor running."

Inside the store they found a man, woman, and boy who were customers, and a woman behind the counter.

"Anything else for you folks today?" the woman behind the counter was asking.

"Do you have some birthday cards, Miz Matney?" the woman customer asked.

"A few," replied Mrs. Matney. "Right back there over the ice cream freezer." She turned to Carl and Wayne. "Can I help you boys?"

"You sure can," said Carl, pulling his gun. "Put all your money in a paper sack for me. And I mean *all* of it, lady."

Wayne had drawn his own gun and turned on the man, woman, and boy. "Get down on the floor," he ordered. "Now! Down!"

Glancing out the window, Carl saw another pickup truck pull up and a man and woman get out. "Hey," he hollered to Wayne, "the door."

Wayne apprehended the couple as they came in. Before he could do anything with them, two more vehicles, cars this time, pulled up. "What the fuck," Wayne muttered. He forced the couple to lie on the floor and waited as three more people came toward the door.

At the counter, Carl's mouth dropped open incredulously. Mrs. Matney had opened a cash drawer and was piling sheafs of currency in a paper bag. The money was banded and marked in denominations: five, tens, twenties. Carl estimated that there was at least three thousand dollars. What in the hell was a little dump like this doing with that kind of money in the drawer? he wondered. But before he could dwell on it, Wayne spoke urgently from the door.

"Hey, man, I need some help over here!"

Carl saw him covering three people just inside the door with their hands up, and five now lying on the floor. And outside, still another pickup truck arrived and two more women approached the store. "Jesus Christ," Carl muttered, "what is this place, a goddamned bus depot? Okay, lady, put both hands on the counter and don't move." He snatched up the bag of 41 money and stuffed it inside his shirt. With Wayne at the door, he said, "Get some clothesline and start tying everybody up. I'll cover the door." Outside he saw another car pull up and a man get out. "Holy shit!"

It took them ten minutes to tie up the twelve people then in the store, and while they were doing it, three others arrived: two on foot from a field across the road, and a third in yet another truck. What had started out with merely a proprietor and three customers, ended up with fifteen people tied up, lying all over the store.

"Come on now," Wayne said tensely when the last one was tied up, "let's get the hell out of here before the goddamned high school band shows up."

They ran out to the car where an almost frantic Billy was trembling nervously. "What the hell happened? Jesus, I saw all those people going in!"

"You might've come in and give us a hand," Wayne snapped as he and Carl jumped into the car. Before Billy could answer, Carl was shoving him over and getting behind the wheel. Punching down on the accelerator, Carl spun the rear tires and sprayed gravel all over the side of the store as he fishtailed onto the highway and sped away.

"Here," he said, tossing the bag of money to Billy, "count that."

Wayne reached over the seat and snatched the bag from Billy. *"I'll* count it. Shit, Carl, he didn't even go in!"

"All right, you count it then!" Carl snapped back at him. Carl was growing weary of Wayne's temperament. The prick took everything so fucking personal, he thought.

Carl sped along Route 83, across the West Virginia line, through the hamlet of Jolo, and past a sign that read: BRAD-SHAW 3.

Back at the store, one of the men managed to work his hands free and untied Mrs. Matney. She went at once to her telephone, which neither Carl or Wayne, suddenly besieged by walk-in customers, had thought to disable. Mrs. Matney put through a call to the Bradshaw constable's office. Clarence Shelton, the constable, answered.

"Clarence," Mrs. Matney said, "they's been a holdup out here at my place. Two young boys that was a' driving a green car with a black top. I seen 'em when they drove up and turned the car around. There was two others in the car with 'em: four in all. One of them was black. Oh, and the car don't have Virginia or West Virginia licenses, neither. I don't know what kind they was, but they was from somewheres else. Anyhow, they're heading toward Bradshaw. I wisht you'd stop 'em and get my money back. They took my whole month's cash, more'n three thousand dollars—"

After Mrs. Matney hung up, Constable Shelton thought the situation over. Four holdup men. And him all alone. Not very good odds. But nothing he couldn't handle. He picked the phone up again and called Sheriff Archie Day up in Welch, West Virginia, twenty miles north.

"Archie, this here's Clarence. We got some holdup men heading your way. Four of 'em. They robbed Miz Matney's store down at the Slate Creek crossroads. Driving a black-over-green car with some kind of out-of-town plates. What I thought I'd do is let 'em go through here, then get on their tail so's they can't double back. Meanwhile, you and your boys can start this way and lay for 'em somewhere. How's that sound to you?"

It sounded fine to Sheriff Day. "I'll throw up a roadblock down around Yukon or War, thereabouts. Now listen, Clarence, don't you go acting the damn fool and trying to be no hero, hear? Not with four of 'em. Just run 'em up here into my little net."

After Archie Day hung up, he had his radio operator send out an emergency call for his chief and all twelve of his deputies.

"Have 'em meet me where Route 16 intersects 83," he ordered.

Then he pulled a shotgun off the rack and went out to his car.

Carl went through Bradshaw doing seventy.

"Got that money counted yet?" he said over his shoulder.

" 'Bout two thousand," Wayne said.

Carl snorted. "Count it again, bro. There's at least three thousand."

Wayne, who had been handing the money to George as he counted it, grabbed it back off George's lap and shoved it into the sack again. He threw it in Carl's lap. "Count it yourself then."

Carl showed him an irritated look in the rearview mirror; but it was only the briefest of looks, because his attention was 43 immediately attracted to something else in that mirror.

They were being followed.

Constable Shelton had been parked at the near edge of Bradshaw, waiting for them. He got on their tail immediately, followed them through town, and stayed with them as they headed straight for Yukon and War, at one of which would be Sheriff Archie Day's roadblock.

The driver of the holdup car, which Shelton now knew to be carrying Alabama plates, had seen him in the rearview mirror when he first fell in behind him, as they entered Bradshaw. He had looked at the officer twice again, both times going through town. Shelton knew the holdup car driver would not suspect anything until he followed them out of town on the other side; then it would be obvious that he was following them. Shelton was thankful that his car was a combination personal car and official car: it had a shield on the side, but the emergency flasher was portable, hanging under the dashboard out of sight. From up ahead, there was no way they could tell he was a police officer.

After the driver glanced back at him the third time, Clarence Shelton took his revolver out of its holster, thumbed the safety off, and placed it conveniently on the seat beside him. Propped against that same seat, its muzzle toward the passenger door, was Shelton's .30–30 slide-action rifle.

As the two cars left the Bradshaw town limits and the driver saw him in the rearview mirror for a fourth time, the holdup car very gradually picked up speed.

So did Clarence Shelton.

"Some son-of-a-bitch is on our tail," Carl said.

Wayne, George, and Billy all turned at once to look out the back window. Clarence Shelton's car was about a quarter-mile behind them, holding steadily.

"How do you know he's following us and not just going the same way?" Wayne asked.

"He picked us up clear back the other side of that last hick town we come through," Carl replied. "He speeds up whenever I do, slows down whenever I do. He's on us, all right."

"Is that shotgun still under the front seat?"

"Yeah."

"Well," said Wayne, "let's stop and teach him a lesson. Don't look like there's nobody in the car with him."

"We may just do that," Carl said. "Let's give him a few more miles first. If he follows us through the next town, we'll do him."

Carl had no way of knowing that they would not get to the next town.

Sheriff Archie Day set up his roadblock with two cars parked in a V, the point facing the direction from which the holdup car was coming. The V was reinforced with a pickup truck parked inside the point. It was set up where a dirt road intersected the highway perpendicularly on the right, but only extended some two hundred yards into the woods and then dead-ended. It was a good place to run the holdup men into, Archie Day thought. No houses or stores or people around to get hurt. And no place to go but up if they decided to run for it on foot.

When the roadblock was arranged to suit him, and his deputies dispersed in what he considered the least hazardous deployment, Sheriff Day, shotgun in the crook of one arm, sat back against a fender, put a fresh chaw of Red Man plug in his mouth, and waited.

Carl saw the roadblock from half a mile back.
"Shit!"
"Oh, Christ—" Billy said.
"Hand me that shotgun!" said Wayne.
George closed his eyes and pulled his knees up on the seat.
Carl had to keep going; there was no place to turn off, not even enough shoulder to pull off on, or turn around on. And the other car was still right on them. It was a trap, all right—nice and neat. The sons-of-bitches.

"I said give me the fucking shotgun!" Wayne stormed, hitting Billy on the shoulder. Billy just stared straight ahead at the cars, the men waiting for them.

Carl's mouth went dry and his face got wet as sweat literally popped from his pores. He could feel his heart going crazy inside his chest. His knuckles were bone-white, he was gripping the steering wheel so tightly.

"Oh, Jesus—fuck—" he muttered. The roadblock was getting closer and closer.

Then he saw the dirt road jutting off to the right, just forward of the roadblock. He was almost onto it already; he had to stomp down on the brake to keep from passing it.

"Hang on!" he yelled. He wheeled the car into a hard right turn, feeling it lean, then tip, feeling the two tires on the right side lose traction and leave the road. *Turning over!* he thought frantically. *Oh, shit!*

But the car did not pitch all the way. It reached a peak with still enough weight on the right side to keep it from rolling over. A split second later its two raised tires bounced back down on the road and its rear end spun out. It skidded on a forty-five-degree angle down to the road's dead end, then slid sideways into a grassy bank and the engine died.

Carl and Billy were out and running first, heading into the trees. Wayne had plunged into the front seat and was struggling to get the shotgun from under the seat. It was jammed in the springs, stuck. George was still cowering on the back seat.

"Get the fuck out!" Wayne shouted at him. "Run!"

George tumbled out, nearly losing his glasses in the process; he ran after Carl and Billy. Wayne, seeing the lawmen hurrying toward him from the highway, finally gave up on the shotgun and took off running himself.

Carl and Billy led the way, running straight into the woods on the left of the dirt road. Carl's natural defense mechanisms were in high gear. He knew he was running on a line parallel with the highway, about two hundred yards into the woods. And he knew that most of the roadblock deputies were now rushing toward the car. His survival instincts told him to cut toward the highway and get on the other side of it.

Carl reached out and slapped the arm of Billy, who was running beside him. "Come on," he said, "this way!"

They ran toward the highway. Behind them, George and Wayne followed. At some point, Wayne caught up with and passed the slower George. "Run faster!" Wayne said, nudging him. But George could not. And Wayne didn't wait.

At the highway, Carl and Billy crouched in a culvert and peered down the road. They were beyond the roadblock now, the V of the cars pointing away from them. There were still several armed men there, standing in the back of a pickup truck, but they were looking down the dirt road, not up the highway.

46   Carl scrutinized the terrain. Across the highway, the woods

were thicker and gradually inclined. High ground, he thought. From there they could keep the deputies in sight.

"We'll cross the highway one at a time," he said. "I'll go first and wait for you on the other side."

Crouching low, Carl hurried over the asphalt and dropped into the culvert on the other side. He looked down the highway; the men in the pickup truck bed were still watching the other way. Carl waved Billy over. Billy crossed as Carl had. Wayne ran up to the culvert then and both Carl and Billy waved him over. Wayne paused, waiting for George to catch up. George, breathing heavily, finally made it.

"We're crossing the road," Wayne said. "Wait until I'm across, then you come, okay?"

"Yeah, okay," George panted. He used his shirttail to wipe the sweat off his glasses.

Wayne slapped him on the ass and stepped up out of the culvert. He was in a crouch, halfway across, when two shots were fired at him. The men in the pickup truck had seen him.

When he got to the other side, Wayne waved George over. Two more rifle bullets whined down the road. Wayne kept waving George over. George shook his head.

"He ain't coming!" Carl said urgently. "Let's go!"

Carl and Billy broke for the thick woods, feeling the ground incline under their feet. Wayne kept waving, shouting at George. "Come on! Come on! You can make it!"

But George shook his head again as another rifle slug whined by.

Finally Wayne saw some deputies moving up in the woods behind George. *That's that, baby,* he thought. He turned and ran after his two half brothers.

George was still in the culvert, trembling with fright, tears streaking his cheeks, when three deputies, two with rifles, one with a shotgun, cautiously approached him.

"Don't even blink your eyes, nigger," the man with the shotgun said, "or I'll blow your belly out."

George stood as still as his trembling would allow.

A thousand yards into the woods and up the hill, Carl said to Wayne and Billy, "You two go on ahead. I'm gonna wait here a few seconds and see if I can hear them following."

Wayne and Billy kept climbing. Presently the sound of their feet rushing over the forest ground faded; where Carl was   47 standing the woods became eerily quiet. He peered back down where he knew the highway was, and listened intently, but he could neither see nor hear anything.

Leaning against a tree, he lighted a cigarette and sucked in a delicious long drag. His shirt was plastered to his body with perspiration; he used a sleeve to blot the sweat out of his eyes. Taking a few more quick drags on the cigarette, he extinguished it against the bark of the tree. He made sure it was out good; they didn't need a forest fire to add to their problems. A final look downhill told him there were no immediate pursuers.

As he was getting ready to start climbing again, a sudden thought occurred to him: a memory of the night he had run away from the Denmarks. He had been on foot and running that night too.

Ain't made much progress in five years, have you, sport? he asked himself.

Shaking his head wryly, he started off after Wayne and Billy.

8

"Hey, kid! You want a lift?"

The driver of a flatbed truck had pulled over to the side of the road which the thirteen-year-old Carl was walking. He was talking to Carl over a half–rolled-down window, leaning over from the driver's seat.

Carl had been walking for two hours; he had gone about five miles, heading south toward Baltimore. His face and head were still throbbing from the beating he had taken from Jennifer Denmark, and he could tell by gently feeling with his fingertips that his lips and nose were swollen and puffy. For a while after he started walking, which was after he stopped running, he had sweated profusely and had to unbutton his Scout uniform shirt to keep going. Now it was after dark and had turned cool; he not only buttoned it back up, he turned the collar up around his neck to keep warm.

"You want a ride or not, kid?" the truck driver asked impatiently.

The Denmarks had always told him never—*never*—to accept a ride from anyone he did not know. He had heard many tales of men who lured young girls or boys into their vehicles and did all manner of unspeakable things to them. But none of the stories had been about a thirteen-year-old who had just taken a beating and was alone, trying to walk twelve miles to his sister's house before his foster parents, or the law, caught up with him.

"Yeah, I want a ride. Thanks, mister."

He got into the cab beside the man and sat there shivering as the truck pulled back onto the road. It was Sunday night and traffic was light. Carl saw a police car up ahead, but it was going the opposite way, past them.

"You cold?" the trucker asked, noticing him shivering. "Here—" He reached over and opened a vent, then turned on 49 the heater. "What are you doing walking down the highway at night by yourself anyway?"

"I was on a camping trip," Carl said. "I got lost and missed my ride home."

"Where do you live?"

"Parkville."

"Well, you lucked out, kid. I'm on my way to Rosedale. Go right through Parkville." He studied Carl in the dim light of the dashboard. "Say, what's the matter with your face? You look like you've been in a fight."

"I fell down a hill," Carl lied. "Hit my face on a rock. That's how I got lost; I guess I was knocked out for a while."

"Oh." The truck driver reached over and patted his knee. "Well, we'll have you back in Parkville in no time flat."

Carl became a little apprehensive when the man patted his knee; he prepared himself to open the door and jump if he had to. But his anxiety was for nothing; the trucker made no further overtures or moves on him. In less than half an hour they were in Parkville. The trucker let him out at Old Hartford Road and Putty Hill. From there he was easily able to walk the rest of the way to Ruth's house.

When he got to Ruth's, he was surprised to find the house dark. At first he thought maybe they went to bed early. Then he saw there was no car parked on the dirt drive at the side of the house. They were not at home. He walked all the way around the house, trying all the doors and windows, but found them locked. He thought briefly of forcing a lock, but he knew Russell, Ruth's husband, would raise hell about that, so he dismissed the idea.

As he came back around front to sit on the porch and wait, Carl saw the headlights of a car turn into the drive. Good. They were coming home. He felt a little inner warmth, thinking how glad Ruth would be to see him. Other people might not care about him from time to time, but Ruth could always be depended on for a hug, a kiss, a kind word. And a welcome.

He had just taken a step toward the approaching car when he saw a red reflection above the windshield—and realized it was a police car. Sucking in his breath, he dove to the ground at the edge of the porch and lay very still. Almost immediately a blinding spotlight hit the house and played across the front door and windows. Carl started trembling. *They're looking for me,* he thought. The Denmarks must have called them, reported him as a runaway.

50   The car moved closer, its spotlight disappearing around one

side of the house. Carl crawled on his belly to the edge of the porch and wiggled around to the other side, where he had the house between him and the patrol car. Getting to his feet, he took off running across a grass field. He ran until he came to a tree. Ducking behind it, he flattened himself and watched as the police car finished inspecting the house and turned off the spot. Then it backed out of the drive and into the street, and drove away.

They'll be back, Carl thought. They would probably *keep* coming back until they caught him.

Sliding down the tree to a sitting position, he drew his knees up in front of him and chewed his fingernails as he tried to decide what to do. He knew now that he couldn't stay at Ruth's. He wasn't sure where his mother was; he had heard from a counselor that she had returned and was living with Ruth. His other sisters—Ann, who was about twenty, and Lois, twenty-two, still lived in the general area, but he had no idea where. Even if he knew, he wasn't sure they would take him in. Ruth was the only one he had ever been completely sure of.

So you've got nobody, he thought. Nobody to run to, no place to go—

Or did he? His mouth dropped open as another thought came to him. He had a *grandmother.* Sure. Mrs. Lennie Jamison. She lived in a little town in Pennsylvania called Fawn Grove. He didn't know exactly where that was—but in an instant he had made up his mind to find out.

Checking to see if the coast was clear, Carl trotted the rest of the way across the field and down the road until he came to a cross-street. He followed the cross-street down to Hartford Road; then he walked until he found a gas station.

"Mister," he asked the attendant, "do you have a road map of Pennsylvania?"

The attendant pulled a map out of a wall rack and put it on the counter. "Twenty-five cents," he said.

Carl bit his lip. "I don't have no money."

The attendant returned the map to the rack.

"Please, could I just look at it?" Carl asked.

"This ain't no library, kid. Shove off."

"I only need to look at it for a minute. Please, mister."

"I said no. Now beat it."

"Well, would you look at it for me? And tell me which way to go?"

"What?"

"Which way to go. I'm trying to get to Fawn Grove, Penn- 51

sylvania, to my grandmother's house. But I don't know which way it is."

The attendant eyed Carl suspiciously. "You a runaway or something?"

Carl nodded. "I ran away from a foster home. They gave me this." He pointed to his swollen lips and nose.

The attendant studied him, moving a toothpick back and forth in his mouth. "You walking?"

Carl nodded.

"Cops after you?"

Carl nodded again.

"Don't suppose there's no reward?"

Carl shook his head. "I ain't worth nothing." Mrs. Denmark had been reminding him of that since he was ten.

"Well, shit," the attendant said. He took the map down again and unfolded it on the counter. After studying it for a moment, he reached back up and took down a Maryland map and opened it. "All right, come around here and pay attention. This here's what you do: go down here to Joppa Road and turn left; you know left from right?"

"Sure," said Carl, slightly indignant.

"Okay. Turn left on Joppa Road and go about three miles until you come to Belair Road. That's also Route One. You turn left again. Stay on that route for sixteen miles, until you get to the town of Belair. Understand?" He waited for Carl's nod. "When you get to Belair, start watching for a sign that says Route Twenty-four. It'll cut right across Route One, so you shouldn't have no trouble finding it. You turn left again—always left, remember—on Route Twenty-four. You stay right on that road for, let's see: five, eight, ten, thirteen miles; then you'll be at the Pennsylvania state line. Fawn Grove is two miles the other side of the line. That means you've got, let's see—" he did some quick arithmetic "—thirty-four miles to go. That's a long way, kid."

"I'll make it," Carl said. He was repeating the instructions under his breath: "Joppa to Route One to Belair to Route Twenty-four—"

The attendant shook his head. "Man, I wouldn't walk thirty-four miles if Barbara Eden was waiting naked for me when I got there."

"Who?" Carl asked, interrupting his memorizing.

"Barbara Eden. The blonde with the nice tits on TV. You know, she plays that genie."

52   "Oh." Carl didn't know what the attendant was talking

about. Television viewing at the Denmarks' had been very restricted.

The attendant stepped over to a vending machine and bought a package of peanut butter-and-cheese crackers. He tossed them to Carl. "Something for the road. Now beat it before the cops find you here. And don't tell nobody I helped you."

"I won't. Thanks a lot." Carl walked out, mumbling, "Joppa to Route One to Belair—"

Behind him, he heard the attendant say, "No-sir-ree-bob. Not even for Barbara Eden. Not thirty-four miles."

As it turned out, Carl did not have to walk the entire distance. It was nine o'clock when he got to Joppa Road and started north. Before he had even gone a mile, some teenagers in an old, modified T-bird gave him a lift all the way to Benson, twelve miles. He was there by nine-thirty, and had walked the remaining three miles to Belair by ten-thirty. That left fifteen miles to Fawn Grove. After finding Route 24, he started hiking north, wondering if he would be lucky enough to catch another long ride. He was not—and ended up walking the rest of the way, alone and in the dark.

It would be the most frightening night Carl would remember for a long time to come. There was a moon, but periodically its light would be neutralized by great dark clouds that had the effect of throwing a shroud over the land. The highway was narrow, with very little shoulder; the asphalt along its edge was cracked and broken, making level walking difficult. When the clouds covered the moonlight, Carl found himself stumbling, tripping, scraping his ankles.

The blackness around him was full of night sounds: in the nearby trees, in the fields, in the culvert next to where he walked. They were rustling sounds, scurrying sounds, screeching, scratching sounds—frightening sounds. They came suddenly out of the night, some of them so close to his feet that he actually cried out and jumped away, startled. Carl wished fervently that he had not left his Boy Scout pack on the Denmark lawn. If he had his Scout flashlight and his Scout pocketknife, he would not have felt nearly so vulnerable.

By twelve-thirty he had reached the hamlet of Forest Hill, which at that hour was closed up tight. Carl decided to rest there and eat the peanut butter-and-cheese crackers the service station attendant had given him. He found another service 53 station, a small one on a corner, its office and islands dark, and sat down between the pumps. Before he had eaten his first cracker, the smell of gasoline became too overpowering and he had to move. He finally sat outside the locked rest rooms and finished the package, wolfing the crackers down, not realizing how starved he had been. When they were gone, he was still hungry; he licked the crumbs from the inside of the cellophane wrapper. Back at the pumps, he used the radiator hose to drink as much water as he could hold; he also washed off his face and hands, feeling refreshed afterward.

Reluctantly, not really wanting to leave the comparative comfort and security of the dark little hamlet, but at the same time still wanting desperately to get to his grandmother's house, he started walking again. Between Forest Hill, Maryland, and the Pennsylvania state line, there were eight miles of nothing. No hamlets, no lights, no traffic—nothing. To Carl it was as if he were walking in a great void. He continued to stumble and trip on the broken asphalt; to be frightened by critters of the night fields: one scurried across his foot while he was relieving himself, causing him to jump so that he pissed all over one pants leg. And he continued to be hungry for the entire rest of the trip. But he kept moving, kept his feet moving like a robot, and slowly, gradually, the long, lonely miles, one by weary one, fell behind him. He kept hoping to pass a road sign that would tell him how far he had yet to go, but for three hours there was not even a route marker. Eventually he came to one, sometime between three and four in the morning, but all it read was ROUTE 165, a crossroad up ahead. Then, a couple of miles farther on, another: ROUTE 136. But still no lights, no people, no traffic. Finally, around five o'clock, although he had not even the remotest idea of the time, he came to a simple road sign out in the middle of nothing else, which read: PENNSYLVANIA STATE LINE. The Parkville service station attendant's words came back to him: *Fawn Grove is two miles the other side of the line.*

Two miles! It seemed incredible to him that he only had that far to go. He actually smiled in the darkness, felt good inside, and for the first time in so long he could not remember when, he was not aware of carrying around inside him the lead weight of being all alone in the world, of not having anyone. He had a *grandmother,* someone tied to him by blood, and she was only two miles away!

In the chill early morning darkness, Carl picked up his pace a step or two, so that he could get there quicker. He was feeling

54

so good that he was not even aware that blood was seeping out of broken blisters on both of his feet.

His grandmother found him at eight-thirty, curled up in a corner of her front porch, deep in exhausted sleep. "Why, I declare! Junior, is that you, boy?" Carl's middle name was actually "Junior," even though he was not a junior to any senior having the same name. It was simply a name Archie had come up with. "Junior, wake up, boy," his grandmother said, shaking him. "Where'd you come from? How'd you get here?"

Slowly, with difficulty, Carl came awake and answered her questions. "I walked, Grandma. All the way from Parkville." He decided not to mention the twelve-mile ride in the T-bird; it sounded better to say he had walked all the way. Besides, he was now aware that his feet *felt* as if he had; they were burning, throbbing, and felt sticky inside his socks.

"Come in the house, boy," his grandmother said. "I'll fix you something to eat. We'll have a look at those feet of yours too; I reckon they'll be blistered raw."

They were. His heels, the outside of each big toe, and the outside of each little toe were rubbed clean of skin and smeared bloody. "I declare," his grandmother said when she got his shoes and socks off. She made him soak his feet in warm water with boric acid in it. It hurt terribly and he cried, but his grandmother told him it was for his own good; she stroked his hair and gave him hot biscuits and maple syrup to eat while he was doing it. When they were through with that, she doctored his beat-up face and listened as he told her what had happened on the Boy Scout camping trip, and at the Denmarks', and at Ruth's house the night before. It all seemed like such a long time ago; he could hardly believe he had run away from the Denmarks' front yard just a little more than twelve hours earlier.

His grandmother ran a tub for him to bathe, and put some salve on his feet, and put him to bed in clean, fresh-smelling linen on a foldaway cot in her spare room. Just before he drifted off, Carl thought how good it felt to be someplace where he could say he belonged; with someone he could say he belonged *to*. He began imagining at once that the spare room might become *his* room; that his grandmother might say to the Denmarks, to his mother, to Ruth, to the *world:* "Junior's going to stay with me now. My house will be his home from now on. Don't nobody bother about us none; we'll get on just fine."

He slept the best, deepest, most restful sleep he ever remembered sleeping that day; got up for an hour to eat some supper his grandmother fixed him; then went back to bed for the rest of the night and slept until six o'clock the next morning.

"I declare," his grandmother said, "I never saw a body sleep so much. You slept like you'd been knocked in the head."

When Carl finally did get up, he could barely walk. His feet were swollen and scabbed. This time it was cold water with boric acid that his grandmother made him soak them in; and after the initial shock, it actually felt good. He had slept in an old nightshirt—his grandmother could not remember whose it had been—and she had washed and ironed his clothes for him. "What in the world kind of shirt is that with all the writing on it?" she inquired of his Boy Scout shirt with its troop and patrol patches, merit badge patches, and national insignia. Carl explained it to her. He hoped there would be a Boy Scout troop in Fawn Grove so that he could join up again, because he really liked the Scouts. This time, he promised himself, there would be no cutting tent ropes or other mischief. He would work hard and do well and make his grandmother proud of him.

For two days Carl hobbled around his grandmother's little house, talking to her, being with her, luxuriating in his new feeling of belonging. For the first time in his life he was excited and enthusiastic about the future; he had positive feelings about what lay ahead of him, instead of the suspicion and dread that he had always felt. There was something wonderful about not being an outsider. In his eager young mind he began to make secret plans for all the things he would do for his grandmother: the yard work, the woodcutting and stacking, the garden weeding, going to the store, any lifting and carrying that had to be done. Why, she wouldn't ever have to do *anything* anymore except cook and sew and clean; he would do *all* the man's work, all the hard work, the heavy work.

He planned to get a job too; maybe working in a service station like the guy who had given him the package of crackers. Carl intended to pay him back for that someday. Maybe in a few years, when he was grown. Drive up in a new car and say, "Hey, remember a kid you let look at a map and gave some peanut-butter-and-cheese crackers to a long time ago? Well, that was me. Here's a little something to pay you back." And he'd hand the guy a ten or even a twenty. Yessir, nobody was going to be able to say that Carl Junior Issacs ever forgot anybody who ever did him a good turn.

Or a bad turn either, he thought darkly, his mind going back to Jennifer Denmark and the beating she had given him. But it had been worth it, he decided, an involuntary smile forming on his lips. For two reasons. One, he had whipped the shit out of that rotten little prick Jacky. And two, it had driven him to finally run away, and had been responsible for him ending up at his grandmother's house.

"What in the world are you grinning at, Junior?" his grandmother asked, noticing his smile.

Carl went over and put an arm around her. "I'm just happy, Grandma," he said. It was the first time in his life he had ever said that.

Carl would always remember those three happy days at his grandmother's house. It was like he was in a new world, like he had stepped out of the old world of strife, tension, uncertainty—stepped into a new world of calm, reassurance, familiarity. Whenever he looked back on those three days he would realize how naive he had been to think that no one would find out where he was; to believe that his new world was secure, inviolable, that because he *felt* good about it his life was now sacrosanct. He was on such a natural high that it simply did not occur to him that his grandmother would notify his mother of his whereabouts. And that Ruth would then know. And her husband Russell. And Lois. And Ann. And eventually the case worker from Welfare. And the Denmarks. And the police.

Carl was stunned when the police showed up at his grandmother's house to take him back. He barely heard his grandmother trying to explain. "I'd like to let you stay, Junior, you know I would. But all I've got is my pension, and that's barely enough for me to get by on myself. Anyway, I'm too old to try taking care of a boy your age; you'd be too much for me. Besides which, you're a ward of the court in Maryland. Why, I could get in all manner of trouble with the Maryland authorities and the Pennsylvania authorities if I hid you. We got to obey the rules, Junior; we got to obey the law. You understand that, don't you, boy?"

Carl did not answer her. He was too numb to answer. Seldom in his young life had he had dreams; then to have them, and see them shattered so suddenly, was as traumatic as being flipped into the air and thrown violently to the ground. He felt dizzy, nauseated, short of breath; felt as if the air had been forced out of his chest by a sudden blow.

"These people know what's best for you, Junior," his grand- 57 mother assured him. "You just mind what they tell you and everything will be all right, hear?"

He heard, but he did not reply. He simply let the policeman lead him away.

That afternoon he was back in Maryland, sitting in the same welfare office he had sat in the day three years earlier when the welfare people had taken Hazel, Robert, Billy, and himself out of school and farmed them out to foster homes. This time there was a different woman behind the desk.

"Well, Carl," she said pleasantly, "let's see if we can mend your fences with Mr. and Mrs. Denmark." She picked up the phone and dialed their number.

Carl sat staring at the floor, having already made up his mind to run away if they sent him back to the Denmarks. Only next time, he decided coldly, he would not run to *somebody,* because there was no one he could trust, no one he could count on not to turn him in. The next time he ran, he would simply run to some*place,* not somebody.

The welfare woman was talking on the phone to Jennifer Denmark. "Well, of course, I understand, Mrs. Denmark," she was saying. "You have every right to feel that way. But the boy *has* been with you and your family for three years. . . . Yes, I know you have, Mrs. Denmark; our records reflect what an exceptionally good home you've given Carl. . . . Yes, there's no doubt that you've done more for him than anyone's ever done. That's why we feel so strongly about returning him to you, reestablishing the relationship. . . ."

The welfare woman fell silent for several minutes and sat listening to what Carl imagined was a long recital of his short-comings and transgressions. Occasionally she tried to interject a "Yes, but," or a "You're right, of course, but," only to be turned back by Jennifer Denmark's refusal to be interrupted, her determination to paint Carl as worthless and undeserving as she possibly could. Listening to the welfare woman's end of the conversation, Carl knew he would not have to run away from the Denmarks again.

"Yes, well, if you're certain that you feel that way," the welfare woman said at last, with a quiet sigh. "If we kept him here a few days or a week, do you suppose there's any chance you might. . . . No. I see. All right. Well, thank you for your time anyway, Mrs. Denmark."

The welfare woman hung up. She sat drumming her fingers

soundlessly on the desktop. Carl kept his head lowered, eyes down.

"Well," she said at last, "the Denmarks don't want you back."

"Good," Carl mumbled. He did not mean for her to hear him, but she did.

"Good? Did I hear you say good? Listen to me, young man: those people gave you a home for three long years! Do you realize how hard it is to place a kid your age in a foster home? Not many families will take a scrawny, homely kid your age, with the problems that usually come along with you: acne, masturbation, eating like a goddamned pony. You were damned lucky to get the Denmarks, people who would be a family to you—"

"They were never a family to me!" Carl suddenly spat. He was unable to contain himself any longer. "They never cared anything about me! They did it for the money the state paid them! And so they'd have somebody to work for them for nothing! How come they never made their own goddamned kid work? Do you think if I'd been part of their family, they'd've made me sleep in a corner of the goddamned basement!"

The welfare woman's eyes were riveted on his. Her face became a spiteful, tight-lipped mask. "Don't you *dare* speak to me in that manner!" she said coldly. "And for your information, I know where there are plenty of kids who would be happy to have that basement corner."

Carl lowered his eyes again. He did not ask where.

"Don't you want to know where?" she asked.

He refused to answer. It was perhaps at that moment in his life that he decided to stop playing the game by their rules.

"I'm going to tell you anyway," she said. Her voice was now flat and threatening. "At the state reformatory, Carl." She hesitated a beat, then added, "Which is exactly where this office is going to recommend that you be placed."

Carl swallowed his fear down a dry throat. He did not care. At least in reform school he would not be an outsider.

9

Sheriff Archie Day paced back and forth at the foot of the hill up which the three fugitives had run. His left jaw was swollen with a fresh plug of tobacco. "How much headstart you figure they've got?" he asked around the chaw.

"Fi'teen minutes," one of the deputies answered.

Sheriff Day squinted up the hill and shook his head. In woods like those, fifteen minutes was a damn good lead.

"Did you take that bag of Miz Matney's money and lock it in your trunk like I told you to?"

"Yessir, I did, Sheriff."

The sheriff walked over to George, who was standing in a small group of deputies with his wrists handcuffed behind him. He stood squarely in front of him, hands on his hips. "I'm going to ask you some direct questions, boy," he said in a neutral, nonthreatening tone, "and I want some straight answers, hear? I got a dozen men out here and I don't want none of 'em killed or shot up. What kind of weapons has them three boys up there got?"

George shrugged. "Guns."

There was an immediate irritable shuffling among the men, but Archie Day held up a hand to quiet them. "I know they got guns," he said to George in the same tone. "What kind of guns? What caliber?"

George shrugged again. "I don't know much about guns."

The sheriff drew his own .38, causing George to draw back slightly in fear. "They have guns like this one?" he asked, holding it out in his palm.

"Yeah," George nodded. "Like that."

A deputy stepped forward angrily. "You better start saying 'yes, sir,' boy."

"Never mind," Archie Day told the deputy. "Do they have any other guns?" he asked George. "Bigger guns? Rifles or shotguns?"

60

George shook his head. "No. Those are still in the car."

The sheriff holstered his pistol. Turning away, he looked at his watch. The three white boys were about twenty minutes ahead of them now. Motioning to his chief deputy to join him, he walked over to his radio car. "I want to try and do this with no shooting if I can," he said. "Them boys don't have no place to go up there. All they can do is wait us out or come back down. If they come back down, it'll probably be here, or at John's Branch, or down near War. What we got to do is get enough men to cover all them places, and patrol the roads between them. I want you to get hold of the four state troopers assigned to the county and get them down here. Also contact the two town officers in War. How many'll that make? Let's see: you, me, twelve deputies, four troopers, two from War— that's twenty." He mulled the number over in his mind for a moment. "Better get up a posse," he decided. "Small posse. Maybe six men. We'll put 'em in the unlikely spots, keep the regular peace officers in the front line."

Archie Day looked around as a speeding sheriff's jeep skidded up to the crossroads and stopped. A reserve deputy that he had left on duty in Welch came running over to him with a sheet of teletype bulletin. "We didn't figure we ought to send this out over the air, Sheriff," he said, a little nervously.

Archie Day read the bulletin. His expression became first a frown, then an incredulous stare, as if he could not believe the words he saw before him. He turned and looked curiously at George, then walked slowly over to him.

"Your name George Dungee, boy?"

George half grinned self-consciously. "Yeah."

"You and them other boys escape from prison over in Maryland?"

"Yeah."

Archie Day shifted the plug of tobacco in his cheek and wet his lips. "You boys been down in Georgia?" he asked quietly.

George shifted his eyes and would not look at the sheriff now. But he answered the question. "Yeah."

"Good God almighty," Archie Day muttered, feeling slightly ill. He turned away from George, revulsed by the sight and proximity of him. Looking at his deputies, he selected two he was certain he could rely on and said, "Take him into Welch and lock him up. One of you stay there with him, the other come on back. I don't want nobody talking to him." He pointed a finger at the men. "And I don't want no rough stuff, 61 understand? This boy's gonna make the papers and TV. I don't intend for us to look bad. Y'all understand me?"

When he was certain he had made himself clear, Archie Day let the deputies leave with George in tow. He read the teletype bulletin again, shook his head in disbelief, then folded it and buttoned it into his shirt pocket.

"All right, men, gather 'round here," he said. "I'm gonna spread y'all out around this mountain so we can keep them other three boxed in up there."

In the car on the way to Welch, the deputy in the passenger seat turned to look at George, who was sitting in the back seat cage. "Say, boy, how come you're running with three white boys? Y'll got yourselves some kind of integrated gang?"

George shrugged, smiled shyly, did not reply.

"Which prison did y'all break out of in Maryland?"

George frowned. "I don't know the name of it."

"Jesus Christ," the deputy said under his breath.

"Better leave him alone," the driver said. "Sheriff don't want us talking to him."

"I ain't hurting him none, am I? Hey, boy, what was it you and them others done down in Georgia anyway?"

George swallowed and looked out the window.

"Must have been something pretty horrible. Sheriff Day looked like he was about to puke when he read that teletype. What'd y'all do down in Georgia, huh?"

George chewed on his lower lip and tried to hold back the tears he felt welling up in his eyes. His hands were still cuffed behind him, forcing him to sit hunched forward and a little sideways. He kept staring out the window, watching the thick roadside foliage stream past as the police car, red light flashing, sped toward somewhere to put him in jail.

What'd y'all do down in Georgia?

The deputy's words clawed at his mind like the talons of an avenging bird, causing visions to explode like flashbulbs in his head. Everything he saw was horrible, and when he saw the woman it was the most horrible of all. As Carl had done in the car, George now closed his eyes as tightly as he could, hoping to blot out the scenes behind the darkness of his lids. But he learned at once that it would not work. If anything, the picture of the woman, her body so stark white—the first white woman he had ever seen without clothes on—was even clearer than when his eyes were open. It was as if the blackness of his closed eyelids provided the perfect backdrop for her whiteness.

62

George shook his head in frustration at not being able to purge the awful visions from his mind. He gave up on the tears and consciously let them flood over his cheeks, and streak warmly, wetly, down to his neck.

"Oh, God," he said, not to the deputy questioning him, but in his own mind actually to *God:* "Oh, God, I'm in big trouble now! They done got me in big trouble now! Those white boys done got me in it now! Big trouble! Big *white* trouble!"

The deputy who had asked all the questions stared at his emotional prisoner and shook his head curiously. What in the *hell,* he wondered, had this nigger and those three white boys done down in Georgia?

Maybe he could find out after they got him in a cell up in Welch.

Archie Day got all his men in place just before dark. Circling the mountain, he made an inspection of each assigned post to ensure that every deputy, every trooper, every town marshal, and especially every deputized volunteer, was in the safest, most secure position should the three fugitives come down in their particular area. He cautioned everyone individually against taking unnecessary chances. "I don't want none of you killed or shot up," he said over and over again that night. " 'Member, we're playing a waiting game; don't nobody go out looking for trouble, hear?"

Later, he sat in his patrol car with the interior lights on, studying a map of the mountain. There was now no way that the fugitives could escape; they were irreversibly trapped. But Archie Day was worried about something else. What was he to do when morning came? The fugitives would still be up there; his men would still be staked out at the bottom—it would be a standoff. Except that with each hour that passed, the three fugitives got a little more of an edge—because they could sleep, and his men could not. By morning, his men would have been up all night: they would be tired, sleepy, incautious; while the fugitives, who would have probably slept, would be rested, alert, and desperate. Sooner or later there would be a confrontation between the fugitives and some of his men. It would happen whether the fugitives came down the mountain and made a run for it, or whether he reached the point where he had to send his men up to flush them out. The standoff between the two sides was of necessity a temporary condition. Archie Day knew he would have to eventually take some kind of positive action; he could not keep the mountain surrounded 63 indefinitely. Besides, if he just sat on the situation, it was going to make him and his department look bad. The FBI would be there first thing in the morning, he knew. They had a tendency to muscle in and take over whatever they were involved in. It was their nature, he supposed: too many TV shows had been made about them. But Archie Day didn't want the Charleston office of the FBI getting any credit that should rightly go to Clarence Shelton, who had called him to set up the dragnet and then chased the fugitives into it; or to the deputies, troopers, and others who were going to be out there in the dark all night subject to being shot down without warning. Archie Day knew he had to do something—but whatever it was had to involve absolute minimum risk to the force he had deployed around the mountain.

It was ten o'clock before he hit on what to do. Through his car radio, he called his office in Welch. "I want you to put in a call to the prison over in Bland. See if you can get a feller named H. R. Call on the line. If you can get him, patch me through. If you can't get him, leave word for him to get in touch with me soon's possible."

Hanging the mike back on the radio unit, Archie slumped down in the seat of the car and listened to the night sounds. Those three boys up there, he knew, were listening to the same sounds.

"What in hell was that!" Billy hissed, grabbing Carl's arm, moving up close to him in the darkness. Carl wrenched his arm away.

"Goddamn it, don't jump on me like that!" he snapped. "Jesus Christ, Billy, you're worse than these fucking animals when it comes to scaring us!"

"I can't help it," Billy snapped back. "These woods are scaring the shit out of me! Why'd we have to run up here in the first place?"

Wayne cleared his throat and spat. " 'Cause there wasn't no bus station handy, man, why do you think? You fucking little asshole."

"Leave him alone, Wayne," said Carl.

"Well, shit," said Wayne. "I mean, why'n the fuck does he *think* we run up here? Because there wasn't no other fucking place *to* run. I mean, shit, Carl."

"All right. Just leave him alone."

"Well, make him keep his fucking mouth shut."

64

"Keep your mouth shut, Billy. Now come on, both of you, we got to keep going."

They trotted along a mountain trail, stumbling, tripping, running into low branches, leaping aside when some animal shrieked and startled them. The moon was bright and they were able to see fairly well except in the shadow of the trees. Carl again remembered the night he had run away from the Denmarks and walked all but twelve miles of the way to his grandmother's house.

"Do you know where the fuck you're leading us, Carl, or are you just walking?" Wayne asked, half challenging.

"I know exactly which way I'm leading you, Wayne," the younger brother answered confidently. "I'm leading you north, that's where. Don't forget, I was in the Boy Scouts, Wayne. I know all about this kind of shit. See that group of stars up there that looks like a dipper with a handle? Well, that handle points to the North Star: see it there, that bright fucker? All's we got to do is follow that star and we're heading north. Which is the direction of Maryland." He paused for effect, to let Wayne and Billy digest just how smart he was; then added, "Wayne, anytime you'd rather do the leading, all you got to do is let me know and the goddamned job's yours. You can have it right now if you fucking want it."

Wayne remained silent.

"Well, what about it?" Carl pressed.

"No, no, shit, no," Wayne replied irritably. "You're leading, so lead. Just get us the fuck out of the Enchanted Forest, will you?"

"Quick as I can, bro."

Carl turned and resumed walking, not following the North Star at all, merely following the mountain trail, figuring it had to lead somewhere.

In Welch, the curious deputy was still trying to pry some details out of George. He stood looking into the cell.

"How 'bout it, boy? Did you and them white boys abuse some little nigger girl? Or some little white girl? You boys commit some rapes and sex perversions down there in Georgia? Is that what made Sheriff Day like to puke back there on the road? You better answer me, goddamn you, boy, if you know what's good for you!"

George was at the far end of one of the bunks, knees drawn up in front of him, head lowered, face hidden. He was shiver- 65 ing, crying, trembling, all at once, and he was dreadfully afraid that the deputy was going to unlock the cell, come in, and do something terrible to him. But still he would not answer; he *could* not answer. No torture on earth would have been able to make him verbalize the deplorable visions in his mind. If they took him out of his cell and threatened to lynch him—which he was aware they very well might do; after all, this was still the South—even then he would not admit to his part in what had happened.

The jailer came into the cellblock and berated the deputy. "Why in hell don't you leave that nigger alone? What in hell's the matter with you tonight anyhow?"

"I want to know what him and those three white boys *done*," the deputy almost whined.

"Good God almighty," the jailer said impatiently. "If'n I show you a copy of the teletype bulletin, will you shut up and let him be?"

"I didn't know there was no copy," the deputy said, his mouth dropping open.

"A copy came in 'bout an hour after the first one. An update, telling 'bout a car that was found down in Livingston, Alabama."

"Lemme see it then."

"Will you leave the nigger alone?"

"If you say so. Lemme see the bulletin."

George watched the deputy follow the jailer off the cellblock and out to the office. Now he'll know, George thought, but at least he'll have to leave me alone. Oh, God, God, God, the trouble I'm in! God, I wish I could talk to my mamma . . .

It seemed like only a minute before the deputy was back. He stood at the cell bars and peered in at George with loathing.

You animal," he said, almost in a whisper. "You fucking black nigger animal."

Just before eleven, Archie Day's radio sounded. "Sheriff, I got Mr. Call at Bland Prison on the line. I'm patching you in." There was a pause, then: "Go ahead, Sheriff."

"H.R., you there?" the sheriff asked.

"I'm here, Archie. Why ain't you in bed, an old coot like you?"

"Lord, I wisht I was. I was just sitting here taking count of how many of my old bones ache from this night air. Listen, H.R., I got me a sticky one over here. Got three fellers caught up on the hill above War. They're armed and from what I know about 'em, they're ready to shoot. Come daylight I don't want none of my men being used for target practice. I sure would appreciate some he'p getting to them before they decide to come down here shooting. If you could he'p us locate 'em so we could come up on 'em unawares—"

"God almighty, Archie, are you asking me to drive all the way over to *War? Tonight?* Why, that's pretty near a hundred miles!"

"I know it is, H.R.," the sheriff said placatingly. "I know it's a lot to ask. I know it's short notice. And I know you work for the prison and aren't obliged to get involved in local matters like this here. But I got a couple dozen men putting it right on the line tonight, H.R. Good men, ever'one of them. I don't want to read in the paper tomorrow where one or more of 'em got shot up or killed. I know you don't want to neither."

H. R. Call sighed wearily into the phone and muttered a curse or two, but finally he said, "All right, Archie, all right. But it's after eleven already; I won't be able to get ever'thing ready to get out of here for at least an hour, hour and a half. If I leave here by one, figuring the roads and all, I probably won't get there until three-thirty or so."

"That's fine, H.R. Long's it's before daylight." Archie Day told Call where to meet him. "I'll be waitin' on you. I appreciate this, H.R."

After he hung up the radio mike, Archie Day felt better. Stepping out of his car, he turned up his collar against the night air, put a fresh chaw in his mouth, and stared up at the blackness he knew to be the mountaintop.

I've got you now, boys, he thought with relief.

In that blackness at which the sheriff was staring, the three fugitives were still running. Laced with sweat, panting for breath, their legs heavy, they flailed blindly through the woods.

"Where—the hell—is that—fucking star you're following, Carl?" Wayne sputtered, forcing the words out in bursts. Overhead, Wayne saw nothing but darkness.

"Gone—" Carl replied. "Clouds—covering. But—but—this must be the—right way. The path—hasn't—turned—"

"We been—running—for hours," Billy said. "I'm 'bout to—give out—man—"

With that, Billy dropped to the ground. Carl, hearing him   67 collapse, turned and went back. Wayne stopped running and draped an arm around a tree for support.

Carl dropped to his knees beside Billy. "You—all right?"

"I—can't—go—another step—" Billy told him, his words little more than a gasp. "Go on—leave me—"

"Yeah—leave him—" Wayne said eagerly. He himself was equally winded, but more desperate, more than willing to press on. "Come on, Carl—let's go—"

"We—ain't leaving him—" Carl said emphatically. "We—got to—stick together. If we don't—we're nothing, man—"

Billy was lying on his belly, one arm bent under his face. Carl stretched out on his back beside him.

"Shit," Wayne said. He stepped over and stretched out next to Carl.

Lying there, their labored breathing gradually returned to normal. Presently, Billy rolled over so that all three of them were then looking up at the black void of sky above them.

"Goddamn, I'm starving," Billy said after a while. "And thirsty."

"Wonder how the fuck far we run?" Wayne said.

"I figure about ten miles," Carl told him.

"I feel like I run fifty."

"Goddamn, I'm starving," Billy said again.

"Shut the fuck up," Wayne said. "You ain't the only one's hungry. There ain't nothin' to eat, so no sense talking about it." Wayne's voice took on a taunting, mimicking tone. "When we get you back home to Mamma, why, she'll fix you one of those good home-cooked meals that she's so famous for. She'll be so happy to see one of her babies come home again—"

"Shut up!" Billy snapped.

"Go fuck yourself."

"Leave him alone, Wayne, for Christ's sakes," Carl pleaded. Jesus, he was sick and tired of those two. One a fucking crybaby, the other a fucking psycho. I ain't never—*never*—running with no relative again, he promised himself.

They rested for perhaps an hour; then, as the perspiration dried on their bodies, they began to get cold and shiver. Carl was the first to get up.

"Come on, we got to keep moving, keep ourselves from getting cold or we'll catch pneumonia."

"I can't," Billy whined. "I can't run another step, Carl."

"Not running, walking," Carl said. "Just enough to stay warm. Come on."

They moved out in single file, Carl leading, Billy hanging on to Carl's belt from behind, Wayne bringing up the rear. For another hour they walked, following the path, Carl still convinced that it had to lead somewhere.

Finally, when the night had changed to morning and the coldest time of all had imperceptibly come round to envelop them; when the lack of food became an acute condition because of the energy they had expended, the lack of water a constant agony; when the pains in their lungs and calves became stabbing reminders, that, while young, they were not in the best physical condition—they smoked and drank beer and otherwise abused their bodies, thus reducing their strength and endurance—when because of all that they felt exhausted to the point of collapse, wasted to the point of physical illness, ready to simply drop to the ground like a cut rope; then they decided that they had to rest. They left the path they had followed for so many long hours and slipped down into a gully that led to the lip of an overhang: a solid sheet of rock that jutted out from the mountainside and formed a natural roof over a cave of sorts. They had no idea where they were or what kind of natural enclosure they were crawling into—it could have been the lair of a wildcat for all they knew—but by then they did not care. The pain, exhaustion, exposure, hunger, thirst, and fear had all caught up with them. At last, they were spent.

In the embrace of the small enclosure, huddled close together, they began almost at once to feel the benefit of trapped body heat. Within minutes they were becoming noticeably warmer, their aching muscles and sore bodies were relaxing and dispersing some of the fatigue, their dry mouths, raw throats, constricted chests were beginning to feel that life might not be over, after all.

Before they had been in the little cave five minutes, Billy laid his head on Carl's shoulder, fast asleep. Carl and Wayne smoked a cigarette. It burned the hell out of their lungs and raised a chorus of indignant protests in their empty stomachs, but they enjoyed it nevertheless. Then Wayne curled up between Carl and the wall, stuck his feet outside the cave about six inches, and promptly fell to snoring.

Man, Carl thought, what I wouldn't give to be able to go right to sleep like they do. But he had not slept well for a number of years.

Not since his first term in reform school.

10

Five of the older boys in the reform school cottage sauntered over and stood around Carl's bunk in a loose half circle. "What's your name, kid?" one of them asked. He was a tall, skinny boy with acne and mean eyes.

"Carl Issacs."

"Well, Carl Issacs, my name's Trump. Me and my friends here kind of run this cottage when the house parent ain't around. We always greet new guys and kind of get to know them, get to know a little about them. First off, you got any folks?"

"I got a mother," Carl said. "I ain't got a father."

"Your mother gonna be sending you any canteen money? Any allowance?"

Carl had to smile. That was funny. He shook his head. "No, she won't be sending me nothing."

"That's too bad," Trump said. He looked Carl up and down appraisingly. "You suck cock?"

Carl blushed deeply. "No."

Trump eyed him suspiciously. "You sure? You *ever* sucked cock? Even once?"

"I said no." Five of them notwithstanding, Carl felt his anger rising.

Trump placed both hands on his hips. "If you ain't got no money coming in, and you won't suck cock, how the fuck you expect to get along in here, man?"

Carl shrugged. "I don't know."

Another of the boys, shorter, stockier, with a vulgar look about his lips, nudged Trump with his elbows. "Maybe he'd like to learn to suck cock."

"No, I wouldn't," said Carl.

"Hey, shithead, I wasn't talking to you," the stocky boy said
belligerently.

"Well, I *was* talking to you," Carl shot back, "and I don't want to learn nothing!"

The stocky kid made a threatening move toward him. Stepping back, Carl brought his fists up to meet him. But Trump stopped the other boy.

"Not now, Jonesy," he said. "Tonight."

The five boys sauntered away, leaving Carl by his bunk. Glancing around, Carl saw that most of the other boys in the cottage were looking at him. But no one made a friendly overture or acted like they wanted to help him. He sat on the floor next to his bunk, back to the wall, and ignored them all.

It was Carl's first day in the Maryland State Training School. After the Denmarks had refused to have him back in their home, the welfare people had remanded him to the court of which he was a ward, with a recommendation that he be placed in the state training school. The court, which processed numerous such cases every week, rarely opposed Welfare's suggestion. After all, the welfare people were the professionals; they had studied the background of the ward involved, knew all the exigencies of the case that the court had neither the time or inclination to learn, so clearly they were best suited to decide where a particular ward should be domiciled. If Welfare said that Carl Issacs belonged in reform school, the court was not about to argue with them.

When he arrived at training school, Carl and two others were given showers, haircuts, cursory physical examinations to check for contagion of any kind, and an assortment of institution-issue clothing. "You'll each be assigned to a cottage," the receiving counselor told them, and then read off their names and told them which cottage they would live in. Later, an older boy showed them all where the cottages were.

The house parent in charge of Carl's cottage was a middle-aged man named Willis, a typical low-paid civil service institution employee who did only what his job description called for and nothing more. As long as his young charges caused him no unusual problems, he left them free to do pretty much what they wanted to do. Which was why Trump and his gang had control of the Cottage.

Carl went to supper that first night thinking that if he got the chance he would make a break for it. He did not relish the idea of going back to the cottage after supper; but he did not want to try running away before supper because he was very hungry. He found the training school food to be plain and a   71 little greasy after being used to Jennifer Denmark's cooking. But at least there was enough of whatever he wanted, and he was not obliged to take anything he didn't like.

When supper was over, Carl walked around outside looking for a way to escape. There was no wall, only a chain-link fence, but that was high and formidable looking. There was no sign of guards, as such, but nearly everywhere Carl looked he saw training school employees coming and going. His brief scrutiny revealed neither an opportunity nor a route to escape from the place. And after a while he was told by one of the counselors to report back to his cottage because evening curfew was approaching.

With some trepidation, Carl returned to the cottage. Willis, the house parent, called him into his quarters. "Only got one rule in my cottage," he said, "and that's a simple one that every boy can understand: Keep out of trouble. Follow that rule and you'n me'll get along just fine. Okay, you've already got your bunk assigned and your things put away. For the next few days you'll be classified to determine where and when you'll work, and how many hours a day you'll be required to attend school. In the morning when the other boys go to their assignments, you just stay in until somebody, one of the doctors or teachers, sends for you. But don't just crap out while you're waiting 'cause that don't look good. Keep busy—get a broom and sweep down the cottage, get a rag and dust the windowsills, something. I'll explain your schedule in more detail after you've been classified and get your assignments. Okay, that's all."

Carl was tempted to tell him about Trump, Jonesy, and the others, to see if there was something he could do about it. But as soon as Willis dismissed him the house parent immediately turned to some paperwork on his desk, ignoring Carl. So Carl left and went back to his bunk.

No one paid much attention to him for the rest of the evening. A couple of kids who bunked on either side of him exchanged a few words with him, but for the most part he was left alone. Everyone knew that Trump and his gang were out to get him that night, and no one wanted to get involved. As the evening passed, Carl became more and more nervous. Whenever he glanced down where Trump and the others had their bunks, one of the kids, usually Jonesy, was looking at him. By the time lights-out came around, Carl's skin was crawling with fear.

72   Carl lay in bed wide-awake after the lights went out. He lay

on his back, very still, arms at his side, eyes shifting left and right as sounds in the night dormitory reached his ears—sounds of coughing, sniffing, bedsprings squeaking, an occasional whisper, a whimper. Carl had no idea what was going on in the darkness around him, and he didn't care. All that concerned him were the boys who had said that they would come and get him "tonight." He was determined to stay awake and alert, to be as ready as he could for them. Several times as he lay there, he had to wipe off the sweat from his palms on the thin blanket covering him. Although his hands were sweaty, his throat had gone dry; he badly wanted a drink of water, but he knew he dared not get up and walk the length of the dormitory to the water fountain. That would have made things too easy for them. If they were going to—well, whatever they planned to do to him—the least he intended was to make it as difficult as possible for them.

Lights-out had been at nine o'clock. An hour later—it seemed much longer—the night noise of the cottage had quieted down. Several boys had gotten up to go to the bathroom or get drinks of water, but that had been earlier; now there was little noise, even less movement. Involuntarily, Carl began to get sleepy. His eyelids became heavy and he could not suppress frequent yawns. Maybe, he began to think, they would not come. Maybe the whole thing had been a bluff, just to test him.

Lying there, Carl thought about his little sleeping corner in the Denmark basement. It had not been that bad, really. Not physically anyway. Only the thought of it had been bad; the *idea* of it, the belittlement, the indignity. And the stigma of every other kid in the neighborhood knowing not only that his mother was no good and didn't want him, but that the people who *did* want him, the Denmarks, would not even convert the spare bedroom—the "guest" room they called it, although no guest ever stayed in it—into a bedroom for him. A nice bedroom like Jacky had, with model planes hanging from the ceiling, and posters of baseball players, and a student desk in the corner, and a world globe . . .

It was while he was thinking about that ideal bedroom he never had that he felt someone's hands grab his right arm and hold it down. It happened so quickly that he did not have time to react before his left arm was grabbed also. A towel was pressed against his mouth and held firmly in place while he tried desperately to shake his face from under it.

"Got him?" he heard someone whisper.

73

Then he felt the blanket being dragged off him, felt hands pulling his undershorts down over his hips, his knees, his feet. His ankles were grabbed and jerked into the air, held up; he felt something firm and round pressing between his buttocks.

Jesus Christ!

Carl managed to get one ankle loose and kicked out, striking nothing, but jerking his body into a sideways wrench that released his mouth from the towel gag.

"Help!" he yelled. "Get away! Get off me! Help! Helllllllp—!"

"Oh, shit!" a voice said in the darkness, and Carl felt his left arm being turned loose.

"Back to your bunks!" came a hushed order from a voice Carl recognized as Trump's. At the same time, Carl felt all the other hands letting go of him. Nevertheless, he continued to yell.

"Help! Get away from me! Help!"

The dormitory lights went on and Willis, the house parent, came rushing in from his quarters upstairs. "All right, knock it off!" he shouted at Carl. "Cut the crap!"

Carl stopped yelling. The entire dormitory fell silent. Willis stood in front of Carl's bunk, hands on hips.

"Nightmare, huh?" he said. "Happens to lots of kids their first night here." He locked eyes with Carl. "Good thing that's all it was. If it was anything else, I'd have to write a report on it, and that's a lot of extra work for me, know what I mean? So I'm glad it was just a nightmare. Think you can go back to sleep now?"

Carl shrugged. "I guess so."

"Let's hear, 'Yes, sir.'"

"Yes, sir."

"Good boy." Willis looked down the line of bunks to where Trump and his boys slept in a group. "I hear any more ruckus in here tonight and I'm gonna do some ass-kicking," he promised pointedly.

The lights were turned out again. The dormitory remained silent. The only sound that could be heard was around Carl's bunk: the occasional chattering of his teeth as he lay there shivering in fear most of the night.

After breakfast the next morning, Carl returned to the cottage as he had been instructed, to wait for a teacher or doctor to summon him. There was another boy waiting also, one who had come in a couple of days before Carl. He was a year older

74

than Carl, but smaller, weaker. His name was Freddy. He and Carl began sweeping the dorm together.

"Trump and those guys'll try again tonight, you know." Freddy said.

Carl shrugged and did not reply.

"You were lucky last night," Freddy said. "Lucky you managed to holler; lucky old Willis was awake to hear you."

Carl kept sweeping, listening but not responding.

"Next time you probably won't be so lucky. Next time they'll probably stuff that towel *in* your mouth to keep you from hollering. Next time—"

"Hey, don't worry about it," Carl interrupted irritably. He stopped sweeping. "How's come they ain't ganging up on you?" he asked tersely.

"They don't have to," Freddy said. "I let 'em fuck me." He looked down at the floor. "It's easier than getting beat on."

"Yeah, sure," Carl said. "Easier." He started sweeping again.

A runner came and got Freddy to take him somewhere, and a little later another one came for Carl. He was taken to the medical section for his psychological evaluation. On his way over, he again scouted possible escape routes, but again was unable to find any.

Carl spent all morning in the medical section, going from room to room, doctor to doctor, answering questions, looking at pictures, working puzzles, drawing nude figures, telling about himself over and over again. At noon he was let go to the dining room to eat; then it was back to Medical for more examinations, the complete physical this time. They finished with him at three-thirty and had a runner take him back to his cottage.

The dorm was empty when Carl got back. Still thinking escape, he walked to each window in the long room and studied what he could see of the institution's grounds. The problem with getting out, as he saw it, was that there was too much empty space: too much lawn, too many sidewalks, too much room between buildings. There was no place to hide, to duck behind or into, no way to keep from being observed by the numerous training school employees who seemed to be moving constantly about the grounds.

Disgusted, Carl returned to his own bunk and sat on the floor. He resigned himself to the fact that he was probably going to have to face the night right there again. Chewing his nails, he tried to decide what to do about Trump and his gang. 75

It never occurred to Carl to complain to the administration over Willis. The administration, to him, represented authority. As did the police. And the welfare people. None of them had ever been on his side; to have gone to them for help was a thought totally foreign to him. As far as he was concerned, he was alone. He had to solve *his* problems *himself.*

Carl knew as he mulled it over in his mind that he had only one of two ways to go: give in—or fight.

He also knew there was no question what his choice would be.

He would fight.

It was as he was sitting there that he finally decided *how* to fight. On the other side of the dorm was an empty bunk with its mattress rolled up at one end. Carl stared at the bedsprings for several moments, then went over and unhooked one from the corner. Taking it into the bathroom, he caught the curled end of it under the nozzle of a faucet and pulled as hard as he could until that curled end straightened out. What he then had was a coiled spring four inches long with a stiff piece of metal sticking out two inches at one end. He took it into the shower room and began methodically rubbing it back and forth on the cement floor, filing the end piece to a sharp point. As he filed, he thought about the previous night.

He hoped it would be Jonesy whose eye he speared with his new weapon.

After supper that night, Carl stayed close to his own bunk. He had the bedspring hidden under his pillow, where he could snatch it out in an instant if anyone messed with him before lights-out. He did not think anyone would, however; Trump and his boys were playing cards in a circle on the floor down at their end of the dorm. They did not seem to have Carl on their minds at all, did not even look in his direction. From time to time, one of the older boys who was not a member of the gang would go up to Trump, whisper in his ear, and slip him some money. Trump would bob his chin at one of two bunks near his own, and either Freddy or one of the other younger boys would accompany the older boy into the shower room. For the entire evening, the only one who even came close to directly paying any attention to Carl was Jonesy. The stocky youth with the perpetual vulgar sneer strolled down to Carl's end of the dorm twice. Neither time did he look intentionally at Carl; but on each trip he stood where Carl could not help seeing him, and with his right hand cupped and lifted his genitals suggestively. Both times the boys in nearby bunks turned and looked at Carl. He avoided meeting their eyes.

When lights-out time came, everyone in the dorm seemed to get into bed with a minimum of delay, as if they were all waiting for what they knew would happen. The usual bedtime horseplay and the barrage of complaints at having to extinguish the lights were both waived, it seemed, in favor of getting house parent Willis out of the dorm and into his own quarters as quickly as possible. There was an undercurrent of agitated anticipation in the air: something was going to *happen*!

Carl climbed into bed in his underwear and pulled the blanket under his chin. He had already sensed the tension in the room, already caught several boys looking at him when they thought he wasn't paying any attention to them; he knew that everybody was waiting for Trump and his gang to grab him again. Earlier, when Jonesy made one of his deliberately casual trips up to Carl's end of the dorm, Carl had seen him whisper to another boy and had caught a few words of it: "— shower room—later—anybody who wants some—" Carl was sure Jonesy was talking about him; he was sure that Jonesy and the others were planning to drag him into the shower room tonight instead of taking him in his bunk.

As soon as the lights went out, Carl pushed the blanket down, reached to the side of the bunk, and got his shoes. They were heavy, hightop brogans, which he put back on and laced up as quickly and quietly as possible. Then he retrieved his bedspring from under the pillow, turned the pillow sideways where his head should have been, and eased himself down to the foot of the bunk. He stretched out, head at the bottom, feet on either side of the pillow, one fist tightly gripping the filed-down bedspring. Eyes wide. Lips parted. Ears straining for sound, any sound.

He waited.

They came twenty minutes after lights-out. Carl knew they were at the side of the bunk: he sensed rather than saw or heard them. The first touch came when one of them tried to throw a towel over his face again, and caught the pillow instead. At that moment, Carl drew his right foot back and shot it forward like a catapult. It connected with a *thud* and someone was thrown back onto the bunk next to Carl's.

"Hey, man get off'n me!" the bunk's occupant growled.

77

Meanwhile, Carl kicked again, toward the opposite side of his bunk, and connected again, though less solidly this time.

"This prick's got shoes on!" Carl's second victim hissed in the darkness. Carl stretched and kicked him again.

Now hands began to search for him, trying to locate and grab him. Carl drew himself into a ball and lashed out with the bedspring, moving it through the darkness in random arcs.

"Ow! Goddamn it!" someone yelled.

"Ouch! What the fuck was that?"

Time and again the hands trying to subdue Carl would meet instead the filed-down point of the bedspring. It scraped open arms, punctured hands, ripped fingers.

"Son-of-a-bitch!" one of them yelled.

"Goddamn fucker—"

When the hands stopped reaching for him, Carl began kicking again. Holding the bedspring between his teeth so as not to lose it, he gripped the foot of the bunk with both hands and steadied himself as he slam-kicked with both feet, moving his knees like pistons. He felt his feet connect with stomachs, thighs, chests, even one guy's balls. Good! he thought. Hope that was Jonesy.

He kept kicking and kept kicking, relentlessly, exhilaratingly, until there was no one left to kick.

When the dorm door crashed open and Willis flipped on the lights, Carl was back in bed the right way, his blanket up under his chin. Willis looked suspiciously at him but said nothing. He stalked down to Trump's area, only to find Trump and his boys also in bed.

"You little bastards are trying my patience," he announced loudly. "This is the second night in a row that I've had my TV interrupted! I warn you, one more time and it's the parade field for all of you—*all day Saturday!*"

Carl would learn later that Willis was referring to the punishment of standing in one spot on the parade field for two four-hour shifts, interrupted only by lunch. It was a miserable, much dreaded punishment, one that never failed, at least temporarily, to make a cottage's occupants behave.

After Willis left, the darkened dormitory was totally quiet for perhaps five minutes. Then a voice that Carl recognized as Trump's said, "Hey, Issacs! I'll stay behind for sick call in the morning. Let's you and me talk, okay?"

Carl did not immediately answer.

"Okay?" Trump persisted.

"Sure, okay," Carl said finally.

He forced himself to stay awake a while longer, in case Trump's invitation to talk was only a ploy to make him let his guard down. But finally a heavy weariness overcame him, a weariness created not only by the few moments of stark desperation as he fought, but also by the extraordinary tension that had drained his young body and mind: tension that was a great weight within him; tension that was loneliness; tension that was fear. When he was finally forced by his own fatigue to rest, he relaxed as if drugged: deeply, warmly, even pleasantly.

Only one part of him remained alert: his right hand still held the sharpened bedspring.

When Trump remained in the cottage the next morning, he and Carl faced each other across a laundry table at the back of the dorm.

"Okay, Issacs, you've proved you're tough," said Trump. "And you've shown us that you've got some kind of weapon to fight with. But how the fuck long do you think you can keep it up?"

"Long as I have to," Carl said.

"What if we manage to take your weapon, whatever it is, away from you? What then?"

Carl grunted softly and tossed the bedspring onto the table. "I can make another one in ten minutes," he said.

Trump picked up the homemade weapon. "A bedspring," he said incredulously. "A fucking bedspring."

"And plenty more if I need 'em," Carl said, waving his arm at the bunks lining the dormitory.

Trump nodded. He tossed Carl's bedspring back onto the table. "You poked holes in three of my guys with that fucking thing last night," he accused. "If you'd have cut 'em any worse, they'd've had to go to the infirmary. Then we'd *all* be up shit creek."

"They're lucky none of them got it in the eye," Carl pointed out. "Especially that Jonesy guy. I *wanted* to get him in the eye."

" 'Course, now *we* can file down bedsprings too," Trump said.

"That won't keep *you* guys from getting cut," Carl told him. "All's that'll mean is that I'll get cut too. I'm willing to take some to give some."

Shaking his head wearily, Trump sat down on the end of the 79 nearest bunk. "So what the fuck are we gonna do about it?"

Carl shrugged. "I don't know. All's I know is that I ain't gonna be getting no money to pay you—and I ain't gonna let you fuck me.

"Forget about the fucking," Trump told him. "My guys don't want to fuck you anymore; they want to kill you now." He thought for a moment, then said, "You sure your old lady ain't gonna send you no allowance?"

Carl grunted to himself. "I'm sure. Look, I'll make you a deal: if my mom sends me any money, I'll give you *all* of it."

"It's just that most old ladies start feeling sorry for their kids when they end up in reform school," Trump explained.

"My mom don't feel sorry for *nobody*," Carl said emphatically.

"Yeah, but most old ladies—"

"Look, man, forget it," Carl insisted. "I'm telling you, *my* old lady's *different.* Just believe me, will you?"

"Okay, okay. But I still gotta figure a way to solve this here problem, you know? I don't want my guys cut up, and I don't want them cutting you up. If word of this gets out, they'll split us all up. I don't want that. But you gotta understand, I got a rep to live up to in this place. If I let you get off with nothing, then my rep is shit from then on. Know what I mean?"

Carl nodded. He understood what Trump was saying; but he did not know how he could help him.

As he sat there thinking, Trump took a pack of gum from his shirt pocket. Unwrapping a stick, he put it in his mouth. Almost as an afterthought, he took a second stick from the pack and tossed it on the table for Carl.

"Thanks," Carl said, delighted. He had not chewed a stick of gum in so long he could not remember when. Gum had been forbidden in the Denmark home.

"Look," Trump said at last, "suppose I *tell* everybody that you're paying off? Suppose I say you're giving me, say, a dollar a week for protection? Would you go along with that?"

"Sure," Carl shrugged, "long as you know you won't be getting it."

"I'll know and you'll know, but nobody else, see? Not even my guys. And if you ever spill to anybody—"

"I won't," Carl swore. "Man, I don't want no more trouble, believe me. Seems like I never have nothing *but* trouble. I won't tell, man. Word of honor."

80   "Okay, kid," said Trump. "Then it's a deal.

The two reform school kids shook hands across the laundry table.

After a week of testing, classifying, and general orientation, Carl was called to a senior counselor's office.

"Well, Carl," he said with a smile, "how do you like it here so far?"

Carl shrugged. "Okay, I guess." To himself, he wondered what in hell the man expected him to say. "I really like it a lot, sir—especially having to fight five guys at once to keep from getting raped." Or, "No sir, I don't like it at all because the older guys want to make me suck cock."

If he said the former, he would be an asshole; if the latter, a fink who would be marked forever.

Easier to shrug it off and say, "Okay, I guess."

"Well, Carl, you're all through with your tests and such. Are you ready to settle down and start earning your way out of here?"

"Sure, I guess," Carl said without hesitation. He knew they would let him out when they *wanted* to let him out.

"All right, we're going to start you in school in a class of sixth- and seventh-graders. You'll go to school half a day, then have a work assignment the other half. How does that sound to you?"

"Okay, I guess. What kind of work will I have to do?"

"That'll be up to your house parent. He has to fill several work assignments from his cottage; he'll decide where you should work."

Carl nodded and asked no further questions.

"Keep your nose clean and obey the rules, Carl," the senior counselor advised. "You can probably get out of here in six months."

Carl thought about that as he walked back to the cottage. Suppose he did get out in six months—then what? Where would he go, what would he do? He wasn't even fourteen yet; they weren't just going to turn him loose. Before he was released from training school, the state would have to find a place for him to go. But where? Not back to the Denmarks, that was for sure. His mother didn't want him. His grandmother? Forget that daydream. Ruth? Maybe; a slight possibility, but not one to really count on. Any place else? Anybody else? No. Not unless it was another foster home.

Wherever they put him, Carl had already made up his mind   81 about one thing: if he didn't like it, he was going to run away. No more bullshit of trying to fit into a family where he didn't belong. That was not for him. No fucking more.

It was past noon when he reported back to the cottage. "School's already over for the day," Willis said, examining the schedule Carl brought back. "But you might as well get started on your work assignment. Go on out back and fall in with the boys lined up there."

Carl found the group, a dozen boys in a loose formation, waiting to be marched to lunch and then to work. Carl fell in at the end of the line.

"What kind of work do you do?" he asked a black boy next to him.

"Gardenin'," the boy replied. "We cuts the weeds and brush around the school; mows the lawns, rakes the leaves. Jus' regular gardenin'."

"Swell," Carl thought out loud. I'm right back where I started when I was a workhorse for Edward Denmark.

The big difference, of course, was that he didn't have to put up with that little prick Jacky anymore. Or call some mean bitch "Mom."

Anyway, it was just for six months. The senior counselor had said he could work himself out in six months.

But at the end of six months, Carl would still be there. With no release in sight.

11

H. R. Call arrived at the rendezvous with Sheriff Archie Day at twenty past four, barely an hour before sunrise.

"Sorry I'm late, Archie," he said, climbing down out of his Scout four-wheeler. "I had to stop at the jail in Bluefield and get some hot coffee to keep awake. Kept dozing at the wheel. Bad habit on these roads."

"You're mighty right about that, H.R.," the sheriff said. "Glad you made it all right. 'Preciate you coming on such short notice." Day peered into the back of the truck. "Who'd you bring?"

"Prince," said Call. "A real sweetheart."

Call turned on the Scout's interior lights so the sheriff could see the dog. Prince was a Rhodesian ridgeback bloodhound the color of caramel candy. His hair was as smooth as glass all over his wiry body except for one place: at the top of his spine just where it curved up to the neck, was a long growth of thick, bristlelike hair, darker than the rest, that grew in the opposite direction, forming a ridge. Thus the name. Prince was four years old, twenty-seven inches high, and weighed a lean seventy pounds.

"A sweetheart," H.R. Call said again. "One of the finest hounds I've ever seen. That dog could track a man through a turpentine factory."

The sheriff and the prison officer walked over to a pickup truck that had a coffee urn balanced on its lowered tailgate. Archie drew coffee for both of them. "Here, this'll warm you up a mite."

As they sipped at the steaming coffee, warming their hands around the styrofoam cups, Archie told Call about the three men trapped up on the mountain. And about the contents of the teletype bulletin in his shirt pocket.

"Great God almighty!" Call said when he heard. "What kind of animals are they, Archie?"

"The worst kind, I reckon. Now don't breathe a word to any of my men out here, 'cause they don't know yet. They just think we're after armed holdup men. But you can see now why I was so anxious to have your help."

"Well, I reckon *so*," Call said soberly. "You say you've got the nigger in jail? Do you think he's safe with you not there?"

"Safe as he'd be anywhere else, I reckon. Don't nobody back there know what they done down in Georgia. And the nigger don't seem like one to talk about it. Fact, he seems like he might be touched," Day added, tapping his head.

"I hope you're right, Archie. God knows, we don't need no lynchings around here."

The two men drank their coffee and stamped their feet to keep the circulation going. A thin fog, with its accompanying dampness, had encircled the base of the mountain by then; that and the thin air made it seem colder than it was. Archie Day knew that up above the fog, where the woods were the thickest, where the three fugitives were, it was warmer. One more thing the three of them had in their favor, he thought.

"H.R., how long do you think it'd take Prince to follow a scent that took him all the way to the top of the mountain?"

"From here? Hell, you're three-quarters of the way to the top already. No longer'n twenty, thirty minutes."

Archie Day looked at his watch. It was quarter of five. He had already had his office check with the weather bureau at the airport in Bluefield, and knew that daylight would break at 5:21, little more than half an hour from then.

"I'd like to be up on the ridge when day breaks," the sheriff said. "What say we take the men I got picked out and ease on up there?"

"You're the boss, Archie," said H.R. Call. "I'll get Prince. You'll admire him, Archie. He's a real sweetheart."

It was surprisingly warm in the little cave where Carl, Wayne, and Billy were huddled together. They were above the fog and sheltered by thick woods and the cave was so small their accumulated body heat warmed the air immediately around them.

Billy was sleeping like the dead: he did not make a sound or a move. Wayne slept a restless sleep: he snored, grunted, snorted, mumbled, twisted, and turned. Carl, when he was able to, merely dozed, drifting into sleep, then quickly began to drift out of it again. He did not lie down or relax, made no effort to make himself comfortable; he simply sat back against the cave wall in the original position he had taken, and waited. And smoked one of his last few cigarettes.

Carl wondered if the men chasing them knew who they were. He decided they probably did not, not yet. But in another few hours, by midmorning, they would; by then they would have fingerprinted George and teletyped his prints to the FBI in Washington. As soon as the answer came back, the posse would know it was after two escaped convicts: Wayne and himself. They would not know for a while who Billy was.

And they probably wouldn't know yet about Georgia.

Then again, he told himself, the law might *already* know everything. Because Wayne's nigger fuck-boy might have *told* them everything.

Carl shifted his weight and let Billy's head rest on his lap. Lighting another cigarette, he held the match for a moment and studied his younger brother's sleeping face. He brushed Billy's hair out of his eyes. Never should have brought him along, he thought. All we've done is fuck up his life like we've fucked up our own.

Carl sighed, deeply, wearily. He knew at that moment that they would not escape. Capture, for them, was as certain as daylight.

Well, one thing was sure, he thought: When they did catch them, he wouldn't be put back into a general prison population where the nigger studs could get at him, the way he had been at the Maryland pen. He'd be a special prisoner this time. Very special.

He'd made damned sure of that in Georgia.

This would probably be the last time he'd ever go inside, Carl thought soberly. The last in a long series of reform schools, jails, and prisons. Carl thought about his first stretch in the reformatory. He was supposed to be let out in six months; they kept him nine because there was no place to send him when he got out. Finally they put him back into the foster home cycle again. This time he was taken to live with a family named Wardlaw. The man was Frank, the woman Edna. Younger than the Denmarks, they had a little girl named Grace, who was six.

"Carl," Edna Wardlaw told him the first night, "we know from your case worker about the problems you had in your 85 previous foster home. We know how you felt about Jacky, and about having to live in the basement. But we think you'll find it a lot different with us. You're going to have your own room here, and we'll try very hard not to show any favoritism between you and Grace." She had smiled and touched his arm. "Although I'll have to admit that Frank and I have spoiled her a little."

"She's a little charmer," Frank Wardlaw said. "Probably have you spoiling her yourself in a week or so."

Carl doubted it. He looked over at the little girl. She was cute enough. But having been number eight in his mother's brood of twelve, he was not inclined to think too highly of other kids. Mostly they were pains in the ass responsible for everyone else getting smaller shares: of food, clothes, everything. But maybe it would be different with just one little girl, he thought.

"We're enrolling you in Arden Junior High tomorrow," Frank Wardlaw said. "It's a nice school; lots of fine youngsters there. You'll like it."

"And I'll take you out and buy you some new clothes, too," Edna said, glancing at his reform school issue: faded, wrinkled denims. "Another thing," she added. "You don't have to call me 'Mom' or Frank 'Dad.' We know you didn't like that before. From now on, you can call me 'Edna.' "

"And me 'Frank,' " said Mr. Wardlaw. "Okay with you?"

"Yes, sir."

"Well now," said Edna. "Did you have supper before they brought you here?"

"No, ma'am."

"We'd better get you fed then. I'll whip up something that's quick. How does hot dogs and potato chips sound? With a Pepsi?"

"Sounds great," said Carl. He could hardly believe his ears. He had *never* had food like that at the Denmarks. Maybe *this* foster home would work out for him. Maybe he had gotten a break for a change.

For a while it seemed like he had. The Wardlaws treated him pretty much like he imagined they would have treated a real son of their own. He tried to show his appreciation by doing what was expected of him: keeping his room and himself clean, being polite and respectful, helping out when he was asked to— and even offering to do things when an opportunity presented itself. And they had been right about little Grace: within a week he was pampering her like she was a princess. When Edna caught him sneaking a stick of gum to her, instead of getting mad she just winked and said, "Told you so."

Frank Wardlaw was an accountant and, unlike Edward Denmark, had no part-time job, so Carl had his afternoons after school free. He asked if he could get a paper route and they said he could. At the end of his first month he had cleared eighteen dollars over and above his collections. Wondering how much, if any, the Wardlaws would allow him to keep, he put it on the supper table that night. They seemed touched.

"Carl, honey, that's your money," said Edna. "You earned it; you keep it."

"Wait a minute," said Frank, taking five dollars of it. "Tell you what: How about if you save five bucks a month? We'll go down to the bank tomorrow and you can open your own savings account. Would you like that?"

"Guy, yeah!" Carl replied enthusiastically. These people, he decided, were *great!* He was really beginning to feel like he had found a home.

If life at the Wardlaw home was perfect for Carl, life at Arden Junior High School was considerably less so. Two things bothered Carl: the lessons and the girls. He was too far behind the class to understand what was being taught; and he was not accustomed to going to school with girls. As far as his lessons were concerned, he did the best he could, faking it in class, borrowing homework to copy, cheating on tests. He did not know what else to do. If he admitted he could not keep up, they would put him back a grade, with the younger kids. That would have been too humiliating, both to himself and, he thought, to the Wardlaws. Maybe if he just hung in as best he could, he would begin to understand the lessons and everything would be all right.

In the meantime, he tried also to cope with the teenage girls all around him. Having not been around girls for a long time, then finding himself thrust into their midst, he was greatly distracted by them. Their tight sweaters and short skirts, bare legs, the makeup they put on at recess and during lunch, all combined to capture most of his attention during class. So attracted was he by their presence that it never once occurred to him that his preoccupation with them may have contributed more than a little to his incompetence in class.

The girl who was to be his undoing at Arden Junior High   87 was Jane. She was very thin and had waist-length blond hair that she kept ruler-straight by pressing it with a steam iron. Jane was a year older than the other students in the class, a grade behind, and she openly smoked cigarettes on her way to and from school. Somehow she heard that Carl had been in reform school and was immediately attracted to him.

"Hey, can I ask you a question?" she said, falling in next to him one day as he walked home after school.

"Sure," Carl answered. Despite everything else, she was one of the few girls in school who did not use makeup. Her face had a creamy, scrubbed look.

"Some of the kids were saying that you'd been in the state training school. Is that true?"

"Yeah, that's true."

"Guy. The reason I'm asking is because I almost got sent to the girls' training school. I'm on probation right now."

"Oh, yeah?"

"Yeah. I got busted for running away from my mom. I was gone three days. When they caught me, I got put in juvie. My mom had to go to court; boy, was she pissed. Anyhow, I got put on probation. What's training school like?"

"Lots of fun," Carl said. "Parties, picnics, movies. I hated to leave but I had to make room for some other lucky kid."

"You bullshitter," she said, shoving him off the sidewalk. Carl laughed. "Come on, what's it really like?" she pleaded.

"It's the shits," Carl said soberly. "I'd try to stay on probation if I was you."

They walked along together, talking about school, discovering that neither of them could keep up with the class. "They've already put me back one grade," she complained. "Guy. If they keep this up, I'll be back in kindergarten."

"I'll probably be there waiting for you," Carl told her.

Finally they came to a corner where she said, "I turn here." She locked eyes with him. "Want to come home with me? My mom's not home."

Carl thought about his paper route. "I, uh, can't. I've got a job I got to go to."

"Oh. Okay." She pulled a long strand of hair over her shoulder and tickled his nose with it. "Well, why don't you come over in the morning? You can walk me to school or something." She pointed down the street. "Fifth house on this side. With the green shutters. My mom leaves at seven."

88

She walked away without waiting for an answer. From the rear she did not look nearly as thin. And her hips kind of swayed as she walked. Man, thought Carl, this is the *real thing!*

He thought about her all during his paper route, after he got home, during supper, after supper, while he watched TV with the Wardlaws, while he played with Grace, while he was getting ready for bed. After he got in bed, it was even worse: then he had unfettered thoughts of her, open, erotic thoughts, and his body coursed with desire. He was a young animal consumed with desire; and it was all he could do to keep his hands off himself. He was sure he had a boner all night long. In the morning he had to run cold water over it before he could even piss.

For the most part, youthful fantasies never come true. Real life never quite measures up to the sometimes incredible scenes conjured up by the imagination of the young. But in Carl's case it did. He left an hour early for school, telling Edna Wardlaw that he had to help his teacher with a science project. From the corner he watched as Jane's mother left for work. He was at her door five minutes later. He could not believe it when she opened the door; she was wearing a hazily transparent nightgown—and nothing else.

"You like it?" she asked, modeling the nightgown for him. "It's one of my mom's; I put it on after she left." She took him by the hand. "Come on, before the bed gets cold."

Carl and Jane never did get to school that morning. Or the next. Or the one after that.

It was stupid. They were bound to get caught, and in the back of both their minds they knew it. But they could not help themselves. They were obsessed with each other, compelled by feelings they could not control; they fixated on each other's young, unspoiled body with a hunger that preempted all, a compulsion oblivious of everything else. In three days they learned every physical act there was to know. When Jane's mother opened the door and walked in on them with Edna Wardlaw and the junior high truant officer, Carl and Jane were locked naked in the sixty-nine position ministering to each other as if possessed.

Edna took him home in silence. Frank had already been called at work and was waiting for them. The two adults held a 89

brief, private conversation. Then Frank took Carl to the basement. "Sit in that chair there," he said, indicating an old
straight-back chair with arms.

"What are you gonna do to me?" Carl asked. Somehow he
could not believe that a nice guy like Frank Wardlaw would
hurt him.

"Just do as I say, Carl, please. Sit down."

Carl sat. Frank Wardlaw strapped his wrists and ankles to
the chair, and for the first time Carl felt fear. "Hey, come on,
what are you gonna do to me?"

"Punish you, Carl. For what you did to that poor girl."

"Hey, I didn't do nothing to her that she didn't *want* done to
her."

"That's not the point, Carl. Not the point at all."

Wardlaw stepped behind him and presently Carl heard a
buzzing sound. As he twisted his head to see what was going
on, he suddenly felt something vibrating across his skull and
saw a thick tuft of hair fall past his face into his lap.

"Hey, my hair—!"

Wardlaw said nothing more to him; he merely continued to
wield the electric clippers in sweeping strokes across Carl's
head, peeling his hair off like a cascading waterfall. While Carl
screamed bloody murder.

In two minutes it was over. Carl was clipped to the scalp.

"You son-of-a-bitch!" he screamed after Wardlaw had un-
strapped him and he had run to safety halfway up the stairs.
"You dirty motherfucker!"

He ran up to the kitchen and confronted Edna. "Bitch!
Whore! Cocksucker!"

Hearing the sound of Frank's footsteps hurrying up the
stairs, Carl fled the house, running bald across the yard, down
the street, leaving curses in his wake.

"Bastards! Pricks! Cunts! Whores!"

He ran and ran and ran. But as usual he could not run fast
enough or far enough.

Within two hours he was caught.

Within two days he was back in reform school.

Carl was a second-timer at the reformatory this time. He
knew how to walk tough and talk tough. He knew the ropes.
Nobody fucked with him this time. Only his senior counselor
gave him a little hassle. And he asked for that.

"Well, Carl, you didn't quite make it on the outside, huh?

Too bad. Well, another stretch in here should help you to mature a little more, to grow up a little."

"How long will they keep me here this time?" Carl asked.

"Oh, six months, I should think."

Carl grunted contemptuously. "That's what they said last time and they kept me nine."

"I'm sure they felt it was for your own good, Carl." The counselor's tone cooled slightly. "Let's see, you were on the gardening detail last time. How'd you like it?"

"I didn't."

"Oh?" The counselor's eyebrows arched. "Well, we certainly don't want you doing anything you don't want to do, Carl," he said sarcastically. His voice then became flat and authoritative. "You're assigned to the garbage detail, Carl. That's all. Excused."

Carl could have ripped his own tongue out. All he had to say was that the gardening detail was okay, and he probably would have been assigned there again. But no, he had to be Mr. Tough. Complain about how long they kept him in last time. Let the man know he had disliked the detail he had been on. Be a wise-ass. And wind up on the dirtiest job in the joint.

Carl worked the garbage detail with Jock Morton, a small, wiry kid from Baltimore's inner city. A year older than Carl, he was nevertheless slightly smaller; but he was far ahead of Carl in street knowledge.

"Wanna escape?" he asked Carl the first day. "We'll run away, steal us a car, burglarize a few places, and head for sunny Florida. What d'you say?"

"I don't think so," Carl said. "I only got six months, you know. I better do it."

Jock shrugged. "Okay." He looked up at the late September sky. "I guess I won't either. Winter's coming anyway. Reform school ain't the greatest place in the world, but at least it's heated in the wintertime. That's more than I can count on in my old man's apartment."

They stuck it out for six months, riding the garbage truck all over the institution grounds twice each day, struggling together to lift the heavy fifty-five gallon drums of waste onto the tailgate, then turning them upside down and emptying them, sometimes having to scrape the contents out with their bare hands. They weren't even given gloves to wear. The dry garbage wasn't too bad: the trash and paper from the offices and school, even the stuff from the few technical shops. It was 91 the kitchen garbage that was bad: the barrels of food slop, vegetable peels, coffee grounds, egg shells—a lot of it already spoiling by the time they got to it. And the hospital garbage was even worse: pails of bandages with pus and blood dried on them; tubes and vials that looked and smelled putrid; sometimes even excrement from a bedpan that got emptied in the wrong place. The garbage detail was the institution's absolute worse job. As Jock frequently said, "This job is really the bottom of the fucking barrel. Know what I mean?"

By the end of March, Carl's six months were up again. He waited every day to be summoned to the administration office for release. At odd moments he daydreamed about walking out the front gate and finding his mother and Ruth waiting for him. In his fantasy he always walked away between them, each of them with a loving arm around him. And he never looked back.

April came and went without the administration office sending for him. He asked his counselor about it, and the counselor replied, "They'll turn you out when they're ready to turn you out, Issacs. Not before."

May came and went. Carl's anger grew and grew. The bastards thought they could do anything they wanted to do to him. Well, *fuck* them.

"You wanna 'scape?" he asked Jock.

" 'Bout time you got ready, man," the wiry boy answered. "I been waitin' all winter."

They got out of their cottage after count one night and dug under the nearest fence. By the time they were missed, at the wake-up count, they were in a hot-wired stolen car across the state line in Pennsylvania. For the next four days they drove in and out of small towns between York and Harrisburg, burglarizing homes and small stores. Jock showed Carl what to do: how to force or trip a lock, spring a window or sliding glass patio door, pry open a coal chute or skylight. Because Jock knew they would be too conspicuous in the better neighborhoods, they stuck pretty much to the blue-collar areas, and their loot was correspondingly small. Most of the time they got only a few dollars, enough for a meal or to fill up the car. Sometimes the house or apartment was so poor they got nothing, not a dime. Over the four-day period they committed an astounding *thirty* petty burglaries. And when they were finally caught, after Jock had drunk some beer and wrecked the car, they had less than four dollars between them.

92

Jock, because of his age and record, was taken to an adult jail, and Carl was returned to the reformatory. Immediately upon arrival, he was put into a solitary confinement room in the isolation building and kept there, alone, for sixty days.

Three welfare workers interviewed him after he got out of isolation.

"We're willing to give you the benefit of the doubt and allow that Jock influenced you in this escape," one of them said. "He's older, has a long record of delinquency, and is considered an incorrigible. He admits to stealing the car and planning the burglaries."

"This is your first serious crime, Carl," said one of the others. "We'd like to erase it like it never happened and give you a chance to start all over. Would you like that?"

Carl kept his eyes downcast. "Yes, sir," he replied quietly. Anything to get out of that goddamned isolation room.

"Carl," said the female member of the trio, "how long has it been since you've seen your mother?"

Carl shrugged. "I'm not sure. It's been a long time."

"Do you want to see your mother again? Would you like to be someplace where you could see her on a regular basis?"

He shrugged again. "I guess so." He wanted to be near his own real mother more than anything in the world; but somehow he could not voice his enthusiasm to these three welfare people. It was part embarrassment, part distrust. They *seemed* to be on his side, seemed to be trying to help him; but every time they put him someplace, he ended up in more trouble than when he started. Some of it, he knew, was his own fault. Jane, for instance. He just had not been able to control himself. Even now, thinking about her as he sat before the welfare panel, he felt an erection starting. Quickly he put both hands in his lap and forced her memory from his head.

"What we have in mind for you, Carl, is a family named Romanski. The man is a very successful architect. They have three sons of their own who range in age from eleven to fourteen, just slightly younger than you. They live in a very nice house that's located just three miles from where your mother and your sister Ruth now live. We've talked to Mr. and Mrs. Romanski about you, gone over your background and problems with them. They're willing to let you come live with them and give you all the freedom you want, within reason, to go visit your mother and sister. How does that sound to you?" 93

Carl's heart was pounding so hard that he was sure the three welfare people could hear it. *This could be his chance!* If he could just be around his mother enough, he was certain she would start loving him again. She probably hadn't liked him before because he was younger and needed a lot of taking care of—not like now when he was older, more grown up, and could do for himself. He could even work; he'd proved that with his paper route: not one complaint, ever, from any of his customers. If his mother would just give him a chance, let him prove himself, he *knew* she would want him back.

"Carl? I asked what you thought of our idea."

"I think it's fine, ma'am," he answered as sincerely as he could. "I'd really like to try it."

When he got to the Romanski home, he wanted to just drop his zipper bag and hurry right over to see his mother and Ruth. But he knew that would not be right. First he had to spend a little time with the Romanskis: get to know them and their sons, and let them know that he appreciated them taking him in. Carl was *determined* to make this new arrangement work.

"I want to thank you for letting me come here," he told Leonard and Virginia Romanski the first night.

"Well, Carl, we just hope you like us," Leonard said, somewhat patronizingly, drawing on an expensive pipe. "We've never taken an outsider into our home before, but since we have the room, well, we all talked it over"—he waved a hand to include his wife and sons—"and we thought, why not?"

"We have so much, Carl," said Virginia Romanski, "that we felt we *should* share with someone less fortunate than ourselves."

Carl lowered his eyes. "That's real nice of you, ma'am." Their words, their attitudes, were supercilious and tactless—not by intent, merely by habit. Carl knew he was being talked down to, but he forced himself not to let it matter. The only thing that mattered was getting through the night so he could go see his mother the next day.

In the room they gave him, as he was unpacking his meager belongings—everything he had fit in just one drawer—he heard the three Romanski sons talking down the hall.

"Do you think he's going to like us?" the youngest boy asked.

"What matters is whether *we* like him or not," the oldest said. "Don't forget, it's *our* house."

94

"Why'd Mom and Dad have to take in somebody like him anyway?" the middle son asked, annoyed.

"They're just showing people how wonderful they are," the eldest said. "They're not doing it for *him;* they're doing it for themselves."

"How long do you think he'll stay?"

"Who knows? I heard that welfare lady say that he had a mother of his own that he'd be going to visit. Maybe when he goes to visit, he won't come back."

"If he's got a mom, how come he doesn't live with her?"

"The welfare lady said she's no good. Called her a 'baby machine' and said she should have been sterilized."

"What's that mean?" the youngest asked.

"It's a way they got of fixing women who keep having babies that they won't take care of. Then they can't have them anymore."

"Wish they'd done it to her," the annoyed middle brother said. "Then he wouldn't be here."

Listening, Carl knew he was red with embarrassment. But he also knew that some of the color in his face was from anger. Dumb little pricks, he thought. Like to see how smart *they'd* be if they got dumped in a strange place where *they* didn't belong.

Later that night, after he was in bed and the house was quiet, he thought about that for a long time. And he decided that most of his problems had resulted from him not having anyplace—or any*body*—to call his own. He had no ties, no real roots, and although his young mind could not put it into those exact words, he nevertheless *felt* the absence of being a part of anything: part of a home, part of a family, part of a circle of love. With him, it was always someone *else's* home, some *other* family, a circle of love that included him but did not really *embrace* him. He was forever the outsider.

But all that's gonna change, he promised himself that first night at the Romanski home. Tomorrow, when he saw his mother, it was going to be the beginning of a new start for him.

He was going to *make* it be.

It was funny, but neither his mother or Ruth looked like they had changed one bit. *He* had changed: grown older, taller, smarter. But his mother and Ruth seemed just the same.

"My God, look at this boy!" Ruth exclaimed when he stepped into the modest little house. She threw her arms 95 around him and squeezed him until he thought he would break. And kissed his cheeks, and touched his hair, and straightened his collar. "My God, look how tall he is!" His sister was delighted to see him again, and her obvious pleasure made Carl feel all warm inside.

"Come over here to me," his mother said. She was sitting across the room, smoking a cigarette, fooling with a worn deck of playing cards. Hesitantly, Carl went over to her. Much more reserved than Ruth, she did not hug or kiss him, in fact did not touch him at all. "You're starting to look a lot like your daddy," she said. The cigarette was between her lips and bobbed up and down as she spoke. "I hear you been a lot of trouble to a lot of people these past few years."

"I guess," Carl said, eyes downcast.

"Think you'll ever learn to be a good boy?" she asked, half in amusement.

He shrugged. Shrugging and downcast eyes were as much a part of him now as any other characteristic. He had learned that they were valuable tools when facing the many formidable opponents that life seemed to have lined up for him. Adults liked to think he was helpless or contrite; they thought he was easier to control that way.

"I hear you're living with a new family not too far from here," his mother said. "Think you'll like it there?"

"I'd like it better if I could come live here with you," Carl blurted out.

"Oh, no. Don't start that," his mother replied flatly. "Everybody's doing just fine the way things are. Don't let's rock the boat." She flicked ashes off her cigarette and began laying out a game of Solitaire.

Carl wanted to plead his case, to say to her all the things he had thought about the previous night, the things he had imagined himself saying, had silently rehearsed. But one look at his mother's expression, that tough frown of hers, one sound of her unflinching, unyielding voice, was all he needed to know that it was no use. She was never going to love him, never going to let him come live with her. She had managed to get out from under all of her younger kids, seen all of them—Hazel, Robert, Billy, George, Wanda, and himself—farmed out by the state to foster homes and training schools. There was no way she was going back to being the mother to a brood like that—or any part of it. It was easier to take care of herself with a waitress job, not be responsible for anyone but her own self, do as she pleased, sit and smoke cigarettes all day and play Solitaire if she wanted to.

No use, Carl thought that day. It was hopeless.

When he turned back to Ruth, she put her arms around him again. "Things'll work out for you, Junior. Really they will. You'll see."

"I know," he said. He forced a smile. *Don't let them see you hurt.* "I got to be going. They're expecting me back."

"Will you come see us again, Junior?"

"Sure."

Ruth kissed him on the cheek. He waved across the room at his mother. She bobbed her chin—and her cigarette—at him, then went on with her card game.

Carl did not look back after he left.

Half sitting, half lying on the ground in the little West Virginia cave, Billy on one side of him, Wayne on the other, Carl smoked his last cigarette as he remembered how hurt he had been that day. It had been a three-mile walk back to the Romanski home, and every step of the way had been filled with hurt of one kind or another. Hurt by his mother's uncaring response to him. Hurt by what he had heard the Romanski boys saying the previous night. Hurt by Mr. and Mrs. Romanski's obvious low opinion of him. Hurt by his own loneliness, his own starvation for something or someone to be *his.* Hurt by every goddamned thing that came his way, every goddamned turn of the road. Hurt, hurt, hurt.

When he got to the Romanski house that day, he had stopped and stared at it for several minutes. It was at that moment, he remembered now in the cave, that all the warmth seemed to go out of him. All the hope, all the caring. He remembered thinking: no more.

No fucking more.

Carl had turned around and walked to a nearby shopping center. He walked through the parked cars, looking for one that was unlocked. It was clear to him now that he would never have a home with his mother—and he was through with living with strangers. One thought burned in his mind as if branded there: get the fuck away. *Far* away.

He had found an unlocked car and begun trying to hot-wire it as he remembered Jock doing. He wasn't really sure whether he could do it or not. And on that particular night he never had the chance to find out. A shopping center security guard   97 had been watching him from the moment he walked onto the lot. The guard had slipped up while Carl had his head under the dash, and dragged him out by the legs. A moment later, Carl was once again in handcuffs.

Smoking his last cigarette down as far as he could, Carl flipped the butt out of the little cave and leaned his head back, closing his eyes. That day, he thought, had really been the turning point for him. From that day on, he simply had not cared what happened.

Feeling sleepy now, he adjusted his position and settled down to see if he could drift off. His eyes very heavy, he felt himself begin to doze. From somewhere far off in the night, he thought he heard a hound bark. But he was just too tired to crawl out of the cave and look for lights.

If they're coming, they're coming, he thought.

12

The bloodhound, Prince, barked only once before its keeper, H. R. Call, silenced it. "You quiet down now, you hear me," he ordered firmly but not harshly. Kneeling, he circled an arm around the ridgeback's neck and scratched him affectionately under the chin. Prince responded with a quiet whine, then fell silent.

Call and the hound were on a ridge with Sheriff Archie Day and six hand-picked men who were getting ready to move in on the three fugitives. Four of them were Archie Day's regular full-time deputies; the other two were state troopers assigned to his county. Archie had a section map unfolded on a large oak stump; he had just assigned each of the men a pie-shaped wedge of land to cover by foot.

"What we'll do soon's first light comes, is all start in a line and move right up toward the crest," he told them. "We only got about two hundred yards to go. H.R. will let go of the hound when we get ready to move. The dog's already been primed with the scent of the things that were left in the car they abandoned. Shouldn't be no trouble at all for him to go right directly to them.

"Couple things I want everybody to remember, though. First off, there's three of them and they might have split up. If'n they did, ol'Prince is only gonna lead us to one of them. The other two is gonna have the opportunity to throw down on us. So we got to be right particular on that score. Second thing is this: if they *do* start firing on any one of us, the others is not to come running over to help out. If we do that, we all end up in the same place, pinned down by the same fire. If shooting starts, I want the men under fire to take cover, and the men not under fire to keep on a'going right up to the top. Try to move in on their flanks or get in behind them. If they ain't on the highest ground, then try to get above them. Don't worry 99 about getting shot by your own men; whoever's under fire will not—I repeat, will *not*—return their fire. Just shoot up in the air ever' minute or so to make 'em *think* their fire is being returned. The ones who work around them to the sides and the rear will wait until they get clear shots—and then take 'em out. Ever'body understand all that?"

The posse understood. Mostly it was no more than backwoods common sense; hunting common sense; the common sense of men who live their lives toting rifles and shotguns.

"All right," the sheriff said, looking off the ridge at the sky, "looks like we got about five or six minutes until first light. Check your weapons; tie your bootlaces good; make sure you ain't got nothing in your pockets that'll rattle; have a last smoke if you want."

One of the deputies finished his last-minute check and started to reach down and pet Prince. "Don't do that," H. R. Call said quietly. "I don't want him to get your scent mixed up with theirs."

The men were mostly silent in those last few minutes; they shifted their weight, wet their lips, looked here, there, everywhere. It was gray up on the ridge; not night, not day; the murky time that is there for only moments.

Then, suddenly, first light arrived.

"All right, men," Archie Day said softly. "Move on out. And be careful."

In the cave, less than fifteen hundred yards from the phalanx of lawmen, all three brothers slept soundly. Billy had now rolled away to his right and was curled up in the fetal position. Wayne had hugged up against the opposite wall; his feet now protruded from the mouth of the cave. In between them, Carl lay on his back, one arm crooked under his head, the other across his chest, hand resting near the pistol in his belt. His lips were parted and he snored lightly, in a deep sleep. He had gone to sleep thinking about the last reform school he had been sent to: a place called the Madison Boys' Home.

Before they put him in Madison, Carl had done two more "six-month" terms at the state training school, on what they called the Senior Side, where the older boys and repeat offenders were housed. Then, because of his age and his record as a runaway—like Jock he was now considered an incorrigible—he had been transferred to Madison.

At Madison, like training school, the boys lived dormitory-style, thirty beds to a room. Also like training school, each dorm had a house parent, male, who oversaw the general conduct of his wards when they were not in school or at work. Carl's house parent was a kindly older man whom most of the boys liked and who made an effort to treat them fairly and make their day-to-day lives a little easier.

"We all call him the 'Old Man,' " Carl was told his first day there by a boy named Cliff. "He's about the best house parent in the place. Some of them are real pricks. You want to especially look out for a guy named Rey. He spells his name with an *e:* R-E-Y. Watch out for him."

"Why? Is he a bad dude?"

"Naw, hell, no. He ain't bad. Son-of-a-bitch is queer. He'll be after your dong."

Carl fell into the routine of Madison easily enough; with all the time he had put in at training school, it was no problem to adjust to a similar environment, a similar routine. All reform schools, Carl decided, must be pretty much alike. He wondered if any of them ever changed a kid, made him better, improved his outlook or attitude. Carl doubted it. It seemed to him that all they did was keep delinquent kids off the streets until they could grow up and commit adult crimes, so they could be put in prison. Warehouses for kids, that's all reform schools were.

Carl and Cliff became best friends. They bunked next to each other in the dorm, sat together in the classes they were assigned to go to, and generally managed to get on the same work details together. Between them there was a tacit understanding that they would back each other if either of them had trouble with another kid. Neither of them did, however. Woodbourne was different from training school in that most of the kids were older, tougher, and smarter. Most of them were equals; there were many peers, few subordinates.

Carl met the house parent named Rey after he had been there about a month. He had a toothache one morning and had gone to the infirmary to have it checked. Rey was in the waiting room, smoking a cigarette, waiting for one of his charges whom he had brought over with a severe nosebleed.

"Hello, there," he said. "I don't believe I've seen you before. Which dorm are you in?" Carl told him. "I don't know many young men from that dorm," Rey said.

Carl noticed two things about Rey that morning. First, he was fastidiously clean: perfectly groomed, powdered, lotioned, even his fingernails gleamed. Secondly, he referred to the residents as "young men" instead of "boys" or "kids." As if allowing them some status. From past experience, Carl knew that 101 was unusual in a keeper. Most of them felt it necessary to keep their charges firmly in their place, as inferiors. Rey impressed Carl with his liberal attitude and friendly manner.

The next time Carl saw Rey was at an institution softball game. Carl was sitting on the sidelines watching while Cliff played. Rey came up and sat beside him.

"Well, how are you getting along?" he asked, smiling.

Carl shrugged. "Okay, I guess."

"You're probably just *saying* that," Rey told him. "But I admire you for it. This place is so depressing, I marvel at how *anyone* can stand it."

"How come you work here if you don't like it?" Carl asked.

"Dear boy, I'm a civil servant. I work where the bastards tell me to work. Besides, it's not like I *live* here, you know. I get to leave every other night. I have an apartment in Baltimore; it's my *salvation.*" Rey looked around cautiously. "Listen, can I trust you?"

Carl shrugged again. "Sure."

"I mean, you're not one of those tattletales that goes running to your counselor with every piece of dirt you hear, are you?"

"I'm no fink," Carl stated unequivocally.

"I didn't think so. Well. We were talking about my apartment in Baltimore. I have two young men from here living there with me. They're supposed to have escaped, but what actually happened is that I *let* them go. Separately. At two different times. One has been with me for, let's see now, about nine months, and the other for about four. The three of us live together very happily."

Carl looked at him curiously. "What are you telling me for?"

"Because there's room for one more," Rey said candidly. "It's a four-bedroom place. Everyone has his own room. Interested?"

"What's the catch?" Carl asked.

Rey's eyebrows went up. "What ever do you mean?"

"I mean, what's it gonna cost me? What do I have to pay?"

"Nothing at all," Rey assured him. "Not in money, at any rate. I take care of the rent and groceries and all expenses. The two boys who are with me think it is a very easy life. All I ask is that they, well, let me be nice to them on the nights that I'm home. Do you know what I mean?"

"Sure, I know what you mean," Carl replied with an edge. "I ain't stupid. They let you suck them off, right?"

102   "Well, yes, to put it crudely."

Carl shook his head. "Thanks anyway."

"You wouldn't have to reciprocate," Rey assured him.

"Huh?"

"You won't have to do it to me. Just me to you."

"No, I don't think so."

Rey sighed quietly. "Well, okay. But I want you to know that I really like you. If you change your mind, let me know."

When the softball game ended, Carl and Cliff walked back to the dorm together.

"I saw you talking to Rey," Cliff said. "What'd he want?"

"You," Carl said easily.

"Me? What do you mean, me?"

"Yeah, he's got the hots for you. I made a deal with him. He gave me twenty bucks and I promised to deliver you to his room tonight."

"What!" Cliff's outrage surfaced immediately.

"He said for me to be sure you took a shower first—"

Cliff took a swing at him and Carl ducked, running away, laughing.

After four months at Madison, Carl was no longer laughing. He became fed up with everything: life in the dorm, Cliff, school, the food, the state-issue clothes he had to wear, the oppressive restrictions. He saw his young life ticking away, one day after another, in a monotonous sameness that was maddening. Everything about Madison began to vex him; he had caught what some of the staff called "outside fever."

"You'll get it from time to time," new arrivals were warned. "You'll think about how much fun it is to go to a movie at night, or hang out at a candy store or pool hall, to put your arm around a nice, soft young girl. That's 'outside fever.' It makes you want to run away. Take some advice: whenever you start feeling like that, get under a cold shower. You're all wards of the state of Maryland. Run away from here and you're fugitives. The next stop is the state penitentiary."

Carl tried for a week to shake his dose of outside fever, but it just seemed to get worse. When he felt he could not stand being in Madison any longer, he went looking for Rey.

"You still got an extra bedroom?" he asked.

"Why, yes," Rey replied, his expression brightening. "What's the matter, got a little outside fever?"

"How do I get out of here?" Carl asked, ignoring the small talk.

"When do you want to go?"

103

"Right now."

"Well, let's use our heads, so to speak, and wait until the end of the day. I have a 1969 Chevrolet, baby blue with a cream top, parked in the administration lot. I'll get something out of the trunk at lunchtime and leave it unlocked. You get a pass this afternoon and go to the library about three-thirty. Slip out the back door of the library to the parking lot. Find my car and get in the trunk. I'll leave at four and we'll be on our way." Rey put his hand on Carl's arm. "You'll like it with me and my other two boys, Carl. We have a good life."

"Sure," Carl said.

His departure from Madison was accomplished without incident. He lay curled up in the dark trunk for the duration of the ride into Baltimore, and before he knew it Rey was opening the trunk lid inside a garage he rented near his building. He led Carl down an alley and up some back stairs to the rear entrance of a third-floor apartment. There, in the kitchen, Carl was introduced to Doug and Hal.

"People in the building think they're my nephews," Rey told him. "The same will apply to you. Come on, I'll show you your room."

It was a nice apartment, roomy and light, modestly but comfortably furnished. Everyone was expected to do his share to keep it clean. Doug and Hal were about the same age as Carl, and generally the same type of youth: light-haired, fair-skinned, lean. They seemed as much at home in Rey's place as if they were living in a normal family. It was all very matter-of-fact.

"Why don't you and Hal go to a movie tonight," Rey said to Doug when he finished showing Carl around. He handed Doug some money.

After they left, Rey sat down with Carl on the couch. "This is new to you, isn't it?"

Carl nodded nervously. "Yeah."

"There's really nothing to it. It's just another kind of love, you know. You may even grow to like it."

He put an arm around Carl and began undoing his trousers.

Carl fit right in with Doug and Hal. It was an easy life. Because Carl was new, he was the only one Rey wanted for the first few weeks, and it was like a vacation for the other two boys. But gradually Rey gravitated back to Doug and Hal, and from then on he pretty much alternated them in sequence. It was the same activity regardless of which boy Rey chose; he performed fellatio on them, but that was all. None of them were ever asked to do anything in return, or required to be used in any other way.

"A lot of people would put us down for living this way," Doug said, "but I'll tell you, man, I don't see nothin' wrong with it at all. We ain't hurtin' nobody, ain't botherin' nobody. Rey's good to us; we got a nice place to live, enough to eat, we stay out of trouble and don't get hassled by the law. Shit, I'll take this life any day instead of the one I had *before* I got busted."

"Fucking-A, man," Hal agreed. "It'd be different if he was fucking us in the ass, or making *us* give *him* blow-jobs. But when all's he asks for is a little cock in the mouth a couple times a week, and for that we get to live decent lives; shit, man, I think we got it knocked."

Carl generally nodded agreement to whatever they said. He did not actively enter into their conversations when they were trying to justify the life they were leading, but neither did he openly disagree with them or tell them they were full of shit. In a way he supposed they were right; it *was* an easy life, and they *were* staying out of trouble. But never was Carl able to rationalize that what he was doing was either right or healthy. Not that he could spell out in his own mind how it was *wrong,* or decide exactly what was *un*healthy about it. But it was constantly in his mind that there was something intrinsically wrong with letting another man suck on his dick. And despite their frequent verbalizations to the contrary, he sensed that Doug and Hal felt the same way.

Still, it was good to be free again, to be away from the restraints and restrictions of state custody. He did not care that he was a fugitive; he felt like he had been one most of his life anyway. Living there in Rey's apartment, Carl felt more emancipated than ever before in his life. Except for the brief physical demands of Rey, he had complete freedom to do as he liked, go where he pleased, and be totally himself without putting on an act for anyone. It had been a long time since he had felt so free; a long time since he had not had to worry about what a house parent thought, or a foster parent, or a teacher, or a welfare worker. For the first few months he reveled in his own autonomy, indulging in his liberation, his new liberty, like it was a drug.

He spent his days going to movies, window-shopping, lying in   105 the park, watching men bowl or play billiards, or simply sleeping. He experimented with a mustache but found that he could not grow a decent one, not yet. He walked along the docks of Chesapeake Bay, looking out over the water at gulls close by and ships in the distance. He tried new foods he had never eaten before. He daydreamed.

And, after what seemed like years of being constantly tense, he let his tired young body and mind rest.

Rey gave a party about once a month, inviting a wide variety of guests, both gay, straight, and in-between. Carl, Doug, and Hal usually acted as cohosts for him, helping serve the drinks and snacks, emptying ashtrays, and in general being polite "nephews" for Rey's friends to admire. Carl was fascinated by many of the people who showed up at Rey's parties: ballet dancers, prize fighters, legal secretaries, models of both sexes, drug dealers, artists, dental assistants, prostitutes, even an occasional policeman. Rey's apartment seemed to be accepted as neutral ground; everyone was friendly with everyone else, regardless of their outside status.

It was at a party of Rey's that Carl met Keen Simmons. A tall, handsome black man, Keen arrived with two teenage white girls on his arms. He hugged Rey and greeted several other guests by name as he introduced the girls around. One, a blonde, was named Bonni; the other, a redhead, was Sharon. It was Sharon who was immediately attracted to Carl, and he to her.

"Keen told me on the way over that all the boys living with Rey were escapees from reform school," she said to him in private. "Does that include you?"

Carl smiled and shook his head. "Keen's just pulling your leg. We're Rey's nephews."

"All three of you?"

"Yep. We came to live with him when our daddy run off and our poor old maw died of grief. Uncle Rey takes care of us."

Sharon nodded knowingly. "Keen says you guys take care of Rey, too."

Carl's smile faded. "Sounds to me like Keen talks too damned much."

"I wouldn't tell him if I were you. He carries a gun."

"What is he, a cop?"

"No," she replied easily, "he's a holdup man."

Carl studied her curiously. "You sure don't seem to care what you tell people," he observed.

Sharon shrugged. "Everybody knows it anyway. Except you, that is. Now you know it too." She took a swallow of her drink. "How old are you?"

"Nineteen."

"Bullshit. *I'm* nineteen. What were you in reform school for?"

"I'm incorrigible."

"Does that mean you do bad things?"

"Every chance I get."

She finished her drink, set the glass down, and locked eyes with him. "Suppose I give you a chance right now. Does your bedroom door have a lock on it?"

Carl wet his lips and nodded.

"Why don't you show me how it works."

"What will your big black boyfriend say?"

"He's not *my* big black boyfriend, he's Bonni's. I'm only staying with them temporarily. Anything else you want to know?"

"Nothing I can't find out for myself," Carl said, taking her hand and leading her down the hall.

Memories of Jane flashed in his mind as they undressed each other. It had been a long time since he had been anything except a passive sex partner to Rey, but the sight of Sharon's bare skin, her nipples, caramel-colored pubic hair; the smell and taste of her, the touch of her fingers and lips and tongue, all drove from his mind any fear that having had sex with another man might have harmed him in any way. He was totally male with Sharon, she totally female with him, and they drove each other's bodies like fine-tuned engines.

For four hours.

Two weeks later, Keen Simmons came to the apartment during the day when Rey was at work. "I want to talk to you, my man," he said to Carl. "Come take a ride with me."

Keen had a late model Lincoln. They got on Route 95 and drove toward Washington.

"Bonni tell me you and Sharon been seeing each other every day. And mos' every night."

"Yeah, that's right."

"She tell me you and Sharon be planning to run off somewhere together."

"We've talked about it." Carl looked out at the passing scenery. "Neither of us has got anybody. We thought maybe we'd be good for each other."

"How you expect to get along?"

"Work, I guess. That's what other people do."

"You ain't 'other people.' You a reform school runaway. You underage. You inexperienced. I doubt if you even got a fucking social security card."

Carl said nothing. Keen was right, all the way. Sharon would be able to get work. She was nineteen, had worked at waitress jobs, at theater candy counters, even as a file clerk. But what the hell would he do—get another paper route?

"Look, my man, I ain't deliberately pissing on your campfire here. It's just that my woman Bonni is real close to Sharon, see, and she worried about what's gonna happen to her if she run off with you, dig? Now let me ask you something, brother: where you and little Sharon planning to split to?"

"Florida. We've talked about Florida."

Keen nodded knowingly. "Cost of living is a motherfucker in Florida. I know; I go down there twice a year. You know what you need, my man? You need yourself a stake, that's what. A little something to like fall back on if the going get rough. I'd say you need about twenty thou."

"Great," Carl said sourly. "Where the hell would I get that kind of bread?"

"It just so happens," Keen Simmons said quietly, "that I might be able to help you in that respect. I happen to be looking for a partner."

Carl moved in with Keen, Bonni, and Sharon. He and Sharon made an agreement between themselves: Carl would work with Keen until he could save twenty thousand. Then he would quit and they would split for Florida and start a new life together.

Keen's specialty was liquor store holdups. "Medium-sized places that can be hit for a grand, fifteen hundred. Out of the way places, side-street places; nothing big, nothing heavy. No violence. Nothing the cops are gonna get all excited about. We take a place down fast and clean, then we *gone*. We move clear out of the area before we hit again. We don't leave no trail, don't set no pattern. We like ghosts, dig?"

Carl dug. Keen acquired a thirty-eight pistol for him, they said goodbye to their ladies, and hit the road. They moved from Maryland to Delaware to Pennsylvania to New Jersey, always leaving from fifty to a hundred miles between jobs. They stayed off the interstate highways and traveled the back

108

roads to avoid roadblocks. They never stayed in a store more than three or four minutes, just long enough to empty the register and cash drawer. They never bothered with safes, never robbed customers: those things took too much time. Hit and run, that was Keen's style, and it worked like a charm. It worked for nine months, through thirty-nine armed robberies in four states. It worked right up to a night when they were on their way back home, crossing the Memorial Bridge between New Jersey and Delaware. It was a toll bridge so they did not think anything about stopping at the toll gate. They never got started again. As soon as they came to a halt, stakeout officers in the toll booths poked shotguns through the windows at them. Their crime spree was over.

For Carl it meant the end of his juvenile crime days. After being sent back to Maryland, where he was still a fugitive, he was sentenced to the Maryland State Prison. In the eyes of the law, Carl Issacs was now a man.

As Carl and his brothers slept soundly in the little West Virginia cave, Prince, the Rhodesian ridgeback bloodhound, padded silently up to the cave entrance and froze, his ears back, one paw up, eyes fixed on the cave.

Moving quietly up behind Prince was state police Corporal Arthur Meadows. He carried a .30-caliber rifle at the ready, a round in its chamber. When he saw Prince stop and go rigid, he himself stopped and dropped to a half crouch. Automatically he thumbed off the safety on his weapon. Then he quickly studied the ground between himself and the cave. He selected a path as clear of twigs and leaves as he could find, and gingerly began to move forward one delicate step at a time.

When Meadows got halfway to the cave, he saw two feet, in shoes, sticking out of the entrance. Prince's nose was a scant two or three yards away. Meadows paused to study the feet for several seconds. They were perfectly still. Drawing in his breath, he continued forward. He moved one careful step after another, as he had learned to do as a boy when his father taught him to hunt. As he moved, his eyes never left the cave entrance except for split seconds to glance at the ground. The muzzle of his rifle never left it even then.

When the trooper got alongside Prince, he took his left hand off the rifle stock long enough to pat the hound's head. Then he moved past him and in four more short steps was at the cave entrance.

Meadows swept the cave with a single, tense glance. All three fugitives appeared to be sleeping. One of them was only a boy; he did not appear to be armed. The one in the middle had a revolver stuck in his belt; Meadows reached down and gently lifted it away. The third person in the cave looked to be the oldest, possibly the leader. Meadows poked him lightly with the rifle barrel. The man's eyes opened.

"No sudden moves," Meadows whispered. "Sit up, and keep your hands together in front of you."

When the man sat up, Meadows saw a second pistol on the ground where he had been lying. In a single, fluid move, the trooper pulled a pair of handcuffs from his belt, snapped them on the man's wrists, and picked up the other pistol.

"Okay, up and out of there. Nice and easy."

As the fugitive stood up outside the cave, Prince growled threateningly. Meadows guided the man up against the outside wall of the cave. Next he nudged the sleeping boy and motioned him out. He patted him down, then had him lie on the ground face down. Then he brought the third one out, doing the same to him.

When he was certain he had the situation and the fugitives fully under control, Corporal Meadows pointed the rifle skyward and fired a single signal shot into the air.

The night-long manhunt was over.

13

The other state trooper was clear around the ridge, and for some reason none of Archie Day's deputies had any handcuffs with them. Archie himself did not even have any.

"All right," the sheriff said to Trooper Meadows, "undo them bracelets and cuff this prisoner to that one. Bert, give me the lace out of one of your boots."

Meadows unlocked the handcuffs, removed them from Wayne's wrists, and cuffed Wayne's right hand to Carl's left. While he was doing it, Archie Day tied Billy's hands in back with the long, thick bootlace.

"One man on each side of them," Sheriff Day instructed, pointing. Two deputies stepped up, one gripping Wayne's left arm, the other taking Carl's right. Day himself held Billy's arm. "All right, let's get 'em down the hill. Arthur," he said to the state policeman, "will you fetch that hound, please?"

Meadows went over and knelt by Prince, rubbing his ears and stroking his neck and back. "Good boy, Prince. Good dog, yessir. Come on now, I'm going to personally see that you get a pound of center-cut steak."

The group made its descent back to the ridge, then on down to the road. Carl, Wayne, and Billy exchanged glances on the way down but none of them spoke. Billy was obviously frightened; his eyes were watery and his bottom lip trembled. Wayne looked like he was in a fog, not quite aware of what was going on. Carl kept a tight control on both his mind and his expression.

"How old are you, boy?" Archie Day asked Billy on the way down.

"F-fifteen," Billy replied, choking slightly.

"God almighty," Archie muttered to himself. Fifteen years old. He ought to be out fishing, or playing American Legion 111 baseball, or learning to drive a tractor. Archie shook his head sadly. God almighty.

Down on the road, other armed men waited. As the posse from the summit got there, two unmarked cars drove up and a quartet of men wearing business suits got out. Archie Day smiled inwardly. Just like he had figured.

"We're with the FBI, Sheriff," one of them said. He turned to Wayne, the prisoner nearest to him. "You're under arrest."

"No shit," said Wayne. Carl could not contain a brief chuckle. What a dumb fucking thing to say to a pair of men handcuffed together and surrounded by an armed posse.

"We'll want to keep them separated from each other," the FBI agent said. "Someone remove these handcuffs."

For several seconds no one moved. The men in the posse all stared at the agent with a common look that clearly spelled *intruder*. The dangerous work was done; now the bureau showed up to glean the glory. Finally Archie Day glanced over at Trooper Meadows. "Take the cuffs off, will you, please, Arthur."

The FBI agents put their own handcuffs on the three prisoners. "We'll take them back separately," the agent said. But they only had two FBI cars. After Carl was put in one, Wayne in the other, the agent in charge said, "Uh, Sheriff, we *would* like to keep them apart—"

"Sure," Archie Day said. "Put the boy in the Scout there with Prince. That all right with you, H.R.?"

"Don't see why not," Call said. "I'll be going through Bluefield on my way back to the prison anyhow." He turned to the agent. "I reckon you *will* be taking 'em to Bluefield, won't you?"

"Right. That's the closest federal lockup."

The prisoners were not taken directly to Bluefield, however; they made a stop at the state police barracks in Welch. There they were locked up in separate cells set apart from one another. During their stay there, which lasted several hours, George was brought over from the Welch jail and also put in an isolated cell. A short time later, a team of officers from the Georgia Bureau of Investigation (GBI) arrived by plane at the Bluefield airport and met with the FBI agents and West Virginia officers to work out the most convenient way to legally get the four prisoners back to Georgia.

112   After a timetable was devised and agreed upon by all the

lawmen involved, the four prisoners were taken in separate cars from Welch to the airport in Bluefield. There they were taken aboard a private airplane and seated as far apart from one another as possible. During the transfer from the cars to the plane, Wayne saw for the first time that his friend George had rejoined the group. He smiled and bobbed his chin at George, but the black man just gave him a slightly sick look in return.

The prisoners were flown to Charleston, West Virginia, 140 miles to the north, and landed at Kanawha Airport. Put into separate cars again, they were taken by motorcade to the Charleston federal courthouse and brought at once before a federal judge. Extradition proceedings were hurried through, after which the prisoners were hustled across the street to a West Virginia state court for a similar hearing. After less than two hours on the ground in Charleston, the motorcade delivered the entourage back to Kanawha Airport where the same private plane flew them back to Bluefield.

At the Bluefield airport, the prisoners remained on board the plane until a second aircraft taxied up nearby. Then there was a formal exchange of extradition writs and a signing of transfer documents, and the four prisoners were officially and legally turned over to the GBI team. The prisoners were brought out of the first plane and led over to the second one.

"Climb aboard," a GBI agent ordered. "You boys are going back to Georgia."

They were not allowed to talk during the trip to Georgia. Wayne and George, seated separately, dozed during much of the flight. Billy, now inconsolably miserable, whimpered and cried from time to time. Carl tried to block everything out of his mind: where he was, what was happening, what *had* happened, and especially what was *going* to happen.

Carl thought of Sharon, whom he had not seen now in more than two years. He wondered where she was, how she was doing. Sharon and Bonni had both been sent to the Montrose women's reformatory after he and Keen had been captured following their nine-month robbery spree. Police officers had found them in the Baltimore apartment, in possession of stolen money, and had charged them with being accessories to robbery.

I almost made it with Sharon, Carl thought. Just a little while longer and they would have had their stake for Florida. 113

Carl had daydreamed about that a hundred times. He and Sharon married, living in a neat little house somewhere near a beach; both of them working, making good money; a car of their own; everything nice, the way normal people had it. He had even thought of someday getting in touch with his mother and maybe sending her a plane ticket to come visit them. He would have been so proud to introduce Sharon as his wife, to show his mother around *his* home, the home he had made for himself after so many homeless years. And his mother would have been proud of *him* too; she would have put her arms around him and *told* him how proud of him she was—

Bullshit.

Carl had blinked his eyes and forced the fantasies from his mind.

It was all bullshit, man. It never had a chance in hell of coming true. You've been fucking doomed since the fucking day you were fucking born. Do yourself a big favor and accept it.

Okay, he told himself. Okay.

Sighing quietly, he looked out the plane's window at the lush Georgia farmland over which they were now flying.

They landed on a private section of the Atlanta airport. A dozen state police cars came up in formation around the plane. Several men of obvious authority came on board and conferred with the GBI agents. Carl, eyes closed and head leaning against the window, pretended to be asleep. He listened to the men as they discussed in hushed voices what they intended doing with the prisoners.

"—obviously can't keep them all in one place. Too much risk involved. The whole damn state's up in arms over what they did. If any lynch mobs decide to take the law into their own hands, we don't want all four of 'em strung up. So it's been decided to split 'em up. The oldest one, the half brother, Wayne Coleman, will be kept here in Atlanta at the Fulton County jail. The kid, Billy, will be kept here too, only he'll be over at Hall Juvenile Center. The other brother, Carl, we're going to take up to Marietta and lodge in the Cobb County jail."

"What about the nigger?"

"He's going over to Decatur, to the DeKalb County jail."

They took them off the plane one at a time and put them in
separate state police cars. Each car had a lead car and a tail

car. They sped away from the airport in threes, red lights flashing, and headed off in different directions.

In his car, heading for Marietta, thirty miles north of the Atlanta airport, Carl stared at the cuffs on his wrists, the chains leading from them down to a chain around his waist, down farther to a pair of leg irons around his ankles. Then he looked out the window as they crossed a bridge over the Chattahoochee River. He and the others had crossed the southern end of that same river the evening they left Seminole County to begin their run for freedom. That had been—how long ago?

Three days!

Was that possible? Only three days?

Or was it a lifetime ago?

Carl shook his head incredulously. Who would have thought it would end this way? In this place?

Georgia, for Christ's sake.

Incredible.

The next morning, Saturday, they fed him and dressed him in his chains again for a trip into Atlanta to GBI headquarters. They took him to an office where several GBI investigators tried to question him. Carl talked as much as he wanted to, playing word games with the officers, trying to find out how much they knew—really *knew,* as opposed to *thought*—while they tried to get him to make a full confession to what they had done in Seminole County.

"We know you were in the trailer, Carl," they told him. "We found your fingerprints."

"Bullshit," he replied easily. "I don't leave fingerprints, man. I wasn't borned yesterday." But his mind automatically and rapidly went back to that time and place, and he tried to remember if he *had* left prints anywhere.

"You might as well cooperate, Carl. Billy is cooperating with us. He's agreed to give us a full statement. About everything. The trailer, the men, the woman—everything, Carl."

"Bullshit," Carl said confidently. But his confidence was all superficial. Worry was seeping through his veneer of self-control and assuredness. *Had* Billy talked? And if he hadn't, *would* he? The kid was only fifteen; he had not been through the wringer like Wayne and he had, did not have the experience they had dealing with the law. Even George was probably better equipped to handle himself than Billy. George was a nigger and a fuck-boy, but at least he had been in the joint and   115 knew the rules about talking to the man. Billy had only done a little state school time; he'd never really had the screws put to him, the heavy pressure put on him.

Maybe Billy *would* talk.

"We want to help you, Carl," the GBI man tried to convince him.

"Sure you do."

"That's a fact now. We don't want to be any harder on you than we have to be. Thing of it is, we got us a right nasty case here. You boys left one hell of a mess down there in Seminole County. But if we could clean it up real quick, find out exactly who did what to the men, and to that woman, why, it'd be a whole lot easier on all of us—"

"Save it, mister," Carl told him flatly. "You're wasting your time."

The men in the room fell silent for a minute, all staring intently at him, their eyes fixed and unyielding, their dislike and utter revulsion at him obvious. But Carl had been through *that* before, too; he looked down at the floor and refused to let their cold, hostile stares bother him.

"Now look here, boy," one of them said, "day after tomorrow, on Monday morning, you gon' be taken back down to Seminole County and formally charged. Thinks'll go a whole lot easier on you down there if we can tell the judge you're cooperating."

Carl looked up at the man. "Mister, there ain't a thing on God's green earth that's gonna make it any easier for me in Seminole County. You know it and I know it. So why don't you stop trying to kid me, huh?"

Silence again. Longer this time.

Then: "All right, boy, have it your own way. Take him back to his cell."

Back in the jail in Marietta, Carl was left locked up the rest of Saturday and all day Sunday. No one questioned him or tried to engage him in even idle conversation. He was kept isolated from the other prisoners, and the only persons he saw were the jailers, clean-up people, and the person who brought his meals. He had his first opportunity in nearly a week to rest, unwind, actually lie back on his bunk and relax, without worrying about his next move. His course was being charted for him by others now; not only did he not have to make his own plans, but for a change he did not have to worry about

116

Wayne and Billy. No more trying to figure out what he and Wayne should do; no more trying to get Billy back to the bosom of their family, such as it was.

And no more running, no more hiding. In a way, it was almost a relief.

On Monday Carl was chained and shackled again, and driven back to Atlanta to a different airport, this one smaller and nearer to Marietta.

"You gonna be treated like a celebrity today, boy," one of his escort guards told him. "They gonna fly you down to Seminole County in the governor's very own plane. What you think of that, boy?"

"Wouldn't have missed it for the world," Carl replied dryly.

At the airport, just as it had been back in Bluefield, West Virginia, Carl saw Wayne and the others being driven up in separate escorted cars and put on board the plane. Carl studied Billy when he had the chance, to see if he could detect anything different about his younger brother's countenance or attitude. Billy bobbed his chin at Carl in greeting as he was led quickly past him. As far as Carl could tell, he seemed the same as always. The GBI men, Carl decided, were full of shit. Billy wasn't going to tell them the fucking time of day. The next time his brother was able to glance over at him, Carl threw him a quick, encouraging wink.

The governor's plane took off for the flight down the length of the state. Resting his head back on the seat, Carl closed his eyes and wondered how it would be in court. Frantic, he imagined. Lots of reporters, flash cameras, lots of security, people pushing and shoving to get a look at them. Not like the last time, he thought. The last time he had been in court was when he was sentenced after his crime spree with Keen Simmons. It had been a nice, quiet proceeding. Escorted into a nearly empty courtroom, taken before a judge, a few legal inanities exchanged between the bench and the lawyers, and then he was committed to the Maryland State Prison—just as calmly as you please.

The Maryland State Prison—where all the nigger studs were just waiting for him.

Carl's expression tightened as he dozed off and the worst memory in his mind became a terrible dream.

He had managed to stay away from the blacks for a while. By always falling in with a group of whites, or making sure 117 there was a corrections officer somewhere close by, or simply by hiding in one of the many places that the prison afforded—the library, dispensary, a counselor's office—he had kept out of their way, out of their clutches, for quite some time.

He knew they were after him; they *let* him know. "Hey, pale pussy! Hey, boy, come over here, I want to show you something. You ever seen a black lightning rod, white boy? Say, boy, you got any hair around your asshole? Or is it just clean and pretty like your mouth? Come here, pretty thing, I gots a chocolate cocksicle for you. Say, little girl, what you got between them sweet little cheeks of yours? Come here, sucker—"

They would make loud, sucking noises whenever he walked by. Reach down and fondle themselves at the crotch and groan. It was as if part of their pleasure was to embarrass and humiliate him; degrade him in any way possible. There were plenty of white boys in there who would do it with them for favors or cigarettes, but the blacks seemed to like it much better when they had to force the act. Only a very few of them bought their sex from the white boys; most of them took it by threat or by strength.

Carl might have been able to stay away from them indefinitely if the riot had not happened. But it did happen. And almost as soon as the convicts got control of the block, five blacks appeared at Carl's open cell door.

"Strip, white boy," one of them said.

"Fuck you," Carl replied defiantly, closing his fists.

"No, fuck *you*," the black said, smiling. He plowed a fist into Carl's stomach, doubling him over.

Two of them grabbed his arms while two others tore off his shoes and pulled down his trousers and shorts. Carl kicked and struggled, but each of the blacks was bigger and stronger than him, and against all five of them at once he was all but helpless. They peeled off his shirt, undershirt, socks, leaving him buck naked. There was a small table in his cell and they swept it clean. Folding his bunk up to the wall for more room, they bent him forward over the table. One of them got under the table and held his ankles in place, legs spread. Two others held his arms out, shoulders pressed down on the table.

"Vaseline," one of them said.

Carl felt something being rubbed on his anus. "You motherfuckers!" he yelled.

"You ain't my mamma, boy," one of them jeered. "But I'se gonna fuck you anyhow."

118

Carl felt the man entering him, a sudden, determined thrust, not slow or easy, not working against the restricting muscles gradually, but right on in, right on up, painfully despite the lubrication, a straight, hard, unrelenting shaft forced into his body like a knife. Carl screamed, then groaned as his attacker began to pump. "Ahhhhh—" the man sighed, "good. Good white pussy. Nice and tight, baby—"

With three men holding him and one using him from behind, there was still a fifth man free. He got in front of Carl, whose head and face were hanging over the front of the table. Dropping his pants and shorts, he grabbed Carl by both ears and lifted his head up.

"Listen to me, pussy," he said roughly. "You feel my hands on yo' fucking ears? You know I can rip yo' ears right off from yo' fucking head? You want me to do it? Do you? Answer me, motherfucker!"

"N-no—" Carl managed to say.

"All right then, boy, you gon' suck my dick then, hear? You gon' let me fuck you in the mouth, hear? An' if you bite my dick, I'm gon' rip bof' yo' ears right off from yo' head. You dig, pussy?"

"Y-yeah—"

"All right then." He stepped closer to Carl's face. "Start sucking, white boy."

They stayed in his cell nearly an hour, each one using him twice, front and rear. When they left him, he was bleeding from the rectum, choking on regurgitated semen that burned his throat and clogged his nostrils from within. He was sick, hurt, mortified, and furious.

"Dirty black motherfuckers," he muttered to himself. "Dirty black motherfucking nigger scum—"

After the riot and Carl's attack by the blacks, the state of Maryland corrections system decided, albeit a bit late, that perhaps the state prison was not the proper institution for Carl. He was, after all, barely eighteen years old. Incarceration in the state prison, in the company of older, experienced, hardened criminals, might conceivably be detrimental to the rehabilitative process by which they hoped to reform him. They decided to transfer him to a medium-custody prison farm.

By then, of course, it was too late. By then Carl had been sodomized and brutalized past reclamation.

On the governor's plane, flying back to Seminole County,   119

Carl woke up laced with sweat. Blinking his eyes, he drove the image of the five black men from his mind. Only when he remembered where he was, did he relax.

It's okay, he told himself. It'll never happen again.

Carl had known from the moment he, Wayne, and George had escaped from the prison farm, that he would someday be sent back to prison. It was his destiny; prison was to be his life. But never—*never*—did he intend to let them put him in a general prison population again. Never was he going to let them subject him to the mercy of the fucking niggers again.

Never.

Interlude:
THE ALDAY FAMILY

14

Jimmy Cecil Alday smiled at the girl sitting next to him in the pickup truck. "It's the nicest library in south Georgia," he said. "That's why I don't mind driving twenty miles to get to it."

"Don't you have a library in your own town, in Donalsonville?" she asked. Her name was Arlene and she was from Mississippi, visiting an aunt in Donalsonville.

"Just a little tiny one," Jimmy said. "It's uptown there in a little store. 'Course, we've got one at the high school too. But neither one of them is as nice as the one in Bainbridge."

Jimmy guided the pickup along the narrow Georgia highway with the steady hand of one who had been driving trucks and handling farm equipment since he was twelve years old. He was twenty-four now in the summer of 1972, a quiet young man with a head of tightly curled hair and a tentative, easy smile that made him instantly likable. The unmarried girls in Seminole County frequently referred to him as "cute." Sometimes, to his utter mortification, his two older brothers did also.

"Why did you make me promise not to tell anyone we were driving over to Bainbridge to go to the library?" Arlene asked.

"I don't want my brothers finding out I go there," Jimmy said.

"Why in the world not?"

Jimmy hunched forward over the steering wheel a bit. "Well, see, if they find out I go there, they're going to want to know why."

"What's wrong with that?"

He flashed her a quick grin. "You don't know my brothers. If they knew why I went to the Bainbridge library, they'd tease me about it until I went crazy. They're like that."

"Why *do* you go over there?" Arlene asked.

"Can I trust you?" Jimmy asked solemnly. "You won't tell nobody?"

" 'Course not, silly. Why, I won't hardly have *time* to tell anyone. My vacation's almost over; I'll be going back home soon."

"I go to the Bainbridge library to look at history books. I study them to see how they're written. I, uh—I expect to write a history book myself someday."

"You do! Why, Jimmy, I think that's marvelous. What's it going to be about?"

"About my family. About the Aldays, clear back to my great-granddaddy. I'm one of the fourth generation of Aldays in Seminole County. My people helped settle this land. We can trace our family back to when there wasn't hardly nobody but Seminole Indians hereabouts."

"Jimmy, that's marvelous!" Arlene said again. "How long have you been thinking about all this?"

"I don't know," Jimmy said. "A long time. The idea come to me one morning while I was out cooking my breakfast on the riverbank. I do that a lot: get up real early and go off by myself somewhere and cook a wild breakfast . . ."

Jimmy Alday always opened his eyes at first light. He never used an alarm clock or had to be otherwise awakened; he simply came awake as daybreak spread over the land, as if he were one and the same with the environment in which he had been born and in which he lived.

He got out of bed quietly so as not to wake the other members of his family. In the bathroom he washed and brushed his teeth in water so cold that it turned his face red and hurt his teeth. He used cold water because he would have had to let the water run a while to get hot water, and Jimmy had neither time or patience to wait for such luxury. Back in his bedroom, he dressed in the garb of a man who lived close to the land: boots and denim and flannel. He pulled on a wool jacket, planted an orange cap on the back of his head, and dropped to his knees to drag an old black purse from under his bed. The purse, which was quite large, had belonged to his mother years ago; he had begged her for it when it was worn out enough to throw away, and she had given it to him. In it he kept a small frying pan and a drawstring bag of salt.

Moving as soundlessly as a hunter stalking prey, Jimmy went into the kitchen and opened his mother's refrigerator. On the top shelf was a platter of wild doves that he and his daddy, and his brothers who lived nearby, had shot the previous day. They were dressed and ready to be baked. Taking several of the birds out one at a time, Jimmy snapped off their legs and put them in the purse with his skillet and salt. He put the legless doves on the bottom of the pile, covering them with the whole ones. Maybe his mother wouldn't notice this time.

Jimmy smiled to himself. Yes, she would. His mother never missed a thing. But she wouldn't say anything. There was something to be said for being his mother's youngest boy.

With the old purse tightly in hand, Jimmy eased out the kitchen door and moved quietly around the house and across the front yard to the road. It was cold that early in the morning, the clear Georgia air thin and moist, the ground under his feet slick with dew. On the other side of the two-lane blacktop road, Jimmy climbed one of his daddy's many fences and set off across a wide cornfield toward a stand of trees in the distance. He walked with a brisk, woodsman's stride, this steady-eyed, serious-looking young man. Normally his eyes had a hint of mischief in them, a sparkle, a gleam that warned all that Jimmy Alday had a devilish streak; but when he was out in the fields and woods, just himself and the land, he became pensive. Sometimes the thought weighed heavily on his mind that he was the fourth generation of his branch of the Alday family to walk here; the youngest male in a line of men that accounted for one hundred years of ownership of south Georgia land, the harvests it produced, the trees that sheltered it. Many had come before him, many would come after him, but he doubted if any would feel any closer kinship to the land than he did. And that was a responsibility that sometimes frightened him a little.

When he had crossed the broad field, Jimmy entered the stand of trees and made his way through their maze, over crunching twigs and dry leaves, to their far side where the riverbank lay. When he got to the bank he stood for a moment, looking down at the still, muddy water; across at the opposite bank; up at the clear, cold sky. The sun had come up by now, and its first warm rays reflected off the sheen of Jimmy's hair. He drew a deep breath, filling his healthy young lungs with the cold, unspoiled air. Then he knelt on the ground, gathered convenient twigs together in a pile, and started a small fire. Pushing dead leaves into a dry place to sit, he made himself comfortable, got out his frying pan, rubbed the salt bag over the wild dove legs, and proceeded to cook his breakfast.

As he sat there in the woods next to the river, eating wild fowl, the young man and the land became brothers. And from somewhere deep in the recesses of his mind came the idea that 123 it might be a fine thing for someone to write a history of the Alday family.

A fine thing indeed.

"That's the first time I ever thought about it," Jimmy told Arlene. He guided the pickup into the shade of a tree across the street from the Bainbridge library, and parked. For a brief moment he felt uncomfortable. "You don't think it's a silly idea, do you?"

"Of course not," she assured him, putting her hand on his arm for emphasis. "I think it's a very special idea, and I think you're a very special person for having it."

Jimmy took her into the library and she saw at once why he was happy here. It was open, airy, modern: a quiet, cool refuge from the long, hot days he worked in the fields with his father and brothers. Being from Mississippi, Arlene knew about farm boys. They were as distinct from town boys as barns were from drugstores. Seldom if ever did the traits or characteristics of one mix with the other. But this Jimmy Alday, whom she had known only a few weeks, was different. He was obviously a young man of the land: he had the deeply tanned skin and supple muscles of a farmer. But he also had keen eyes that were alert to *more* than the land, and a yearning, searching mind that instinctively knew the importance of tradition, and of the significance of each individual in the scheme of things. Arlene herself was not old enough or mature enough to understand exactly what it all meant; but she did realize that Jimmy Alday was an unusual young man.

"Show me some of the books you've looked at," she said.

Jimmy led her to the section on Georgia history and pulled out a few books for her.

"There's already some family histories here," he said, "but most of them are about families up around Atlanta, or over east around Augusta and Savannah. Hardly anything at all's been written about our little corner of the state." He opened a large book with a double-page map of the state as it had been when the Civil War ended. "See here," he said, pointing to the farthest southwest corner where Georgia met Florida on the south and Alabama on the west. "This is where my great-granddaddy rode into Georgia from Texas . . ."

It was a hundred years before Jimmy. His great-grandfather was Math Alday, whose name may or may not once have been

Matthew. The story had come down through generations of the family that he had been a short, stocky man with a full beard that hid a neck like a tree stump. Great-chested, they said he was, so thick in the torso that his weight bowed his legs. He wore rawhide like a lot of Texicans, and carried pistols at his waist, and you could tell by his direct gaze that he was a serious man not given to trifles or dalliance. He said a thing just once, never repeating himself. And once he set a goal, no force on earth could dissuade him from it, and few could delay him.

Math Alday had crossed the bottom of Louisiana, the bottom of Alabama, and part of the panhandle of Florida, before turning north and riding into the southwest corner of what, just ninety years earlier, had become the fourth of America's original thirteen states. No one remembers why Math had ridden up into Georgia. Probably it was because he was looking for land, and in the settlements along the way he would have heard that the land around the big lake in Seminole Indian country could be had cheaply—if a man was willing to pay the second price of standing up to those Seminoles, who were likely to try to drive him off. Indians, however, were no problem for Math Alday. Where he had come from, the Texican country, there were *real* Indians: Creek, Cherokee, and the bloodthirsty Comanche. Anyway, no one, white *or* red, was likely to drive Math Alday off land that was rightfully his.

In one of the settlements near the big lake, Math located a man who had title to more than a thousand acres bounding the water. Math had ridden into the settlement on a fine mustang mount, leading another one behind him. In those days, prime horseflesh was at a premium in south Georgia. Math had immediately guessed that from the scarcity of good animals around the settlement. He began negotiations with the landowner: horseflesh for acreage. When the bargaining was done, the landowner had Math Alday's spare mustang, and Math had 250 acres of the rawest, wildest land he had ever seen.

With the title to the land in his pocket, Math found an itinerant Baptist preacher who had no church but held prayer meetings on a clearing at the edge of town. "Brother," he said, "how'd you like to have yourself a real church, with a roof and a floor on it?"

"The Almighty's sky is my roof," the preacher said, "and His sweet green earth is my floor. I need nothing else."

"That's fine when the weather's good," Math said pragmati-   125 cally. "But when it ain't, your roof leaks and your floor turns to mud. Seems to me that people are more apt to listen to His word when their feet ain't wet." He pulled out a free-hand map drawn on settlement-store wrapping paper and pointed to the land he now held by the big lake. "I've got two hundred fifty acres down there that I aim to clear and plant."

"There's Indians down there," the preacher warned.

"There's Indians everywhere," Math said. "Don't worry about 'em; if they're on my land, I'll tend to 'em. Now then, I'd like to get more people to move down there, enough to start a settlement of our own. Best way I know to draw people is to have a church and a school. If you'll agree to settle there and preach, I'll give you the land for a church and help you build it."

"*Give* me the land, you say? How much land?"

"Four prime acres. Enough for any church. I can start clearing it tomorrow. When the church is built, it can double as a schoolhouse during the week. We'll worry about somebody to teach later." Math cocked his head. "What's your answer?"

The preacher stuck out his hand. "Done," he said.

The next day, Math Alday rode down into his wilderness land with a newly purchased Concord ax and felled the first tree for a little church and schoolhouse that would be used by his people for more than a hundred years.

"That little original church later did become the very first schoolhouse in the county," Jimmy told Arlene with a touch of pride in his voice. "It's still down there today, right where my great-granddaddy built it. I can take you down and show it to you if you want me to."

"I'd like to see it sometime, Jimmy," the girl said. "I really would."

When they left the library, Jimmy drove back to Donalsonville and parked uptown near the post office. It was Saturday and Second Street, the main commercial street, was crowded with shoppers and traffic.

"You've probably already seen the old-fashioned soda fountain down at the drugstore, I guess," he said.

Arlene nodded. "My aunt took me there."

"Want to go get some ice cream?"

"All right, if you do."

They walked down Second, not holding hands as some
126 young couples were, and feeling a little awkward because of it.

Several people exchanged greetings with Jimmy along the way, but none of the people knew Arlene so they just nodded and smiled at her. At the marble-topped soda fountain, where Jimmy's father had once bought ice cream for Jimmy's mother, the young man purchased two double-dip cones, and he and Arlene walked down Second eating them. In front of the Western Auto store, two men loitering in the shade appeared to Arlene to be paying particular attention to them.

"I think those men are talking about us," she said quietly to Jimmy. He looked over at them, then shook his head, suppressing a grin.

"My brothers," he said. "Just don't pay no attention to 'em. Maybe they'll leave us alone."

"Don't you like your brothers?" she asked.

Jimmy looked at her with slight incredulity. " 'Course I do. I love my brothers. I just don't want to listen to none of their teasing right now."

"What would they tease you about? Me?"

"For sure."

"What would they say?"

"Oh, they'd ask me if Mother knew where I was at, and if Daddy said I could be uptown by myself, and was I old enough to be walking with a girl. Just anything at all that they believed was clever."

Arlene glanced back and saw that the two men were still watching them. "Put your arm around me," she said.

"What?"

"Put your arm around me—" She took his arm and pulled it around her waist, and put her own arm around him. "Might as well give them something to really tease about," she said impishly. They walked on down the street with their arms around each other.

Oh, Lord, Jimmy thought. Sunday dinner tomorrow was going to be mighty interesting.

That was the summer of 1972, in Donalsonville, Georgia, when Jimmy Cecil Alday was twenty-four years old, full of life, full of plans, and full of the future.

15

Math Alday had taken a wife during the early 1870s and during the next decade fathered seven children. He lived his life, grew old, and died near the big lake in the southwest corner of Georgia. His seven children spread out over the land, some staying, some leaving. One son who stayed was Joell Alday. When Joell reached manhood, he too took a wife, from another clan that had put down roots in the land around the big lake: the Johnsons. Gertrude Johnson became Joell's bride, and the second generation of Math Alday prepared for the third.

Joell and Gertrude brought nine children into the world. Little Guy only lasted six years, but the others grew to adulthood. The girls were Dollie Mae, Merle, and Esmeralda, the boys Stion, Ned, Paul, Aubrey, and Everett. With them, the seeds of Math Alday spread even farther over the Georgia land, and the Alday roots sunk deeper. Then, suddenly, the land was swept away from the family by something a lot of them did not even understand, something called the Great Depression. What Indians and nature had not been able to accomplish, economics had. The Aldays, like tens of thousands of other Americans, lost everything.

Recovering from the Depression was slow, hard work.

Ned, the eldest living son of Joell, went to work for others. Like his father before him, he courted a Johnson girl, a pert, pretty young woman named Ernestine, to whom he proposed marriage.

"I don't have nothing to offer," he made clear, "except myself. I got two good hands to work with and I mean to use them to get back my family's land. But right now, well, I'm going to be working for the folks who've got the sawmill. I'll be living wherever the camp is; when it moves, I'll move. It won't be the easiest life in the world for you, but I promise to make it better someday. What do you say?"

Ernestine said yes. She wanted Ned and she wanted a big family like the one he had come from, nine children, and the even larger one she herself came from, ten children. They married and moved into a little wooden sawmill house that could be dragged on a sled from lumber camp to lumber camp as the cutting dictated.

The year was 1935. Ned was twenty-four, Ernestine twenty-one.

"You won't be seeing a whole lot of me except on Sundays," Ned told her early on. "I work a lot more'n most men."

That had been an understatement. Ned worked *constantly*. At the sawmill, he was the first one up in the morning, even before daybreak, to fire the big boiler used in the cutting operation. Then he worked twelve hours logging. At night, when other loggers were relaxing, Ned would finish supper, load his rifle, and be off to the wilderness around the lake.

"I'll be out until I get something," he would say. The "something" would be a raccoon or 'possum, occasionally a wildcat or even a panther, which still roamed the marshes at that time. After a kill, Ned would skin the animal and on the weekend take the hide into town to sell. When game was scarce, he would set fish baskets to trap fresh fish in the lake, which he would also take to town and sell to restaurants. Ned Alday was working when the sun came up, working when it went down. He knew no such thing as an eight-hour day; all he knew was that there was Alday land around the big lake that needed buying back—and he was bound unto himself to have that land.

Ned *was* home sometimes, however. That became clear to all the first time Ernestine began to swell up in front. "Well, well, well," Ned said when he slowed down long enough to notice. "Well now, that's just fine." Like every Alday before him, he loved young ones. And besides, when he got the land back, he would need heirs to pass it on to.

When Ernestine gave birth to the first of their nine children, a boy, they named him Norman.

For a time, one of Ned's younger brothers, Aubrey, lived with him and Ernestine. Unmarried, Aubrey worked as a logger in the same sawmill where Ned worked and lived. Aubrey was quieter than Ned, more thoughtful. Ned was a storyteller who would spin a tall tale for anyone who would listen; uptown on the courthouse steps on Saturday afternoons, he could often be found in the center of a group of farmers and 129 other loggers, enthralling them with the wildest yarn he could concoct. But Aubrey was more reticent; he was a watcher, an observer. He was also fearless—absolutely fearless. People around the big lake said that Aubrey would walk alone in the deep woods as if wildcats did not exist; wade in the marshy waters as if there was no such thing as a water moccasin snake. Perhaps it was his prowess with a rifle that gave him such confidence; he was a crack shot and could split a marble thrown into the air.

As restrained as he was, there was one thing in life that Aubrey could not resist: western movies. Picture shows, they were called in south Georgia. In the little community of Donalsonville, twenty miles north of the lake, a fellow named Dunn had opened a movie house, calling it Dunn's Theater. That was where one could find Aubrey every Saturday, from the time it opened, often until the time it closed. It was not unusual for him to go in and sit through the first show of the day, leave, go have supper somewhere, and later go back in and see the same show over again. The western picture show, to Aubrey, was the most wonderful thing ever invented. He *loved* these movies, with a fervor and a passion. His heroes were men like Buck Jones, Charles Starrett, and Johnny Mack Brown.

Sometimes he got teased about his love for the westerns. Ned would say, "Well, it's Saturday. I reckon you'll be going to the picture show with the other kids."

"I reckon," Aubrey would reply impassively.

"The other single boys from the camp will be going to the square dance out on the edge of town."

"That so?"

"They'll be meeting girls and dancing and having a fine ol' time."

"Good for them."

" 'Course, you'd rather be settin' up there in Dunn's picture show lickin' an ice cream cone and watching some fool make-believe cowboy ridin' some fancy Hollywood horse. I bet you even stomp your feet and holler, just like the little kids does."

"Sometimes," Aubrey would admit, "when it gets real exciting." He would smile and head out the door.

"You won't never find a wife in that blamed picture show!" Ned would yell after him as he left.

"Ain't looking for no wife!" Aubrey would yell back, laughing.

130   Aubrey loved to go to town on Saturday afternoons, not just

for the picture shows, but for the atmosphere of excitement. Saturday was the big day in Donalsonville. *Everybody* came to town: farmers, loggers, hunters, fishermen, wives, sons, daughters, girl friends—the main street literally teemed with life. Aubrey, the watcher, the observer, liked to walk around and look at people. Sometimes he would pick a spot and, as he put it, "set a spell." Ned knew that if he wanted to find Aubrey, he should first check Dunn's Theater, then start walking up one side of Second Street and down the other. He would either bump into his wandering brother somewhere along the way, or else find him "setting a spell" in front of the Cash Drug Store, the Dollar General Store, the Piggly Wiggly grocery market, or the Merchants and Farmers Bank. Aubrey would be sitting there with a Dr. Pepper in his hand, watching the world go by.

"That boy won't never find no wife," Ned would complain to Ernestine. "He'll live with us 'til he's old and gray. You'll be cooking for him for the rest of your life."

"Let him be," Ernestine would reply quietly. "He'll do all right. You'll see."

Ernestine was right and Ned was wrong. Aubrey did find a wife.

One Saturday, between picture shows, Aubrey ambled over to the Donalsonville hospital where his younger sister Dollie Mae worked as a practical nurse.

"Hey, Aubrey," she greeted him. "Picture show over?"

He nodded. "Let out a little bit ago. Good one today. Hoot Gibson picture. And a chapter of *The Painted Stallion* serial with Crash Corrigan."

Dollie Mae shook her head in amusement. "You and your picture shows, Aubrey, I swear."

"I like picture shows," he said simply. Down the hospital corridor, another practical nurse was just returning from delivering meal trays. She was a slim, attractive girl with bright, pretty eyes. "Who's that?" Aubrey asked.

"Inez Runnels. She works here with me. Isn't she cute? You want to meet her?"

"I reckon not," Aubrey said, suddenly shy. "I'd best be going. Got some bin'ess to attend to."

"I know what kind of business you've got," Dollie Mae said, grabbing his shirt-sleeve. "Settin' in front of Piggly Wiggly, that's your important business. You just wait a minute—"

Inez, the other practical nurse, had pushed the food cart up to them by then, and Dollie Mae stepped in to relieve her of it. 131

"I'll do the rest of this, sugar. You stay here and talk to my brother for me. This is Aubrey. Aubrey, this is Inez."

Before either of them could say a word, Dollie Mae was pushing the food cart away and they were alone. They glanced awkwardly at one another, not knowing what to say.

"Is it crowded in town today?" Inez finally asked.

" 'Course it is," Aubrey said with a frown. "It's crowded *every* Saturday."

Awkward silence again. Then: "You from around here?" Aubrey asked.

"I'm from Miller County. Up Colquitt way." She studied him for a moment. "You farm hereabouts?"

Aubrey shook his head. "Log. But I aim to have me a farm someday."

Inez looked away and it was his turn to study her. He liked what he saw. She was as pretty as Ned's wife Ernestine, and that was saying something.

"Listen," he said almost urgently, "do you like picture shows?"

"I'm crazy about them," Inez replied.

"No fooling," Aubrey said with a pleased smile.

There was never another awkward moment between them.

Aubrey and Inez were married in 1938, in a simple ceremony in the Donalsonville courthouse. They arranged for rooms in a boarding house in Bainbridge, a nearby community. Aubrey's job as a logger at that time had him working at The Forks, a point where Spring Creek, the Flint River, and the Chattahoochie River all came together. As his brother Ned did by hunting and fishing, Aubrey also sought to earn extra income by training bird dogs. He had a natural ability to handle dogs and he put it to use the first time for a big landowner named T.B. Bradshaw in Canton, Georgia, up north of Atlanta. Every day after work, while it was still daylight and without even eating supper, Aubrey would run the dogs into the thick woods and teach them to point for quail and other game birds. With infinite patience and an uncanny instinct for the way a dog thought, it was only a matter of time before Aubrey was ready to return to Mr. Bradshaw a brace of the best hunting dogs he could have asked for. After that, Aubrey's reputation as a dog trainer spread and hunters from all over the state sought his services at one time or another.

132   In addition to training dogs, Aubrey eventually began or-

ganizing hunting trips for northern Georgians who wanted to come down to the big lake and go for quail in the thicket woods. Aubrey would serve as their guide on the trips; after he and Inez got some land and a house, he would bring the whole group back for supper. He delighted in showing off Inez's cooking.

While all this was going on, the young couple was also starting a family of their own with their firstborn son, whom they named Benny. They would eventually have five other children, the youngest of whom, Curtis, would come when Aubrey was in his middle forties.

Life was good for Aubrey Alday, as it was for his brother Ned—and they both worked hard to see that it remained that way.

They both looked ahead to many more long years of the good life they had made.

16

Before Arlene went back to Mississippi that summer of 1972, Jimmy did take her down one Sunday afternoon to see the original old Baptist church, later a one-room schoolhouse, that his great-grandfather Math Alday had helped build. Afterward, they drove around the back roads that ringed Lake Seminole, and Jimmy showed her all the land that Ned, his daddy, now owned.

"It comes to five hundred and thirty-eight acres," Jimmy said proudly. "He started buying it a piece at a time back before I was born. It taken him twenty-five years to build it up to what it is now."

At one point he parked his pickup at the side of the road and took Arlene walking along a fence line.

"This here parcel was the first one Daddy bought. When he got it back, it was just like it had been the day my great-granddaddy Math found it: all trees and marshes, scrub weeds, wild flowers. The whole section had gone completely wild again. Daddy had one little ol' John Deere bulldozer and nobody to help him with the work. Only my oldest brother Norman and my next oldest brother Jerry had been borned at that time, and they was both just little kids who couldn't do no heavy work. So it was left up to Daddy. He had to clear the land all by hisself . . ."

Those first hundred acres, Ned was fond of saying, had been the hardest he had ever worked. By day he would ride the little bulldozer like it was a rodeo bronc, raring and kicking over the rough, raw ground. He bulldozed that ground by blade and shoveled it by hand, dug rocks out of it with a pick, roots with an ax, and leveled the acreage by sheer force of will and back muscle. At night he would walk up to the porch tired to the point of exhaustion, aching with the pain of his labor.

134   "It's the hardest, toughest land I ever seen," he would say to

Ernestine. "It's land rough enough to break a man. But it ain't agonna break me. No, sir. Not me. *I'm* agonna break *it.*"

And break it, he did. Cleared it, he did. Plowed it and planted it, he did. He put half of it in corn, half in peanuts. It was his first own crop. A prouder man never lived.

"The only thing I'm prouder of than my land," he once said, "is my family."

His and Ernestine's family, like their land holdings, was growing every year. After Norman, they had Jerry, Chester, and Jimmy; and the girls: Patricia, Jeannie, Nancy, Mary Elizabeth, and the baby of the bunch, Faye. Four sons and five daughters. And both parents doted on every one of them as if each was an only child.

One by one as his sons were born and grew, Ned introduced them to the land he so loved. It was his ardent hope that all four of them would remain there where they had been born, and work the land with him as men. He got his wish with three of them. But with Norman, the eldest, it was not to be.

"I don't want to spend my life in Seminole County, Daddy," Ned's firstborn told him. "I want to get out and see the world."

Norman stayed at home and worked the land with his father until his three younger brothers were big enough to shoulder their share of it; then he joined the Army and eventually made it his lifelong career.

But the three younger ones—Jerry, Chester, and Jimmy— would all, to Ned's delight, stay with the land.

While the three boys who remained at home were growing up, Ned spent many hours with them in the backwoods. Paul Shingler, a townsman who owned a Pontiac dealership, also had three sons, and the two fathers and six boys frequently hunted together.

"Ned, get those boys of yours up early on Saturday and let's us all go hunting," Paul Shingler would say. He was a stout, friendly man who thrived on the hunt. "I've leased me the hunting rights to three thousand acres of wild land down by the lake. We can go after dove, quail, some of those migrant ducks that come down from Canada, and who knows, we might even get us a deer now and again." In southwest Georgia, men hunted anything that could be cooked and eaten.

So the Shinglers and the Aldays ventured forth, fathers and sons, taking to the thicket in search of game. For the six boys it was heaven, pure and simple: there was nothing more wonderful than hunting with their daddies.

135

"Those young'uns of ours," Ned said to Paul Shingler, "are like steps on a ladder." And they were. Standing in a straight line for a shoot, each was about two inches shorter than the one next to him. Jerry Alday was the eldest; Edwin Shingler was a year younger; Chester Alday was a year younger than Edwin; and so on down the line: Marty Shingler, Jimmy Alday, Ted Shingler. Steps on a ladder.

Once they had a shoot to see who was best among them with a shotgun. Mr. Shingler won. But Jimmy, the youngest Alday, was a close second.

"My two brothers couldn't hardly believe it," Jimmy told Arlene. "Everything at my house had always been according to age, you know. Jerry was the oldest boy at home, so Jerry was supposed to be the best shot. And Shugie next—that's what we called my brother Chester. Then me, see, 'cause I'm the youngest. And 'course Daddy was Daddy, so he was supposed to be better'n all of us. I tell you, you ought've seen their faces when I come in second to Mr. Shingler. They like to died."

He did not tell her that although he was an excellent shot with almost any firearm he detested the killing of any living thing except wild game to be eaten. He had first demonstrated that quality when he was only twelve and he and three school friends were target-practicing in the woods with BB guns. Their targets were paper bull's-eyes that came with the tubes of BB pellets. For a while the boys were satisfied to test their aim at those targets stuck to trees. But later one of them decided that birds would be more of a challenge.

"I won't stay if y'all are going to shoot birds," Jimmy said.

"What's the matter with shooting birds?" the boy demanded.

"Birds is part of the forest," Jimmy said. "They're harmless. And they sing pretty. Ain't no need to kill them."

"Well, hell, your brothers kill doves. And quail."

"That's for eating. If you kill a robin or a bluejay, you gonna eat it?"

"No, I ain't."

"Then you oughtn't to kill it."

"I'll shoot birds if I want to," the boy declared. The other two joined with him.

Jimmy took his targets and BB gun and went home.

As the youngest boy, Jimmy frequently tagged along after Ned wherever he went. Ned by now had become a great storyteller. Whenever two or more of his friends were with him, Ned could not resist the temptation—nor was he ever encouraged to—to spin a tale. As he grew older, his stories became longer, more detailed, and more and more incredible. His reputation for exaggeration increased with every adventure he related. By the time he reached the age of fifty, he was referred to fondly as "Lyin' Ned." He thoroughly enjoyed his fame, and as his sons grew up he used them, one by one, to substantiate his tales. Jimmy was the last of Ned's verifiers. With the boy at his side, he would tell any outrageous lie that he fancied, and immediately turn to his son for corroboration.

"Ain't that right, Jimmy?" he would ask.

"That's right, Daddy, it sure enough is," Jimmy would un-hesitatingly testify, even though he might be hearing the story for the very first time. Jimmy grew to manhood vouching for and ratifying his father's boundless imagination. Eventually a story spread all over the county that Ned had to take Jimmy with him when it came time to call the hogs in at night. Word was, the hogs wouldn't believe Ned unless Jimmy was there to back him up.

Such play helped contribute to a deep bond between them. Jimmy was proud of his father. He once said, "My daddy is the best man I know. If I grow up to be half as good a man as he is, I'll be satisfied with myself."

Jimmy felt he had legitimate reasons to admire his daddy. Love and blood aside, the young man had a high opinion of Ned as an individual. Not only had he bought back his family's land parcel by parcel, and single-handedly reclaimed it from the wilderness, but without any advanced education and purely by means of his own creativeness, he had become one of the most innovative farmers in south Georgia. It was Ned who purchased the first cotton-picker and brought it into the county. Ned who privately experimented with crop rotation to make his land work for him as close to year-round as possible. And Ned who was the first farmer to deliberately overplant watermelons—and then haul them 150 miles to Columbus, Georgia, to market.

So the pride Jimmy felt for Ned was not just founded in the family tie; Jimmy admired Ned man-to-man.

It was Jimmy who first recognized that his daddy was beginning to slow down. Ned's hard work and diligence had paid him handsome dividends, but it had also taken a toll on his health. Severe arthritis eventually set in and he found that he could not keep up with his sons any longer. He who had sired and raised them could now be outworked by them in the field. He admitted as much to Jimmy one night in a moment of privacy.

"You and your brothers are better men than I am now, Jimmy. You know that, don't you, boy?"

Jimmy had shaken his head. "That's not so, Daddy. We're younger men, stronger men, healthier men. But we won't never be better men."

Jimmy's comment had touched Ned, fueled his pride, given him pause to think and reevaluate. They were *his* boys, sons he had brought up from infancy to manhood. Whatever they did, it was just as if *he* were doing it. His land was theirs, their labor his. That was the Alday way.

And that was one more thing of which Jimmy Cecil Alday was proud in that summer of 1972, when he was twenty-four years old and had his whole life ahead of him.

2

WAYNE COLEMAN
and GEORGE DUNGEE

17

Wayne Coleman's alarm sounded at five A.M. He had one of those cheap windup clocks that had an alarm like a fire signal. Wayne hated it. He swore every morning that he would throw it away and buy a better one, a quieter one, just as soon as he had a little extra money. Trouble was, he never seemed to *have* any extra money.

Groaning, he reached out from the bed and slammed the alarm button down, shutting off the grating noise. Son-of-a-bitch, he thought sleepily. Looking over at his curtainless window, he saw a gray, dreary Baltimore day. I can't make it this morning, he decided. Can't get up this morning. Pulling the covers over his head, he buried himself in the warm darkness.

The thought of getting up and going out to his construction job was totally repugnant to him. He hated getting up, and he hated that goddamned job. Back-breaking labor, that's all it was. Pick-and-shovel work. Not fit for a dog to do.

But fit for you, my ignorant friend, he told himself. Fit for stupid people who can't read well or write any better than a fifth-grader. Fit for someone who couldn't apply for a decent job because he wasn't even smart enough to fill out a detailed employment application. Oh yeah, pick-and-shovel work was just your speed, old buddy.

Shit, Wayne thought, throwing off the covers. He sat up on the side of the bed, wearing his underwear, the same underwear he had worked in for two days and slept in for three nights. He stank but he was not aware of it. Getting up, he went across the room to a two-burner hotplate and put on a pan of water to heat some coffee. Then he turned to a wash basin, urinated in it, rinsed it out, and washed his face in cold water.

Wayne's room was seedy and shabby. Plaster hung down in two places from the ceiling, several strips of wallpaper were peeling, and the squeaky wooden floor was unwaxed and bare of carpet. There was a single twin bed in one corner; he slept 141 on a bare mattress, used a bare pillow for his head, and his covers were wool blankets from a surplus store. He had an ancient wooden table and two mismatched chairs, and an old club chair with a floor lamp behind it. That was it. Plus the hotplate and sink. It was called a light housekeeping room, and it rented by the week. The bathroom was at the end of the hall.

While he waited for his water to boil, Wayne dressed. Grungy jeans, khaki shirt, heavy work shoes that laced up over his ankles. After he got the shoes on, he sat on the side of the bed with his face buried in both hands, wishing to God that things were different, that life wasn't the way it was for him. Goddamn, he thought, what made life so good for some people and so fucking bad for others? How did a thing like that get decided anyway? What was it that put *him* at the bottom of the fucking totem pole?

Wayne sat there brooding sleepily until he heard the water boiling and bubbling in the pan. Then he got up and fixed himself a cup of instant coffee. He carried it to the lumpy club chair and sat down, holding the steaming cup between both hands. He stared down at the ugly floor. Jesus, how he dreaded going out on that goddamned job! He would actually rather take a beating—a physical beating—than go out there.

Putting the cup on the chair arm, Wayne looked at his hands. They were lined, cracked, calloused, imbedded with dirt that would probably never come out. I'm twenty-five years old, he thought, and my hands look like I'm fifty. Old before my time, he thought. But, hell, that shouldn't surprise him. He'd *always* felt old; sometimes he thought he'd been *born* old.

Picking up the cup and blowing on the steaming coffee, Wayne thought of his family, wondering where they all were. He had one older brother, Jimmy Coleman, who he thought was living down in North Carolina, working as a carpenter. Three older sisters: Ruth, Lois, and Ann. The latter two, he believed, were still around the Baltimore area somewhere, married probably. The eldest, Ruth, was probably still in Parkville, probably still worrying herself sick about what was happening to all those younger Issacs kids that his old lady seemed to have had one after another. Jesus, what a baby machine that woman was. He himself was the last offspring of Carson Coleman. He did not even remember his father—the man was just a name, somebody who had been there before Archie Issacs came along; someone who had fathered five kids and then walked away and left them like they were so much garbage. Wayne never really thought of Carson Coleman as his father.

142

He knew he *was,* but the man who had *acted* like a father toward him had been Archie Issacs.

Wayne, the last of the Coleman brood, and Roy, the first of the Issacs children, were less than three years apart in age, and had grown up close, as brothers should. When they reached their teens, they had worked alongside Archie in the fields, worked with him when he hired the three of them on at a dairy farm, worked with him at nearly everything he did. They had been Archie's main helpers; he said so many, many times, and praised them for it. Wayne had enjoyed working with his step-father and half brother. He had been part of a team, pulling his own weight, doing his share, and he had felt good about it.

What the hell had happened to all the good feelings he used to have? he wondered. How had life turned out to be so much shit for him? Sipping his coffee, he tried to figure out the turns his life had taken. Archie had left, of course, driven away, Wayne thought, by his mother, her drinking and running around. Then Ruth had tried to take care of the younger kids and hadn't been able to make it. The kids had been taken away by the state and farmed out to foster homes. Roy had gotten away from it all by joining the Army. Wayne himself had drifted off on his own.

Wayne had tried life both ways—crooked and straight. Being crooked had not worked out too well for him. He had been arrested for breaking-and-entering and given two years for it. He served a year. Not hard time; easy time. But still time, and he had not liked it.

Out of prison, he worked at whatever he could find, mostly menial work, common labor, day jobs that paid you at the end of your shift and hired you again the next morning—if you showed up. Pick-and-shovel work, Wayne called it.

Sighing wearily, Wayne drank his coffee and set the cup on the floor beside the old chair. Damn, he thought. Damn, damn, damn! He wondered how the younger kids, his half brothers, were doing. Roy was probably still in the army. Carl, he had heard, had run away from a foster home and been sent to the state training school. Robert, Billy, and George were all in foster homes somewhere, he supposed. Goddamn it, there ought to be a law that kept men like Carson Coleman and Archie Issacs from running off and abandoning their kids like that. Ought to be a law that made a man take care of little kids that he causes to be borned. Hell, if he'd had a father to help him grow up, if all the other kids'd had a father, somebody to help them, teach them, guide them, then maybe life would be a lot different for all of them. I know it sure would be for me, he thought fervently. *I* would have made something of *my* life if I'd had somebody to point the goddamned way and give me a little shove. Then maybe I wouldn't be the kind of fucking misfit I am now. Fucking clod. Don't know nothing, can't do nothing, ain't got nothing, won't *ever* have nothing. I'll be fifty by the time I'm thirty, and when I'm forty I'll be dead. And my whole fucking life will have been just so much shit going down the fucking toilet.

Wayne got up and went over to a small medicine cabinet above the sink. He looked at himself in a faded, stained mirror on the cabinet door. His face was gaunt, his eyes mirthless and dull. I'm *old,* he thought. Jesus Christ, look at me! Twenty-five fucking years of age and I'm *old!*

Worse than that, I'm *nothing.*

Turning from the mirror, a look of utter rage and frustration came over his face. His eyes lost their flatness and took on a wild gleam. Inside, he could feel a desperate surge of *something,* telling him to *move.* It was like a last summons to survival: do something now or perish. And never be missed or remembered.

Wayne walked to a small closet and pulled a brown paper-wrapped parcel from the shelf. Laying it on the bed, he peeled the paper away and hefted its contents in both hands.

It was a .410-gauge double-barrel shotgun.

Wayne had an old beat-up Chevrolet that looked like hell but managed to get him where he wanted to go. On the day that he absolutely, positively could not make himself face another shift at his pick-and-shovel construction job, he took the shotgun, got in his old car, and drove out into the country. In the deep recesses of his mind, he knew what he was going to do; he just did not know exactly where, or exactly when. But something told him that at the right place, at the right time, he *would* know. And he would do it.

He drove around outside the city, cruising random country roads, turning when he felt like it, enjoying the scenery, the day, the freedom. Not going to work at the job he hated had filled him with a buoyancy that he had never known before. That simple decision not to go to work, to cast aside his rotten job, to free himself once and for all from that weight on his mind and body and spirit, seemed to have done wonders for him. For a change, he felt like he was worth something, that he, his life, his future, actually had value.

144

Wayne did not attempt to square his bountiful new feeling with the fact that he was about to commit a serious crime. It did not occur to him that his newfound self-esteem was negative in nature, conjured up by the false bravado of shunning his responsibilities; and that by committing the crime he would merely be undermining his already shallow character. His good feelings were counterfeit, but there was no way for him to know that. It had been so many years since he had experienced legitimate good feelings, and they were buried so far down in his memory, that he was unable to summon them for comparison. So he accepted the fraudulent for the genuine; he could not tell the difference.

He found a little country store that day, in an out-of-the-way place on the back road. One old man and no customers. Robbing it could not have been easier. The old man did not resist, did not panic, did not get hurt. Wayne made him lie on the floor, thinking he could get in his car and be gone before anyone would see him. But he had trouble starting the god-damned car. He had to sit in front of the place a full minute to get it running. By then, of course, he was being watched by the old man: the make and color of his car was being noted, his license number memorized, a telephone call to the police being made.

Wayne got away from the little store—but not far away. About two miles from there, at a crossroads stop sign, his old Chevrolet stalled. Before he could get it started again, a county police car pulled up behind him. The officers, who had already received a radio call about the holdup, were on him with guns drawn before he even saw them. In seconds he was in custody, his good feelings gone, dissolved into the sick, sick feeling that accompanies arrest.

In court the case against Wayne Coleman was basic and simple. He had been caught with the stolen money, identified by the store owner, and was in possession of the deadly weapon with which he had committed the crime. And he was an ex-convict with one felony conviction already on his record. The court sentenced him to ten years in prison.

Wayne was miserable. Ten years was a hell of a price to pay for a scant few hours of feeling like he had some worth. He could barely believe his bad luck. The robbery had only netted him a few hundred dollars. At least, that was what they had told him; he had not had time to count the loot. He realized, of course, that the amount of money involved did not really mat- 145 ter; what had sent him up for ten years was the goddamned shotgun, plus the fact that he was an ex-con.

Unlike Carl, Wayne had no problems with other convicts when he got to prison. One look at Wayne's dull eyes and emotionless face was warning enough not to mess with him. While he was not physically intimidating, there nevertheless was an aura about him that said: *Fuck with me, man, and you better be prepared to kill me. 'Cause you'll have to.* The black studs left him alone, the prison yard ripoff artists left him alone, and—as long as he behaved himself—the administration left him alone.

And behave himself he did. Wayne may have been slow, but he was not stupid. On a second-term ten-year sentence, he knew he could be granted parole after two years and actually get out in thirty months. That was what he determined to work toward: the earliest release possible. He did the best he could on all the aptitude and psychological tests they gave him; was on his best behavior during every staff interview; accepted all his counselor's recommendations as to group therapy, prison work programs, and self-improvement studies; and in general played whatever game the prison administrators wanted to play, by whatever rules they established. He was not a model inmate, since he always lacked an attitude of sincere enthusiasm, but at least he was not a troublesome prisoner. He went through the administration's step-by-step rehabilitation process like a robot, doing everything by the numbers, going from one square to the next as if a pawn in a chess game. He did not complain, agitate, or talk back. He did exactly the amount of work assigned to him: not a whit more, not a whit less.

When his two years were up, Wayne felt certain he would be paroled. He faced the board with the supreme confidence of an honor student interviewing for a scholarship. On the table in front of the parole board were copies of his unblemished prison record. He went smoothly through the brief interview, giving stock but acceptable answers to the board's few questions. When he left the interview room, he felt certain that an early release date would soon be forthcoming.

Returning to his cell three nights later, Wayne found his parole hearing notification waiting for him. He quickly opened the envelope and read the slip of paper inside. The news stunned him. He had been given a two-year set: he had to serve
another twenty-four months before the board would consider

him again. Wayne dropped forlornly to his bunk, devastated by the shattering disappointment. Burying his face in his hands, he cried for the first time since he was a child.

The next morning, Wayne was summoned to the office of the associate warden in charge of custody.

"Coleman, I know you must be very disappointed by the parole board's decision in your case. But I want you to know that you came very close. And your good record here did not go unnoticed. The board has recommended that you be considered for transfer to a minimum security facility where you'll have more freedom of movement and more opportunities for self-improvement. I'm going to endorse that recommendation. Within the next month you can expect to be transferred to Poplar Hill Correctional Camp. You'll like it there."

"Yessir," Wayne answered mechanically. Poplar Hill or wherever, he would still be locked up—for another two long years.

A week later, he was taken by prison bus along with several others across the state to Poplar Hill. The correctional camp was a lot different from the big walled prison; it consisted of dormitory buildings, cyclone fences, and lots of open spaces. To Wayne it looked like some kind of hospital or convalescent home. But shortly after his arrival, that illusion was dispelled.

"Well, Coleman," the assignments officer said, "from your record I see that on the outside you did day labor in construction work. You'll be happy to know that we can give you some very similar work here. We're going to put you on one of our road maintenance crews. It's good, healthy outdoors work. You'll like it."

"Yessir." He spoke mechanically. Lethargically. Helplessly.

The next morning when he lined up for work, he was issued a shovel. He looked dejectedly at it, his whole being overcome by apathy, indifference. He was back where he started: pick-and-shovel work.

Only now he did not have a choice of going to work or not.

18

Fannie Dungee sat looking across the kitchen table at her son George. He was a grown man, well into his twenties, but for the life of her Fannie could not help thinking that in reality, in his head, he was still such a boy.

"This girl you say you gon' to move in wid, what you say her name is?"

"Elizabeth, Mamma. Elizabeth Lincoln. Her family was named after President Abraham Lincoln. He freed the slaves."

"Yes, he did," Fannie said. Sometimes she wondered about *that,* too. What, she wondered, had freedom done for her people? She had grown up dirt-poor and black, just like three generations of her family before her. And now her only son apparently was going to do likewise. Here he was, full grown and ready to start living his own life, and he didn't have much more future than today's newspaper. He'd never held a decent job, had not finished school, had not learned very much even while he *went* to school. Why, the boy couldn't even write: he still printed everything except his scrawled signature.

"Son, how you think you and that girl gon' get by?" Fannie asked. "You can't seem to hold no job for very long, and you say she ain't even working."

"She got a job promised to her, Mamma. As a maid at the Holiday Inn. An' I be able to find work if I keep looking."

"Are you two fixin' to get married?"

George looked down at the tabletop. His mother was a devout Baptist. "We, uh, thought we best see first do we get along living together, Mamma."

"Lord, Lord, Lord," Fannie said quietly, more to herself than to a deity. "Young peoples, young peoples. What the worl' coming to?"

Things were so different now than they had been when she was a girl. Back in her day, young people had a set of rules that they tried to live by. Oh yes, sometimes they failed, but at least the rules were there, the young folks *tried.* Nowadays they seemed to make up their rules as they went along. Fannie sighed and thought of her dead husband. George, poor little fellow, had never known his daddy; Fannie's husband had died of consumption when the baby was just six months old.

Fannie had done her best raising the boy; and by the standards of the Baltimore ghetto where economics dictated that they live, she had done an exemplary job. The apartments in which they had lived were always extremely modest, often downright poor, but they were always immaculately clean. Fannie saw to it that every wall, every baseboard, every inch of floor, every windowsill was spotless. scrubbed clean with bleach within hours after they moved in. After George reached a certain age, he always helped his mother, both to make their quarters clean and to keep them clean. As a teenager he often cleaned and waxed the floor for Fannie without even being told, just to save her from having to do it after work. George knew that his mother worked very hard to support them while he was growing up. She put in long, hard hours at a vegetable canning plant, for wages far below what the labor deserved. But it was the best work she could find. An uneducated black woman could not be overly selective about jobs; especially if she had a fatherless son to raise.

George had given his mother very little trouble while he was growing up. There were often times when he did not obey her, but he was always polite and respectful about it. If Fannie told him to be sure and go directly to school, he would smile and say, "Yes, Mamma," and then go do whatever he wanted to do. To his credit, he managed most of the time to avoid getting into trouble over his indiscretions. He seemed instinctively to know when he should stop breaking the rules and start being a good boy again; he had a sixth sense about just how far he could go, and invariably he checked himself before reaching that point. So even though he was a truant, a petty thief, and a drinker during his adolescence, Fannie never knew it. To her he was an almost perfect boy. A little slow, to be sure, but certainly not bad.

"Lord, Lord," Fannie said again. "If you bound and determined to move in wid' this girl, George, I am not about to say nothin' against it. You grown, she grown, you two got to do whatever you think be right for you." She reached across the table and took his hands. "An' you know, George, that your mamma gon' be praying for you every day. You know that, don't you, son?"

"Yes, Mamma, I know it."

"All right then." She patted his hands. "You go on and get your things together; go on and move in wid' your Elizabeth. An' I'll pray to Jesus that ever'thing be all right wid' both of you. Go along now."

Elizabeth was the first girl that George ever slept with. They had met while working at a small coffeeshop near the docks, Elizabeth as a counter girl, George as a dishwasher. Elizabeth had been attracted to George's quiet, slow ways and soft, almost lazy speech. And the fact that he was not very big. She herself was small, barely five feet tall, and she had always felt out of place with men considerably larger than her. With George, who was only about five-four, she felt comfortable.

They took their coffee breaks together, talked when business was slow, and once in a while she helped him with the dishes, although she was not obliged to do so. Once when he broke his glasses, she used a hairpin to wire them together until he could afford to get them fixed. "Say, thanks," he told her gratefully. "I don't know what I'd do without my glasses."

"Are your eyes very bad?" she had asked.

George smiled his lazy smile. "Yeah, pretty bad. I've had to have glasses since I was just a little kid."

"You should try to take better care of them," she had scolded lightly. "Be more careful."

"Okay, I will. Thanks."

They had only known each other a couple of weeks when Elizabeth invited him home one night at closing. "Want to walk me home, George?" she asked.

George, ill at ease, had shrugged. "Sure, I guess so. If you want me to."

"I want you to," she said. She took his hand and they walked off together.

An hour later, in bed in the little housekeeping room that Elizabeth rented, she propped herself up on one elbow and said, "George, have you ever been with a girl before?"

"No," George admitted, looking away.

"Well, it's not anything to be ashamed of," she said. "You just a little late getting started, is all. But we can fix that." She put her tongue in his ear and drew one of his hands over to the warm place between her legs. "Do you like that, George?" she asked, her words tickling the wetness in his ear. "Like what you feel there, hmmmm? Here, let me show you something—"

George never did become an accomplished lovemaker. The best Elizabeth could say for him was that he *lasted;* he would keep right on going until she indicated that she'd had enough. He made up in quantity what he lacked in quality. And for Elizabeth that was satisfactory.

After they began living together, they settled into a kind of limbo relationship that got no better or worse, did not expand and grow nor deteriorate and die. They seemed to fit together; if they were not complementary, they were certainly compatible. They almost never argued. If George wanted to watch an Orioles game on television—and he followed the team religiously from season beginning to end—then Elizabeth usually watched it with him. If he wanted to go to a movie, which he also liked very much to do, she would go along with him, seeing whichever picture he selected, seemingly having no preference of her own. Wherever George led, she followed; and when he did not lead, she did not move.

Elizabeth stayed employed most of the two years they were together, but George was not as fortunate. He managed to get several jobs as a dishwasher, but none of them lasted very long. George's slow, easy ways, his extremely casual approach to anything that needed doing, did not serve him well when there was a sinkful of dirty dishes and a restaurant full of people hurrying to eat during their lunch hour. The same slowness hindered him when he tried to move up a step to short-order cook; he simply could not keep up with the orders.

For the most part, George and Elizabeth lived off whatever she was able to earn. When George was not working, Fannie would occasionally give him a few dollars out of her meager income; but with rising costs and what she felt bound to give to her church, she barely got by herself. It did not particularly bother George that he could not keep a steady job; it seemed to him that unemployment was just part of everyday life in the Baltimore ghetto. As long as Elizabeth had a more or less steady income, and in a pinch there was always Fannie to fall back on, he was not going to worry about going hungry or having a place to sleep. Some days, when Elizabeth gave him lunch money and carfare to go job hunting, George would buy a pint of muscatel and sit nursing it in a movie all day, seeing the same picture over and over. He liked the movie theaters; they were dark and peaceful, and there was no one there trying to make him hurry and do something. He hated hurrying.

Living life slowly and easily, that was the way for George. The only way.

When George and Elizabeth had been living together for   151 about a year and a half, she came home one night with a very serious look on her face.

"I went to the welfare clinic for an examination today," she said. "I'm going to have a baby, George."

George stared at her without commenting.

"Well, say something," Elizabeth said.

George shrugged. "I never counted on no baby," he said.

"Neither did I. But we been having our fun in bed, now we gots to pay for it. You gon' have to find you a good, steady job, George."

"I been looking," he claimed. "There jus' ain't no openings."

"You got to look harder, George." Her voice took on a slight edge of harshness that he had never heard before. "I'll be able to keep working about six or seven months, I expect, but after that it's going to be up to you to support us. We gon' be your family, George; you gon' have to take care of us."

All the next day, George remained in the shabby little apartment they shared, not going out at all. He sat on the couch and stared into space; lay on the bed and stared at the ceiling; sat in the kitchen and stared at the tabletop. The thought of being responsible for a little baby frightened him. He was not at all ready for such a heavy responsibility. He felt as if he were being asked to hurry again.

"Ain't there nothing you can do about that baby," he asked Elizabeth later. "Some way you can not have it?"

"If you mean will I go get an abortion somewhere, George, the answer is no," she said firmly. "We made this baby and we gon' have it and take care of it. You hear me?"

"Yeah, I hear."

In the months that followed, as Elizabeth's belly grew bigger and bigger, George continued to look for work, but with no more dedication than he had earlier. The impending arrival of his child served as no incentive for him at all. He found jobs from time to time, delivering circulars, distributing telephone directories, unloading vegetable trucks in the summer market; but they were all part-time or temporary work, nothing that had any permanence or stability. And even at those menial occupations, George remained incredibly slow.

There were times when he put his preferences aside and actually tried to do better: to move faster, work faster, produce more, to *hurry;* but he did not seem to be able to do it. His mind would say *move! Go! Get it done!* But his body would not respond at once; his mind would then forget it and go on to some other, more pleasant thought, such as a movie or an Ori-

152

oles game or a bottle of muscatel. Whatever the job was would never get done. George would still be thinking about it when the boss came around to check. And often that would be it; George would be fired.

When it came time for Elizabeth to stop working and take it easy for the last couple of months until their baby came, George still did not have a steady job; in fact, he was hardly working at all, at anything.

"I'm just gon' have to go to the Welfare," Elizabeth told him. "Ain't nothin' else I can do. An' you know they gon' come round here and ask you questions an' all."

George shrugged as if it did not matter to him, but it did. He was not good at answering questions; people were too quick for him, they made him feel stupid. He was not stupid, he was slow, but people who asked questions never allowed for that. They asked the questions fast and they expected fast answers. It was *hurry* all over again.

On the day that Elizabeth went to the welfare office, George put his few meager belongings in a grocery bag and left. He was waiting on Fannie's apartment stairs when she got home from work that night. "The welfare peoples gon' be after me for not working to support Elizabeth and the baby," he told his mother. "Can I come back and stay wid' you again?"

He could, of course. Fannie, good-hearted soul that she was, would not have turned away a stranger, much less her own son. Besides, she thought, it was better for him to be there with her than off alone somewhere, or with strangers who would take advantage of him. If he was there with her, Elizabeth would know where to find him; Fannie was sure that the young woman would be able to talk George into coming back to her. After the baby came, George would see for himself that it was nothing to be afraid of. A little tiny baby didn't really take no money to care for, it just took time. Fannie was sure that everything would soon be all right with George and Elizabeth again.

She was wrong. Elizabeth did not come looking for George— but she did send the welfare investigators around to talk to him after the baby was born.

"Mr. Dungee, you're the natural father of the infant girl that has been born to Miss Lincoln," they told him, "and that means that you are legally liable for that child's support. Since you have made no voluntary effort to provide for the child's care, we're going to have to issue you a summons to appear in family court and have the matter heard by a judge." 153

George appeared in court and explained to the judge that he had not been able to find steady employment and had no dependable income. The judge was sympathetic but bound by certain laws. "I can understand your dilemma, Mr. Dungee; it is not easy to meet one's obligations when employment is scarce. But the law nevertheless dictates that a natural parent aid in the support of an indigent minor child for whom the county or state has taken over responsibility. I'll make it as easy as I can on you, however. You are hereby ordered to pay the sum of five dollars per week in partial support of your minor daghter. The court feels that you should be able to do at least that much. Bear in mind now that failure to comply with this order will put you in contempt of court. That's all. You're dismissed."

George paid the five dollars a week as long as he had a job of some kind and had the money. But he made no *effort* to do it. If he had five dollars in his pocket on Wednesday, Elizabeth would get it; if he did not have it, he did not worry about it. Nor did Elizabeth. She got by with her new baby as best she could on her welfare check and, when it was forthcoming, the five dollars from George. But when she occasionally had to borrow money from her relatives, they scolded her for not being firmer with George.

"Why don't you make that worthless nigger give you your money every week, 'stead of jus' when he feel like it?" she was asked. "Set the law on that boy; they'll see he pays!"

But Elizabeth would not do it. From time to time she *threatened* to do it—but that was as far as she ever went. Her case worker, however, had no qualms at all about doing it. She knew Elizabeth was not receiving regular payments from George, and she pressured the young woman to admit it.

"He's not paying you, is he, Elizabeth? That's why you have to borrow money, isn't it? Why do you let him get away with it?"

"It jus' don't seem right to put a man in trouble over something like that," she said. "It's only five dollars a week—"

"It may be *only* five dollars a week," the case worker pointed out, "but when you don't receive it, you have to borrow money to supplement your welfare check. That five dollars could feed your baby for a couple of days."

The case worker pressured Elizabeth until she finally agreed to sign an affidavit stating that George had failed to make prompt and regular payments in compliance with the court order.

George had just started a job as a box boy in a neighborhood market when a welfare investigator and a policeman came to pick him up. "What you gon' do with me?" George asked as the policeman handcuffed him.

"You'll have to stay in jail until you can see the family court judge. The court calendar is pretty full; it usually takes a few days for your name to come up on the docket. When you get to court, the judge will decide what to do with you. He'll either give you another chance or send you away for a few months to teach you a lesson."

In George's case it turned out to be the latter. The judge he saw was influenced by two things in his case: George had been working when picked up, and he was under an order to pay only five dollars a week. "A kid with a paper route could pay that much," one of the welfare workers told the court. And the court agreed. It appeared that George had flagrantly violated the payment order out of sheer disrespect for the court.

"Let's see if a few months of incarceration will inspire you to help support your daughter a little more regularly. I sentence you to six months at Poplar Hill."

Back in the lockup, George asked another prisoner, "What's Poplar Hill?"

"Prison camp," he was told. "Not too bad a place, really. Better than going behind the walls."

George was transferred there two days later. He and some others from the city jail arrived by bus just as a group of state prison transferees were being processed in at the camp reception area. While George was being issued his clothing, bedding, and toilet supplies, he bumped into another prisoner and dropped some of his things. As he was trying to pick them up, his glasses fell off. Someone almost stepped on them but one of the state prison transferees saved them for him.

"Hey, thanks, man," he said gratefully. "I'd be lost without them. Thanks."

"Forget it," said Wayne Coleman. "You're gonna have to move a little faster, man. These motherfuckers will run over you."

"Yeah, sure," said George.

Back to hurrying again, he thought.

He watched Wayne Coleman easily juggle all his issue and move into the next room for a barracks assignment.

Nice guy, George thought. Saved my glasses. Maybe I can get to be friends with him.

19

The state dumptruck edged back to the culvert along the side of the highway, elevated its bed, and let slide a full load of number-two gravel. The gravel poured into the culvert, forming a six-foot pile the peak of which came up even with the elevation of the road. Twelve convicts, all with shovels, stood in a line and watched the dust of the dumped load settle. As soon as it had, the corrections officer in charge yelled, "All right, go to work! Six men here, six men over there! Spread it out in both directions!"

A shovel and a rock pile, Wayne Coleman thought dismally. Welcome to Poplar Hill.

The work crew divided and formed on each side of the gravel into two lines of six men each, standing at intervals of eight feet apart. They moved the gravel chain-fashion, the man nearest the pile passing a shovelful to the next man's shovel and so on down the line. Not a very scientific method but it eventually got the job done, spreading the gravel out fifty feet in each direction from the original pile.

Wayne was the last man in his line, on the end; he took gravel from the shovel of the fifth man and spread it out at the end of the culvert. As he worked, he became aware that the line was not functioning smoothly; there was no rhythm to it. When Wayne held his shovel out, number five should have been turning to fill it at the same time. But like as not, Wayne found he had to stand there, empty shovel held out, for four or five seconds, until number five caught up. It was not number five's fault, Wayne saw at once. The hitch was being caused by number three, the third man in line. He was too slow to keep up the tempo of the line.

"Come on, boy, for Christ's sake!" number four yelled. "You draggin' on the line!"

156   "Yeah, okay," number three said.

Wayne looked up the line and saw that number three was the black boy who had dropped his glasses in the receiving area. One of the reasons he was not able to keep up the speed of the line appeared to be those same glasses; they kept slipping down number three's sweaty nose and he would have to pause and push them back, which meant taking one hand off his shovel.

"Come on, boy, goddamn it!" number four yelled again. "Pick it up!"

"Yeah, get with it, boy!" number two joined in. "I thought all you coons had natural rhythm."

"I'm trying," George Dungee said, half shyly, half embarrassed.

"Try harder," number four ordered. Number four was a white con, six feet tall and muscular. He had a skull-and-crossbones tattooed on one bicep. Guess that means he's tough, Wayne thought dryly.

They worked for an hour, with George under constant harassment by the men on each side of him. Then the boss blew his whistle for a break and the lines fell out.

"Jesus H. Christ," number four said loudly, "you the slowest bastard I ever did see! You move like a fucking snail!"

George shrugged good-naturedly and did not say anything.

"You better speed it up when we start again, snail," said number two, "or I'm gonna start pitching the gravel on your fucking feet. I can't stand there and hold it all day, you know."

Two and four sat down together. George sat down by himself on the bank of the culvert. He used the tail of his shirt to try and clean his glasses. Wayne sat down near him and lighted a cigarette. When George put his glasses back on, he saw Wayne, recognized him, and smiled. Wayne bobbed his chin at him.

After ten minutes, the whistle blew again and the convicts stood up to go back to work. Wayne picked up his shovel and stepped over to George. "Don't pay no attention to them assholes," he said, nodding at two and four. "Just try to keep up as best you can."

His advice did not work. George could not keep up; he simply did not have the required coordination, the necessary physical balance, the reflexes between mind and body. It took too much concentration for him to hold his shovel steady to allow number two to fill it up; too long for him to pivot from number two to number four; too steady a hand for him to turn his shovel over and pour the gravel into number four's shovel. He   157 could do it—if allowed to do it slowly. But when he rushed, the cycle broke down completely: he did not take a full shovel load from number two, or he lost half of it in turning too quickly, or he poured half of it on the ground by missing number four's shovel.

"Jesus Christ, man!" number two yelled in frustration. "Can't you *move,* you fucking snail!" Angrily he tossed a shovelful of gravel on George's feet.

"Come on, come on, come on!" number four was yelling at the same time. "Man, you must be fucking *stupid!*"

Number two received another shovelful from number one, and threw it too on George's feet while George was being chastised by number four. George looked down helplessly as sand from the gravel went into his shoes.

Finally Wayne had enough of it. "All right," he said, "hold it just a fucking minute." He walked up to George. "You go on down to my place at the end of the line. You can be as slow as you want down there, it don't make no difference." George hesitated, looking from Wayne to the two white boys who were riding him so badly. He was clearly frightened of doing the wrong thing. "It's okay," Wayne said, "go on down there."

George trudged down to the end of the line while Wayne took his place between two and four.

"All right," Wayne said tonelessly to number two, "I'll try to keep up with you, hear? But if I can't, don't throw no gravel on my feet 'cause that'll make me mad. An' if I get mad, I'm gonna hit you in the face with my shovel. We understand one another?"

Number two stared open-mouthed at Wayne. Who did the little shit think he was? Number two started to challenge what Wayne said, but something suddenly made him check his words. Maybe it was that hollow, almost lifeless look in Wayne's eyes—a look that clearly was dangerous, threatening. Number two got the distinct impression that it would not really be necessary to throw gravel on this man's feet; he got the impression that if he so much as opened his mouth, that this creepy-looking little prick would haul off and bash him in the face with that shovel just for arguing with him.

"No sweat, man," number two said. "I'll work at whatever speed is good for you. We just wanted to get the nigger out of here, you dig? Me an' my buddy here"—he indicated number four—"we like to work with white men. Know what we mean?"

"Sure, I know what you mean, man," said Wayne. "Come on, let's shovel gravel."

The line went back to work. At the far end of it, George Dungee did just fine all by himself. As the tough little white guy had said, he did not have to rush at all.

That night after supper, Wayne was lying on his bunk in the dormitory when George came over and knelt on the floor next to him.

"I want to thank you for what you did today, man," George said. "Those guys were really starting to lean on me pretty hard."

Wayne shrugged. "Forget it. Those guys are assholes. If they give you any more trouble, wait 'til they're not looking an' bash their fucking heads in with your shovel. You don't have to take no shit from guys like that. They ain't nobody."

"Yeah, I know, man. I just like to try and get along, is all." George smiled his soft, lazy smile. "Living is lots easier when everybody gets along. You know?"

"Sure," Wayne agreed, shrugging again. "There's just some people you can't get along *with*." Wayne fingered a cigarette out of his shirt pocket and stuck it between his lips. As an afterthought, he took the whole pack out and offered one to George. "Yeah, thanks," George said. "I'll pay you back next week; my mamma's sending me five dollars."

"Don't worry about it."

There was a book of matches on the windowsill next to Wayne's bunk. George reached for them, struck one, and lighted both their cigarettes.

"How are your hands after that work we had to do today?" George asked.

"My hands? Hell, they're all right. I've done pick-and-shovel work before. Why? Your hands sore?"

"Sore as hell," George admitted sheepishly. "I've never done no labor work like that before."

"You're smart," Wayne said. "That kind of work is no fucking good. It ages a man, you know. But don't worry about your hands; they'll be okay in a few days. Tomorrow'll be rough, though; second day's always worse than the first." He studied the quiet black man for a moment. "Listen, stick by me tomorrow, hear? I'll help you out if I can 'til your hands get tough."

"Hey, thanks, man, I really appreciate it." George stood up. "We're allowed to go outside until seven-thirty. I was going to walk around. You want to come?"

"Yeah, sure," said Wayne. "Why not."

They went outside and walked along a sidewalk that circled 159 the dormitory. It intersected another one that led to a softball diamond backed by a rise of bleachers. A number of inmates were loitering around the field and in the bleachers; others were playing catch or generally horsing around in small groups here and there.

"Guess it's all right to go over there," George said. "Every-body else is doing it."

Wayne and George strolled down to the bleachers and sat down. It was a pleasant evening, warm, with the slightest of breezes. They each smoked another of Wayne's cigarettes, looking up at the sky, watching it darken. George was such a soft, reposeful person that Wayne found himself wondering what the black man was in prison for. Finally he asked him.

"Contemp' of court," George said, and told Wayne the whole story.

"What a lot of shit," Wayne said when George finished. "Send a man to fucking prison for five lousy dollars a week. Man, sometimes I think we'd be better off living in fucking Russia." This from the same Wayne Coleman who soundly condemned Carson Coleman and Archie Issacs for not sup-porting *their* children. It seemed not to occur to him that George Dungee, whatever his reasons, was of a kind with them.

As Wayne and George sat there, the night beginning to close around them, they noticed some of the men come over from the ball field and wander off in couples under the bleachers. Others went into the bleachers and climbed to the last row, to sit together with their backs to the top rail where no one could get behind them.

George glanced timidly at his new friend. Wayne looked away self-consciously. But even as he did, he could not help realizing a sudden warmth that seemed to course through his body. He swallowed and sat very still, waiting, as it got darker by degrees. When it was finally too dark to see anyone else in the bleachers, he heard George say quietly, "I really want to thank you for helping me out today, man."

Wayne reached over and put his hand lightly on the black man's slim shoulder.

"Well, go ahead, why don't you," he whispered.

Wayne and George worked side by side the next day, and every day after that; and every night after supper they walked over to the bleachers and waited for it to get dark. Neither of them had ever felt close to another male before, and they were

160

both caught up in the excitement of it. To Wayne, George was as soft and gentle as any of the very few women he had ever been intimate with; and to George, Wayne represented the first white person he had ever known who treated him as if they were both the same color.

George had experienced occasions in his life when white people had been nice to him or given him something—white teachers, white customers, white salesclerks. But always it had been after George had done something for them: after he'd been good in school, or served them properly, or bought something from them. But Wayne had befriended him *beforehand,* when George had done nothing to deserve it. Befriended him twice, in fact: the first time when George dropped his glasses in Reception, and again his first day on the gravel line. Wayne could easily have ignored him both times; everyone else had. But both times Wayne had stepped in to help him, just like—why, just like a *friend,* George realized.

Friend.

The word had very little real meaning to George. He had used it most of his life, to describe someone he *knew:* on the school playground, on the block where he lived, at places where he worked. But the people to whom he had applied the word had not really been friends—not in the way Wayne had become his friend. For the first time, after that day on the gravel line, George thought he knew the meaning of genuine friendship.

With Wayne the feelings were different. He did not try to analyze his relationship with the easygoing black man; he did not sanctify the word "friend" and hold it above George and himself like some holy umbrella. With Wayne it was much more basic. He had discovered another human being with whom he felt compatible both physically and mentally. Wayne had been intimate with women now and again, but he had never really felt *right* about it. Whoever the woman was, Wayne had come away from her feeling inadequate—either in what he said or how he performed. Something about every one of the few women he'd had always left him with a desire to leave quickly and hide somewhere. He did not want to be *seen* when it was over, as if he feared that a finger would be pointed, a ridiculing laugh directed at him. But with George it was not so. With George he felt confident, in control.

Wayne's one regret was that he had met George in prison, and that their respective sentences controlled their futures.   161

George had only six months to serve, and would then be turned loose; he would not even be on parole. Wayne had at least two more years, and probably up to another six months after that before he would actually be released. There was no way, he was sure, that their relationship would survive a separation of eighteen to twenty-four months. Even if they both wanted it to.

It was like everything else in his fucking life, Wayne thought: if it was something good, he was sure as shit going to be deprived of it. Life, Wayne was convinced, was all figured out for him. He wasn't going to have *anything* good for very long.

And that was fucking that.

Three weeks after Wayne and George established their friendship in the bleachers, they were working one day on a crew at the side of a highway, cutting away weeds and brush, when a camp truck pulled up and delivered four new convicts.

"These here just transferred in from the state pen," the truck guard said. "They'll be on your detail."

The road guard checked the men in and issued them hoes from the tool trailer. "Fall in with the others and hoe up them weeds on the shoulder," he ordered. "Keep in a straight line. No talking. No stopping work without you raising your hoe for permission. Get to work."

There was a slim young man with light hair among the newcomers. Wayne stared at him, frowning. George, seeing that Wayne had paused in his work, glanced anxiously at the road guard.

"Hey!" he whispered urgently.

Wayne, preoccupied, looked at him. "Huh?"

"Keep working, man," George said. "You want the road boss on your ass?"

Wayne started throwing his hoe again. "Yeah, okay." He worked for a couple of minutes, then said, "Hey, thanks, George. Thanks for waking me up."

"What happened to you, man? You looked like you was touched or something."

"I'm not sure," Wayne said. "I'm not sure what happened."

Wayne kept working until the break whistle sounded. Then he put down his hoe and said, "I'll be back in a minute."

Wayne walked over to where the new men were working. He looked closely at the fair-haired young man he had noticed earlier. After a moment, the young man looked back at him.

"What the fuck are you staring at?" the young man asked, trying to sound hard.

Wayne stepped up to him. "What's your name?"

"What the fuck do you care?"

"I think you're my brother. My name's Wayne Coleman. Ain't you Carl?"

The young newcomer's eyes grew wide. "Yeah, man! Hell, yeah! I'm Carl. Wayne? No shit, is it really you?"

"It's me, all right. I'll be damned. Carl. Junior."

They shook hands, almost self-consciously. Each of them wanted to hug the other, but they were afraid how it would look to the other men. It was part of the convict mentality that Wayne could go to the bleachers every night with George, while every convict who saw them knew what they were doing, yet would be ashamed to embrace his own half brother in front of those same men. And Carl, having recently been sodomized in prison, would not embrace Wayne for fear that the men on the gang, whom he did not even know yet, might take it the wrong way.

So they stood facing each other awkwardly, having shaken hands in the accepted fashion, and each tried to think of something to say, something that would *establish* himself with the other. Their crimes were the only bond they could think of.

"What are you in for, man?"

"Armed robbery."

"Me too."

They had transferred to Poplar Hill from different state prisons, and had not seen each other in years. Before they had a chance to talk about their family, the whistle sounded ending their break.

"See you tonight after supper," Wayne said. "Come down to the bleachers by the ball field."

"Okay," said Carl, "see you."

When Wayne went back to where George was and resumed working, George was pouting. "What's the matter?" Wayne asked, glancing over from his hoe.

"Who was that white kid?" George wanted to know.

"Shit, man, that was my brother," Wayne said.

He smiled. It felt kind of good to have somebody care enough to be jealous of him.

That night Carl came down to the bleachers.

"This here is George," Wayne said. "Him and me is like partners."

"Oh. Hi," Carl said, bobbing his chin but not offering to shake hands. *A fucking nigger*, he thought. *My own brother has got a fucking nigger for a partner. Shit.*

"Sit down," Wayne said. "Let's talk."

For the next hour they talked about the family, where everyone was—as far as they knew—what they were doing, and what all had happened to them over the years. And they exchanged stories about themselves: how time and circumstance had treated them, why they had ended up where they were.

"Bad luck, that's what it's been for me," Wayne declared. "Just plain old bad fucking luck. I mean, man, I never—fucking *never*—get a break. Everything I touch turns to shit. Let me tell you something, bro: if I ever get my hands on that cocksucker Carson Coleman, I'll kill the son-of-a-bitch for causing me to be born. That's the truth. I swear it."

"Sometimes I feel the same way about Archie," Carl admitted.

Neither of them openly blamed their mother for any part of what had happened to them over the years. They both *felt* that she was to blame, at least partly; but those were deep, private thoughts, too painful to be shared. Secret, shameful thoughts.

"Anyway, it's great that you're here," Wayne said, and immediately laughed at himself. "No, man, I don't mean that it's great that you're here in this shithouse; I mean it's great that you're *here*, that we're together, you know."

"Yeah, I know what you mean," Carl said. It was clear that he and Wayne felt something toward each other; not love exactly—both would have denied that outright—but a kinship of sorts, a familiarity in spite of not having seen each other in years; or perhaps a common bond as orphans of the same storm. Carl could not define or classify it; he only knew that it was there and he felt it. And he knew Wayne felt it too.

"Be kind of nice getting to know each other after all this time," Wayne said.

"I don't think we'll be able to," Carl told him. "I ain't staying."

"What do you mean?"

"I mean I'm escaping, bro. First chance I get. I'm gonna run away and I'm gonna get as far away from here as I can. And I ain't never coming back."

Wayne stared at his brother. There was a grim determination in Carl's eyes that discouraged argument of any kind. Wayne had no way of knowing *why* Carl was so resolved to

164

run; he did not yet know of the brutal rape Carl had recently suffered behind the walls, at the hands of blacks. He did not know that Carl now associated that humiliating experience with being locked up. Had he known, it would have explained Carl's reserve when meeting George.

"Listen, Wayne, come with me," Carl said. "Let's split together."

"I don't know, Junior," said Wayne. "I mean, escape is serious business."

"Jesus Christ, so is armed robbery with a shotgun," Carl said with an edge. "What the fuck, Wayne, do you want to spend two more years in this shithouse?"

"No, 'course I don't, only—"

"Only, shit," Carl said. Somehow he knew instinctively that he could dominate Wayne, lead Wayne. "Look, bro, we can make it out of here easy. Steal us a car. Rob us some money. Then take off for sunny Florida. Come on, Wayne. We'd make a good team, bro. What do you say?"

Shrugging, Wayne looked at George. "Hey, man, want to split this place?"

"I was just talking about you and me," Carl told his brother.

"Can't George come if he wants to, man?"

"I was just figuring on the two of us—"

"Well, figure on the *three* of us," Wayne said flatly. He reached over and shook George's knee. "What do you say, Georgie? Want to get out of this shithouse? Hit the open fucking road?"

"I don't know," George replied easily. He grinned at the two white brothers. "I only gots five more months to serve, you know."

"So what?" said Wayne. "When you get out, you won't *stay* out. You'll fuck up with them support payments and be right back in here again. You know fucking well you will."

George continued to grin. "You probably right."

"I'm for splitting," Wayne said. Escape was the answer to his two main problems: serving another two years, and losing George when his friend got released.

"I guess I'll do whatever you say," George told him almost lazily. For all the impact it had on George Dungee's mind, he might have been agreeing to go to a movie.

"We're in," Wayne said to Carl. "We're with you."

Swell, Carl thought. Now he was saddled with a fucking nigger. But he could take care of that later—after they got 165 out. Once they were all on the run, Wayne would see things straight and drop George. In the meantime, Carl would just act as if nothing were wrong.

"All right!" he said, slapping Wayne on the back. "Come on, it's getting dark. We can talk about it walking back to the dorms."

"George and me are gonna stay down here for a little bit," Wayne said.

"Huh?" Carl looked around at the men pairing off in couples. He felt himself blush and was glad it was too dark for Wayne to see it. Inside, he felt sick.

His own brother had a nigger fuck-boy.

Swallowing with difficulty, Carl kept himself under control. "Yeah, right. Well, we'll talk about it tomorrow then. I'll, uh—see you guys in the morning."

As he walked away alone, Carl thought: Jesus Christ, you just couldn't trust *nobody*.

Interlude:
THE ALDAY FAMILY

20

Fess Baker could tell by the frown on Jimmy Alday's face that the young man was troubled. "Sit down there, young feller," he said. "I'll be with you soon's I grade these last few papers. How's the old classroom look to you?"

" 'Bout the same, I reckon, Mr. Baker. You don't look no older."

"Well, I *feel* older." Fess Baker had been teaching agriculture at the Seminole County High School for more than thirty years. A tall, lean, Gary Cooper-type, he had long ago lost count of how many young men had passed through his classroom. Some he had forgotten for years, only to remember them when their sons came along. But he always remembered the exceptional ones. Like Jimmy Alday, whom he looked up at now. "What can I do for you, son?"

Jimmy sat in the front chair, facing the teacher's desk. "I've got kind of a problem, sir. See, I, uh—I've got this chance to go down to the Everglades in Florida and become a park ranger. A friend of mine's uncle is in charge of the ranger service down there. He's putting on two new rangers for the summer, and he's pretty sure he'll be able to keep them on in the fall. My friend and me can have the jobs if we go down there. My friend has already decided to go, but, well, I haven't quite made up my mind yet."

"I hope you didn't come in here thinking I'd make it up for you," Fess Baker said without rancor. Jimmy looked down and said nothing. "How long have you been out of school now?" Baker asked.

"Six years, sir."

"Been working the land with your daddy and brothers the whole time?"

"Yessir."

"You mentioned this ranger thing to your daddy yet?"

"No, sir."

Baker rose and walked to the window of his classroom. He thought of Norman Alday, the eldest son of Ned's who had left the land and gone off to the Army. He knew how much that had hurt Ned.

"Jimmy," he said, turning toward the room again, "you were one of the brightest pupils I ever had in forestry and wildlife management. I never saw a boy who had more of an instinctive *feel* for the woods and its inhabitants than you had." Baker walked slowly back to his desk and sat down. He put the tips of his fingers together in a tent. "Rangering is a fine occupation," he said. "It's an occupation, like farming, that a man can be proud of. It's an occupation that a father can be proud to have his son go into."

Jimmy was looking down at the floor. Swallowing, he raised his eyes to his former teacher. "How do you think my daddy would take it if I was to tell him I was going?"

"You want the God's truth?"

"Yessir."

"All right. Your daddy's a proud man, Jimmy. I think he'd shake your hand, pat you on the back, and wish you the best of luck. And he'd brag to everybody in Donalsonville about what a fine ranger you made. But inside it would tear him up. Nobody would ever know it but your mother, but a little bit of him would die if you was to leave home, Jimmy."

The young man sighed quietly. "That's what I was afraid you'd say."

"How badly do you want to go, son?"

"Pretty badly, sir."

"And how much do you love your daddy?"

"Why, I—more than anything in the world, I reckon, except Mother."

"I expect that's your answer, then," said Fess Baker.

Jimmy thought about it for a moment, then slowly nodded his head. "Yessir, I reckon it is."

When Jimmy left the high school that day, he went directly to tell his friend that he would not be going to the Everglades with him.

For a while, Ned Alday thought he might have the same problem with his three sons that he once had had with his brother Aubrey: they seemed to be interested in everything 168 *except* settling down and starting a family.

"Slow, that's what they are," he complained to Ernestine. "All three of 'em: slow. Jerry and Shugie both ought to be daddies by now. You don't reckon there's anything the matter with them, do you?"

"Oh, Ned," Ernestine said impatiently. "There's not a thing in the world the matter with those boys. They're just taking their own good time, is all."

"They're sure enough doing that, all right. Take much more of it, they'll be too old to have young 'uns."

"They will not!" She was sitting opposite him on their front porch, shelling peas in the last light of day. "Why are you just picking on Jerry and Shugie anyway? Don't you want Jimmy to get married too?"

"Jimmy's too young," Ned said at once. "He needs a little seasoning first."

"I see," Ernestine said, glancing knowingly at him, suppressing one of her soft smiles. She knew that if Ned had his way, Jimmy would stay at home permanently. Jimmy, more than any of their other sons, had become Ned's "buddy."

"Who do you figure will go first, Jerry or Shugie?" Ned asked, directing the conversation away from their youngest son.

"I don't have the slightest idea," Ernestine said. "And I don't thing it makes a bit of difference. I don't even know why we're talking about it."

"Way I look at it, it'll probably be Shugie. Jerry's too much of a fussbudget about everything. Doubt he'll *ever* find a woman who'll please him."

"Why, Ned Alday, that's not so and you know it! There's not a thing in the world the matter with Jerry. Just because he likes everything neat—"

"Blamed perfectionist, that's what he is," Ned said, working tobacco into the bowl of his pipe. As he lighted up, he nodded sagely and concluded, "Yessir, it'll be Shugie, all right. Shugie'll be the first one to marry."

Ned was right.

Chester Alday was never called by his given name. There was not one person in a hundred who knew that his name *was* Chester. To most people, he was "Shugie." That was the doing of one of Ned's sisters. When Chester was a baby, crawling around on the floor, she had picked him up once and nuzzled his neck and said, "This is my little sugar." For a while then he   169 had been "Little Sugar." Gradually he became "Little Shugie." Then just plain "Shugie." By the time he was in elementary school, the name "Chester" was all but forgotten: he had become Shugie Alday.

Shugie was unaware that he was his daddy's prime candidate for marriage. Ned, crafty as ever, had not said a word to the boys about settling down; he knew if he tried to influence them, they might oppose him just out of stubbornness. He had raised them to be independent thinkers, even where he was concerned, and they had developed their stubbornness naturally over the years, mostly as a defense *against* him. While they were growing up, Ned habitually put them up to mischief against one another. Ernestine tried to head off a lot of it, but Ned was too sly, too subtle for her. He would go to Jerry and tell him Shugie said this or that; then go to Shugie and tell him that Jerry was going to whip him for one thing or another; and presently he would have the two boys going at each other like young cubs. Then he'd holler, "Ernestine, these boys of yours are scuffling in the house again!" Ernestine would have to come in from the kitchen and discipline them while Ned, looking as blameless as the day he was born, would sit innocently stuffing black cherry Paladin tobacco into his pipe. When it was all over, of course, and the boys realized what their daddy had done, they would all have a big laugh over it. Except Ernestine. The best she could manage was a resigned smile.

Shugie got to be twenty-five years old before he proved Ned right about being the first to settle down. It was May 1968, a cold, bitter winter at last over, and south Georgians were out and about enjoying a pleasant spring. Shugie pulled his pickup truck into the local Tastee Freeze and got himself a strawberry cone. While he was standing there enjoying it, the Hall sisters from Bascom, Florida, across the state line, drove up. Shugie knew Mary Hall; he had dated her a few times over the years, nothing serious. But he had never met Barbara Hall, her younger sister. Barbara was a short, pretty girl with a quick smile and an hourglass figure. She looked at Shugie, standing there with his strawberry cone, and he looked at her, in her tight jeans and blouse, with her ready smile, and it was love at first sight. They locked eyes and fell for each other, hard and heavy, at exactly the same moment. They would talk about it later: how they had both known they were in love the moment they met. It was like a movie, except they were both so surprised that things *did* happen like that in real life.

170

Barb Hall was twenty-two and not a bit shy. "You're the Alday boy ever'body calls 'Shugie,' aren't you?"

"That's me," said Shugie. "How come I never met you before? Mary keep you hid away?"

"No," Barb said, shrugging, "I'm just not around much. I spend a lot of time up in Mariana. I work up there, at Sunland. I'm a recreational counselor."

Shugie nodded. Mariana was a small city across the line in Florida. Sunland was a children's center.

"What are you girls up to?" Shugie asked, licking at his cone.

"We had to come over to the Town and Country grocery to get some sour cream for mother. She's fixing to make a cake."

Shugie kept looking at Barb, and her at him. It was almost eerie, like they could read each other's mind. They would later admit to each other that they both knew, in that instant that they locked eyes, not only that they were in love but that they would someday be married.

They started going together, seriously. Neither of them dated anyone else. In March of the following year, on Barb's twenty-third birthday, they officially became engaged, making plans to marry the following August. When Shugie went home and told his family, none of the other Aldays could figure out why Ned sat back with such a self-satisfied look on his face. Only Ernestine knew why.

The old storyteller had been right again.

It was the summer of 1972 that Jimmy had been offered the chance to become a ranger in the Everglades. That was the same summer Arlene had visited from Mississippi. For a brief time the excitement of the prospective ranger job had pushed to the back of Jimmy's mind his secret desire to write a history of the Alday family. Then, when he met Arlene and shared his secret with her, it assumed its former prominence. Throughout the summer, whenever he saw Arlene, they talked about the history book he would write, and how important history was to just about everything. Arlene was almost as enthused about his plans as Jimmy himself; she made him promise faithfully to send her the very first copy that came off the press.

When summer ended and Arlene was gone, and the lure of the Everglades died, and the history book project was all talked out of him, Jimmy went back to the land, went back to concentrating on being a farmer with his daddy and two brothers. He seemed to settle down then, to throw off some of the itchiness that had been noticeable all summer.

Ned had known, of course, that something had been bothering Jimmy during the summer months. He had automatically assumed it was a girl. And just as automatically assumed it would pass. His youngest son had given no sign at all of wanting to marry and settle down. And Ned was in no hurry for him to; he liked having Jimmy at home.

Ned knew that all his boys would eventually marry and start families of their own. They had become young men of the land, and the land dictated that there be new generations to grow up on it, work it, inherit it. As he approached his sixtieth year, Ned often gave silent thanks that three of his sons shared his own feelings for the earth. Those feelings had begun to evince themselves when the boys had been in their early teens, in Fess Baker's agriculture class at the high school. Before they ever got to that class, of course, they had already begun learning at their father's side: learning the labor of it, the ache of it, the sweat of it. Fess Baker taught them the science of it. Like a doctor keeping abreast of all the current medicines and cures, Baker kept up with the latest fertilizers, insecticides, crop rotation theories, and methods of planting. He taught his students the one thing that so many farmers had forgotten: that record-keeping was the key to successful farming. Record-keeping. What was planted, where, when, what kind of seed, how much rain it had taken, how much sunshine, what was the last crop in that field, what would be the next.

The young men entered Fess Baker's class as "Green Hands." They were the rookies, the plebes, of the farming program. After a year, they became Junior Farmers; after two years, Georgia Planters. In their fourth and last year, those who were good enough, proficient enough, those who had enough feeling for the land and whom the land responded to, were promoted to American Farmers, the highest agriculture degree awarded to a student by the Future Farmers of America (FFA). On the way to that honor, a young man would have learned about corn and peanut crops; about soybeans and cotton; about every edible vegetable imaginable; about the best-tasting watermelons grown in America; and even about cows and hogs, which were also grown on the land. He would have learned scientifically from Fess Baker what he was learning practically from his father. And sometimes, in a rare moment, he would learn something in class, take it into the field with him, and his father would learn it too.

Jerry, Shugie, and Jimmy all excelled in Fess Baker's class.

The dedicated agriculture teacher was to say after his experience with them that in his entire career he had never encountered three young men from the same family who were so similarly attuned to the needs of the land, so instinctively aware of what was right for the land, and so quietly and personally dedicated to a respect for the land; a respect, Baker felt, that had to have been hereditary. It had to have come from Ned. And Joell. And Math.

All three Alday boys were eventually selected to travel to Kansas City to attend the annual FFA convention. Jerry won the trip for planting a prize-winning acre of corn. Shugie won it as state speaker for Georgia. Jimmy won it for outstanding achievement in forestry and wildlife management.

When Ned heard about the awarding of the trips, he went uptown and walked up and down Second Street telling everyone he knew how proud he was of his sons. Then he stopped in at his friend Paul Shingler's showroom and bought a brand-new Pontiac. That evening at the supper table he said, "You boys tell Fess Baker he'll be taking you to Kansas City in style, in a new car."

It came as a surprise to his two younger brothers, but the next to marry after Shugie was Jerry. Shugie and Jimmy had long since decided that Jerry was too discriminating, too demanding, to ever find a woman who would suit him. The newly married Shugie frequently remarked that Jerry was "too particular" about things. Everything had to be just so with Jerry: his tools had to be in exactly the same place all the time; his truck engine had to be tuned just so; his clothes, even the way he combed his hair, had to suit him just perfectly. Shugie said he was a "fussy old man" and once told him to go look for an old widow woman to marry, "somebody about seventy or eighty years old."

Shugie and his bride Barbara, whom he had married in August 1969 at the Circle Hill Baptist Church, had returned after a honeymoon in Panama City to a brand-new twelve-by-sixty-one-foot mobile home that was set up by the side of Ned's large front yard. Barbara had left her job in Mariana and gone to work in Donalsonville at the Thomas Five-and-Ten. Barb fussed at Shugie to let Jerry alone, but Shugie would have given up eating before he stopped teasing his older brother.

Jerry did not let Shugie's remarks bother him. He knew Shugie was just trying to get his goat. As youngsters they had   173 become so accustomed to Ned putting them up to mischief, so used to being pitted one against the other, that they had grown up with a natural inclination to act that way. But it was always in the right spirit, always done good-naturedly, never with malice. The Alday brothers loved each other: quietly, deeply, just as they loved Ned and Ernestine. It would have been unthinkable to any of them to do anything rancorous to one of their own.

Jerry knew he was in for some heavy teasing when he finally did pick out someone to marry, so when it happened, he went directly to Shugie with the news.

"I've found me a girl," he told his brother seriously. "Her name's Mary Campbell. She's from up Bainbridge way, works in the bank there. I'm fixing to take her out to supper this coming Wednesday night. Like to invite you and Barb to come along and meet her."

"How can she work in a bank if she's blind?" Shugie inquired with a straight face.

"She's not blind, Shugie. Do you want to come along or not?"

"Not blind? What's the matter with her, then? Wait a minute, I know. She's backward, is that it? Touched?"

"There's nothing wrong with her, Shugie—"

"Then why's she going out with a fussy old man like you?"

"I'm only two years older'n you are, Shug."

"I know, but you *act* like you're an old man. You act older'n Daddy and Uncle Aubrey and Uncle Paul and Uncle Bud—"

"I do *not* act like an old man, Shug," Jerry replied patiently. "I am just a little bit more particular than some, is all."

Shugie narrowed his eyes suspiciously. "How old is this Mary Campbell anyway? Seventy? Eighty? She a widow woman?"

"She is twenty-three years old and she is *not* a widow woman."

Shugie had just been given fresh ammunition. *"Twenty-three*! Kind of robbing the cradle, ain't you. I mean, you're in your *thirties,* Jerry."

"Just barely," Jerry replied self-consciously. "I'm not thirty-one yet."

"Well, still, I don't know if me and Daddy can give our blessing with you being so old and all—"

Jerry had taken enough. "I'm going now, Shugie. Do you and Barb want to come out to supper with us on Wednesday, yes or no?"

"We most definitely do," Shugie said cordially.

On Wednesday, Jerry, Shugie, and Barbara drove over to Bainbridge and picked up Mary Campbell. She was a pretty girl, a little taller than Barb, dark-haired, with freckles over every inch of her that could be seen. Shugie and Barb saw at once that she was a sweet, pleasant person; they liked her immediately, so much that Shugie refrained from teasing Jerry about her—in her presence anyway. Jerry was pleased that they all got on so well together; it was important in a family like the Aldays that everyone like everyone else. He already planned to marry Mary Campbell, if she would have him, and he knew that he and Mary would live in close proximity to his parents, as Shugie and Barb did. It was doubly nice that Mary and Barb liked each other from the very beginning.

The following Sunday, Jerry brought Mary Campbell to dinner to meet Ned and Ernestine. He knew beforehand that his parents would like her. Mary was the kind of girl his own sisters were: good-natured, decent, cheerful, always ready to help, interested in everyone's problems, everyone's children; a sweet, gentle young Southern woman who did not smoke, drink, or use profanity, and who had accepted Jesus Christ as her savior and regularly gave thanks to Him for her blessings in life. If Ned and Ernestine could have personally designed someone for their eldest son to marry, their creation would have been Mary Campbell. They could not have been happier with her.

Jerry and Mary were married later that year and drove to Dothan, Alabama, for a brief honeymoon. Then, like Shugie and Barb, they came back home to a brand-new mobile home, green with white trim, which had been brought up from Tallahassee and installed on a small clearing facing the road just a quarter of a mile from Ned and Ernestine's house and Shugie and Barb's trailer.

For Ned, the marriage of Jerry and Mary, only six months after Shugie and Barb's wedding, meant that his boys were at last putting down their own roots in this land he had worked so hard to buy back. He could sit on his front porch and see Shugie's mobile home off to the side of his yard, and look down the road and see Jerry's new place close by, and it gave him a deep sense of satisfaction.

It was a good feeling, he thought, for an old man to have.

The fact that the Alday brothers turned out so well in Ned's estimation does not mean that they were perfect in every re- 175 spect. Like all growing boys, they covered much rocky ground on the road to maturity. Jimmy, the youngest, was a good example. No youngster in Seminole County was subjected to more whippings than Jimmy got. Being adventurous by nature, he was, it seemed, *always* in trouble. Not bad trouble; not big-city trouble: no drugs or stealing or gang activities. Just mischief trouble. Things like popping .22-caliber cartridges together and exploding them—in school—which frightened teachers and students alike half to death. Shugie was no angel either. He was caught shooting craps in the school gymnasium one time and sent home to his parents for it. But for the most part any trouble the boys got into was minor. Whenever they seemed to be on the verge of anything serious, there was always Ned or Ernestine to straighten them out.

Like the time Jerry and Shugie joined the Ku Klux Klan.

"You have done *what?*" their mother asked in her coolest voice.

"We've done joined up with the local branch of the Klan," Jerry said, trying his best to sound proud and determined.

"Well, you can just go right back and *un*-join," Ernestine told them. "No son of mine is going to be part of the KKK."

"Oh, we can't do that," Shugie said, a little self-consciously. "See, once you join, you ain't allowed to quit."

"And just who says you're not allowed to quit?"

"Uh, the Grand Wizard or somebody like that."

The boys exchanged nervous looks; it was obvious that their mother was beginning to seethe.

"You can go and tell the Grand Wizard, whoever he is under that sheet," she said icily, "that your *mother* has said that y'all are both to quit. You tell the Grand Wizard that if there's any objection to it, from him or anybody else, that they can come here and talk to *me* about it. Tell him he can bring his whole gang if he's a mind to, hoods and torches and all, I don't care. I'm not afraid of him *or* his gang. But you two are *not* going to be part of no such foolishness as that! Do you hear me?"

"Yes, ma'am," they said in unison.

"Do you understand me?"

"Yes, ma'am."

"Well, then get on out of here and go make it plain that you're both quitting. Right now!"

"Yes, ma'am!"

They scampered out of Ernestine's house and hurried off
into the night. Neither of them ever mentioned the Ku Klux

Klan again. And always, whenever there was any Klan activity in the county, parades or rallies or such, Jerry and Shugie always made sure they were at home where Ernestine could see them. They did not want her to have even a suspicion that they had not obeyed her.

While Ernestine and Ned might invoke their parental authority to prevent the boys from doing something they ought not to, so also did they refrain from pushing them into decisions that they felt the boys should make on their own. Decisions such as joining the church and accepting Jesus as their savior. Ernestine herself was a God-fearing, church-going woman, Baptist to the core. Ned, on the other hand, had never been saved, never baptized, and was far more informal in his relationship with the Almighty. Neither of them encouraged the boys to go forward or stand back when the preacher called the unsaved to the altar in the little church that, four generations earlier, Math Alday had donated the land for and helped build. Both decided to let nature take its course with the boys. If they were destined to be saved, Ernestine was certain, they would be.

It was Reverend Fred Hill, pastor of the Spring Creek Baptist Church, who eventually led the boys to God. He knew of Ernestine's devotion, just as he knew of Ned's restraint. He sensed that the boys might easily step in either direction; he hoped that he could get them to come forward, and, if successful, it might bring Ned formally into the fold.

It was on one of those rare warm days in November, in 1968, that Reverend Hill went to see the boys. Brother Hill, as he was called, was a small bulldog of a man, with a square-jawed, no-nonsense face, and he carried his belief in Jesus with gritty determination. On the Saturday afternoon that he visited the Ned Alday home, he found all three brothers in the back yard, working to get an old car running again.

"Good day, boys," he said, planting both fists on his hips as though preparing to do battle with Satan, which, in a way, he was.

"Afternoon, Brother Hill," said Jerry, and Shugie and Jimmy answered accordingly.

"Boys, I've got something to talk to you about," Brother Hill said solemnly. "Will you sit with me over here under this tree?"

The reverend and the three young men sat in a loose circle on the ground. Brother Hill looked from one to the other and 177 finally said, "Boys, y'all have to make a decision for Christ." Then he began to talk to them, quietly but forcefully, never raising his voice, yet capturing and holding their undivided attention with the sheer force of his own belief. He spoke of God, of Christ, of heaven and hell; he said everyone on earth, sooner or later, one way or another, had to make their life right with God.

It was Jerry whom he brought forward first. "I feel a need for Christ, Brother Hill," Jerry said, his head bowed. Shugie and Jimmy followed their older brother's example: they bowed their heads and admitted that in their own lives they too felt a need.

Brother Hill told them to pray about their need, to think about it, consider it, examine it; then, if they were certain it was a need for Jesus Christ, to come forward and embrace Him.

The boys pondered their feelings for six weeks; then on a cold Sunday in January 1969, the three of them, along with a friend of theirs named Roy Barber, all came forward at Sunday services and asked to accept, and be accepted by, their savior. Brother Hill asked if they had heard the call from Jesus; they each said they had.

"You are sowing the seed," the minister said, "and God will give the harvest."

Watching from the audience, Ernestine felt tears streak her cheeks. All three of her boys, reaching out to Christ together. It was a glowing moment for her.

A week later, the Alday brothers and Roy Barber went to the Bethany Baptist Church, which had the nearest baptistry, and were immersed in the holy water of baptism. When they returned home that night, Ned went to each of them in turn, privately, and said simply, "I'm right proud of you, son."

The three Alday brothers took to their religion as if they were born to it. Each of them eagerly participated in all church activities, volunteered for any work that had to be done, attended every service and prayer meeting, joined in every religious community undertaking. They became three of the most devout and conscientious young men in the county. In just three-and-a-half years after formally joining the church together, all three of them, again together, were ordained deacons of the church that their great-grandfather Math Alday had helped build. Jerry became the church's treasurer, and Shugie the church's song director. Jimmy became director of the Church Training Union.

All three were noticeably proud of their appointments. Their only argument was among themselves, about which job was the most important.

Jimmy at last felt that his boyhood days were over. His two older brothers were married, and now all three of them had joined the church. The business of serious living appeared to be at hand: marriage, children, taking over the labors of the growing farm from their aging father, utilizing their free time to serve their church and their community.

Jimmy was glad he had remained at home, glad he had not gone to Florida and become a ranger. He often thought of his eldest brother Norman, away making a career in the Army. Norman was not all that different from him and Jerry and Shugie; he had his family, his work, his religion, just like they did. But to Jimmy, Norman never seemed settled. One year he might be stationed in California, the next in Germany. The family all loved Norman and shared a mutual excitement when he came home on leave with his uniform and medals and stories of exotic places; but deep down they were all glad they were not him.

Jimmy knew he would not be a complete man, at least in the eyes of his peers, until he married and produced children. It was of great importance in the scope of life in south Georgia to bring forth the next generation. The previous generation depended on it. Jimmy could only imagine how hollow Ned would have felt his life to have been if none of his sons had remained to work the land, if they had *all* gone away, found other careers as Norman had, and Ned had known that the land he had dedicated himself to getting back would, after him, pass to *strangers*. What a terrible thing to contemplate.

Almost equally bad would it have been for Ned to approach the twilight of his life without the assurance of a *new* generation. With three of his own sons staying at home, that generation was accounted for. But before Ned Alday could lay his head down in final peace, the *next* generation would at least have had to begin. There would have to be grandsons. Alday grandsons.

Jimmy gave a great deal of thought to that in the fall and winter of 1972–73. It was evident in the way he spoke to his mother and to others about the importance of carrying on the family name, the family tradition. Evident in the way he quietly chided Jerry and Shugie about the fact that they had not yet produced any children.

179

"Y'all *do* know how it's done, don't you?" he would ask, always making certain Barbara and Mary were not around to hear. He would not have embarrassed his sisters-in-law for anything in the world. But he showed no mercy with Jerry and Shugie.

"Y'all two are something, I swear. Two great big healthy bulls can't even make one little tiny calf. I reckon it's just gonna be up to me. I hate the thought of making y'all look bad, but *somebody* has got to carry on the Alday name in this branch of the family. Looks like I'm gonna have to find me a woman, get married, and give Daddy his first Alday grand-baby."

For the most part, Jerry and Shugie ignored him—or tried to. But they both knew, without even discussing it between them-selves, that Jimmy was only half joking. They were aware of the deeply serious streak in their youngest brother, and they knew it was weighing more and more on his mind every day that no one had begun the fifth generation yet. There were grandchildren, of course; their sisters had married and pro-duced babies. But those grandchildren were Millers and Hor-tons and Blizzards and Purvises; they weren't Aldays.

On New Year's Day in 1973, Jimmy Alday made a resolu-tion: before the new year was over he would have himself a wife, and a baby would be on the way.

Barely twenty-five years old, the young man was carrying the heavy burden of Math and Joell and Ned.

3

BILLY ISSACS

3

BILLY ISSACS

21

Billy stood in a doorway in the Baltimore ghetto and watched daylight come. Drizzling rain darkened the sidewalk in front of him, the day around him. His hands were shoved deep in his jacket pockets; one shoulder leaned against the doorjamb; his eyes flicked, darted, searched, scrutinized. The street lay before him like an ugly painting done in watercolors from a sewer: no lights, no brights, no cheer. All grays and blacks, dirty reds, dirty browns. Everything the color of shit, vomit, scabs. The ghetto was the city's wound. Billy hated it.

An old drunk came by, clutching a bottle of Thunderbird wine to his chest. Stopping in front of Billy, he glared defiantly at him, opened the bottle, and gulped down a long, gurgling swallow. "I don't give a shit if it does kill me!" he said belligerently.

"I don't either, old man," Billy replied tonelessly. "Come here—"

Billy pulled him close enough to quickly go through his pockets. He found eighty cents.

"You're almost as bad off as I am," he said, taking the money.

"Tha's my money," the drunk said. "Give it back."

"Beat it," Billy told him, "or I'll take your bottle too."

The drunk clutched the bottle to his chest in sudden fear and hurried off.

After Billy had been standing there a little while, the dampness brought up a strong smell of stale piss from the stairs behind him, so Billy walked down the street to an open storefront and stood there. In a little while a young black man staggered into the storefront with him and sat down at his feet. His head was nodding and he scratched at one forearm as if vermin were attacking it. In his shirt pocket, Billy could see a twenty-dollar bill.

The nodding man remained in the storefront for ten minutes. Billy ignored him the whole time. Finally he dragged himself up and shuffled off down the street. "Have a nice day, officer," Billy said quietly to himself. Fucking decoy cops must think everybody on the street is stupid.

Later the rain stopped and the squalid neighborhood spewed its dregs onto the street. An ancient yellow bus, once used for school children until it had been condemned as unsafe, pulled up at the corner and parked. As the driver got out, an Hispanic woman leaned out an apartment window above him and yelled, "Is that the welfare bus?"

"Not today, lady," the driver yelled back. "Unemployment office today!"

"Shit," the woman said, and disappeared.

Across the street, a huge black woman opened a makeshift, unlicensed cafe, and a while later the smell of greasy pigs' feet in boiling water reached Billy's nostrils. It reminded him again how hungry he was. If he didn't score soon, he told himself, he would use the drunk's eighty cents to buy a loaf of bread, some junk food, something; he had to put something in his stomach or he was going to get sick again. Nothing, he was certain, was worse than getting sick from being hungry. It was the most awful kind of sickness.

Down his side of the street came a tall, slim figure in a tight sheath dress cut low in front and slit up one side. Nice, Billy thought, forgetting his hunger for a moment. He took one hand out of his jacket pocket and put it in his trousers pocket. The slim figure swayed tantalizingly nearer—and then Billy saw it was a punk in drag. Shit, he thought, grunting contemptuously. A fucking weirdo. He put his hand back in his jacket pocket.

A couple more winos wandered past him. Then a trio of black boys around eleven or twelve, who glared meanly at him but did nothing more because he was bigger than they were. Billy was fifteen and filling out nicely for his age. He had broad shoulders and long arms, both good attributes for a street fighter, which he had to be from time to time. And, like his older half brother Wayne Coleman, whom he hardly knew, he had a certain set to his jaw and mouth and eyes that warned people away, that said, "Look, I don't want no trouble. But don't try to walk on me, see?" It was the look of a hardhead.

A radio car cruised down the street from the corner. When it passed Billy, he pretended to be looking in the store window. It went on by. Some 1950s rock and roll began to play somewhere, wafting out over the street in muted tones. People came out of nearby buildings and walked toward bus stops where they stood together but apart, their expressions insipid, looking like wind-ups waiting to be pointed in a new direction. Billy watched them closely, appraisingly, trying to think straight in spite of the hunger impulses being sent relentlessly from his stomach.

Finally he chose one. A short, stocky white woman wearing a raincoat, with a *babushka* on her head. She carried her purse like a running back carried a football: in the crook of her arm, held close to her body, wrist and hand curled protectively around its end. She walked in long, determined strides, like a peasant woman negotiating a furrowed field.

Billy crossed the street and approached her on an angle from behind. He timed his interception to be made just as the woman crossed an alley in midblock. One second she was alone, plodding forward; the next she felt a slight bump from the side and her purse was being wrenched from her grip—was gone—and a figure was running at breakneck speed down the alley. She screamed, ran after him a few feet, stopped, returned to the street, screamed again. Several people stared curiously at her but no one moved to help her or even see what was the matter.

Billy stuffed the purse under his shirt as he ran. His eyes were wide open with fear, mouth dry, heart exploding in his chest. *Last time,* he told himself wildly. *Last time, man. No more of this shit!*

He was fifteen years old and he had said that to himself many times before. But this time he meant it.

Two hours later, Billy was in the northern part of the city in a coffee shop, finishing his second breakfast. He had eaten until he could not stuff another forkful of food in his mouth. Now he sat there, bloated, drinking Boston coffee, looking out the window when traffic went by, thinking he might see Kelly's mother driving her to school. They would probably know by now that he had escaped from reform school; the juvenile cops would have made routine inquiries at his old high school, and Kelly would surely have heard. He could just imagine what she and her mother would think of him when they heard. He only hoped they would give him a chance to explain why; hoped they would not condemn him without at least hearing his side. 185

In the meantime, he had other, more pressing matters to think about.

" 'Scuse me, mister," he said to the counterman, "you wouldn't need a dishwasher by any chance, would you? Or a clean-up or delivery boy or anything?"

The man shook his head. "Got a full crew, kid. Sorry. Say, you ain't gonna tell me you can't pay for them two breakfasts, are you?"

Billy pulled the eighteen dollars he had gotten out of the purse. "I can pay for what I ate. I just need a job, is all."

"Listen, somebody was saying yesterday that the Quality Inn Motel down the street is looking for a janitor. They may want an older man—"

"I'll try 'em anyway," Billy said eagerly. "Thanks, mister."

Before he went to apply for the job, Billy found a K-Mart discount store and bought a new shirt and a comb. He cleaned up in a gas station washroom and made himself as presentable as possible. Then he walked to the Quality Inn and asked the owner for a job.

"I was looking for an older man," the owner said. "Somebody reliable, steady."

"I'm reliable," Billy pleaded. "Honest, I am. And I'll be a good, steady worker. I really need the job, mister."

"How old are you?"

"Seventeen," Billy lied.

"Don't you go to school?"

"Yeah, but I gotta go nights on account of I gotta support myself."

"Where are your folks?"

"My dad ran off a long time ago. And my mom's dead."

"No brothers or sisters?"

"No, sir." That, he thought, was probably the biggest lie he had ever told.

"Well, I don't know," the motel owner said reluctantly.

"Look, mister, just give me a chance. Let me work one day. If you don't think I'm any good, don't pay me. How's that?"

"Sounds like you really do want a job. All right. Work the day out. If I like what you do, I'll take you on."

Billy did the work of two men that day. He cleaned the pool and pool area, raked out all the shrubbery, mowed the lawn in front of the office, cleaned up the garbage can area behind the kitchen, and performed a variety of other tasks both assigned and simply because they needed doing. At the end of the day,

186

Mr. Shenk, the owner, said, "All right, young man, you've convinced me. I'll give you two-fifty an hour for full-time work. That's six days, forty-eight hours. Sundays off. Want the job?"

Billy did. And when he inquired about living there also, Mr. Shenk gave him permission to sleep in the room that was used for supplies for the maids. "There are a couple of rollaway cots stored there; you can sleep on one of them. The room has a bathroom and a shower too. Just don't get in the way of my maids."

"No, sir, I won't. Thanks, Mr. Shenk. You won't be sorry."

Billy worked at the motel for a week before he went to see Kelly. He collected his first paycheck, cashed it, and bought himself some new jeans and shirts. Kelly Nash and her mother lived in a small house a couple of miles from the motel. Billy went over there after dark and walked past the house a couple of times. There were lights on but Mrs. Nash's car was not in the drive. As badly as Billy wanted to see Kelly, he did not go up and ring the bell because he was afraid Kelly might have one of her girl friends over. If he expected to have any chance at all of succeeding in his new life, he had to remain completely out of sight until the juvenile cops stopped looking for him.

Finally, Billy decided against seeing her at all. He left the neighborhood and walked to a bowling alley. Finding a phone booth, he dialed the Nash number from memory. Kelly answered on the first ring.

"Kelly, it's me," he said.

"Billy! My god, where are you?"

"Never mind where I am. Are the cops looking for me?"

"Are they! They've been around school two days in a row. Billy, are you all right?"

"I'm fine. Hey?"

"What?"

"I still love you."

"I still love you too, Billy. Can I see you?"

"Not now. Not for a while. Is your mom home?"

"No, but she will be any minute. She just went to the grocery store. Billy, what are you going to do? Aren't you afraid they'll catch you?"

"Sure, I'm afraid. I'd be stupid if I wasn't."

"You shouldn't have run away, Billy."

"I *had* to," he told her almost fervently. "You don't know how it is in that place, Kelly. It's like being in jail. You're locked up like some kind of—crook or something. I'm not a   187 criminal, Kelly. I don't deserve to be locked up just because I don't have no home or family. That's been the cause of every problem I ever had, all the trouble I ever got into: everything was just because I didn't have nobody who gave a damn about me."

"I give a damn about you, Billy."

"I know you do."

"I wouldn't ever have let you do what you did to me if I didn't love you."

"I know. I'm not talking about you, honey. I'm talking about having a family and a mom and a dad. That's my problem. But I ain't gonna be locked up for it!"

He could hear Kelly begin to cry softly into the phone. "Oh, Billy, what are we going to do?"

"What you're gonna do is just keep loving me," he said. "What I'm gonna do is lay low for a few months until the heat's off me. Then maybe we can run away or something. Would you run away with me?"

"You know I would. I'd do anything for you, Billy. Haven't I already proved that?"

"Yeah. You have." Briefly he remembered the night she was talking about—a night when her mother was going to be out very late, and she had let him come over after the neighborhood was dark and quiet. He had climbed over her rear fence and she had let him in the back door. She was just out of the tub, smelling of bath oil, her hair damp at the back of her neck—

Knock it off, man, he told himself. Don't start thinking about that or you'll drive yourself nuts.

"Listen, I've got a job and a place to stay," he told her. "I'm not gonna tell you where, 'cause if the cops ask you, it'll be better if you don't have to lie. But I'll be okay. And as soon as I can, as soon as I think the heat's off, I'll call you again. Will you wait for me?"

"You know I will, Billy. Listen, my mom just drove up."

"Okay. I'll see you soon."

He hung up.

Leaving the bowling alley, Billy walked the two miles back to the motel. He felt lonelier than ever before in his life. Talking to Kelly had made him feel worse, not better. He wanted so badly to go to her, put his arms around her, hold her hand, touch her hair, sit with her and talk to her. She was the only person in the world that he trusted totally and completely. He felt a desperate need to keep in very close touch with her, a need to reassure himself that she was there, that she was still his.

I'm going to make it, he kept telling himself every block or so as he walked through the quiet night. I am going to do everything right, I am going to *think* and plan ahead and figure things out, and I am going to *make* it. Other people made it. There was no reason why he couldn't.

As he walked, Billy had his hands shoved into the pockets of his new jeans, his shoulders hunched forward, his head down. There was a determination to his step, almost an offensiveness, as if he knew there would be many formidable obstacles in his way. Sometimes it seemed that everything and everybody was against him, that life's deck of cards was so stacked against him that he couldn't cut anything but a joker—and then the laugh was on him.

But he had made it this far. He had got away from the foster home, got away from the reformatory, and was making it completely on his own. He had a job, a place to sleep, some new clothes, and a few bucks in his pocket. Up ahead he saw the warm glow of the Quality Inn sign. He straightened his shoulders, lifted his chin a bit.

Home, he thought.

22

Billy Issacs's life up until the time he escaped from reform school was not a great deal different from his brother Carl's. It was a life that started with strangers in strange houses: foster homes. Billy was thrown into the foster home cycle at the same time Carl was. His first home was with the Scanlans of Roysterville, Maryland. Art and Rosemary. He was five years old. The Scanlans had no other children. They did not know how to deal with or treat a child. For six months they nervously tried to adjust to him, and he nervously tried to adjust to them. He cried a lot; he wanted his mother and his big brothers and his big sister Ruth. He could not understand why he had been snatched away from his family. Five years old is a rough age to be uprooted.

Art and Rosemary did not know why he was so unhappy. They were being good to him, treating him as if he were their very own, taking the best care of him they could. What he had with them was so much better than what he had come from—at least according to the welfare worker's story of the poor kid's plight. It never occurred to the Scanlans that what he came from had been *his;* and this new life, however much better it might be, was completely foreign, therefore frightening, to him. Nor did he have any idea that it was meant to be permanent. For all he knew, he might be snatched away from *there* too.

Billy would recall years later that the thing wrong with his first foster home, and with *every* foster home, was that he was never sat down and told *why* and *for how long.*

Why was he being sent there? He never knew, not really. He was only told that "this is going to be your new home, and you're going to like it here." It was never explained to him, at any age, that his mother simply was not capable of supporting her brood of children. To him, early on, he thought he was there because his mother did not want him—which presupposed that she did not like him. Later, as with Carl, the reason was because his mother was "no good."

How long was he going to stay? He never knew. Not once was he told, at any age, that the people to whom he had been given were interested in keeping him a month, a year, ten years. Never was he given any indication, even with the Scanlans when he was five years old, that they might want to keep him, raise him, make him their own or one of their own. Never was the element of love included as part of the arrangement.

The Scanlans gave up after six months. They could not cope with a sad little five year old who whimpered a lot. From there Billy was sent to the home of Harold and Marge Hudson in Butler, Maryland. The Hudsons had a large home out in the country, where they had two other boys whom the child welfare department boarded with them. Billy was six when he went to live there. It was with the Hudsons, two years later when he was eight, that he learned how much the element of money was involved in being a foster parent.

"I've got jobs for you boys," Harold Hudson announced one Saturday morning. "Put on your old play clothes, we're going for a ride."

He took Billy and the other two boys, both of whom were older, about a mile away to a horse farm.

"You boys are going to be working here from now on. Cleaning out the horse stalls. You two," he said to the older boys, "will get ten dollars a week; and you, Billy, because you're so small and can't do as much work, will get seven-fifty. The money will help Mrs. Hudson and me make ends meet."

They worked all day on Saturdays, and for three hours after school every day. It was dirty, freezing work in the winter, and hot, filthy work in the summer. Because Billy was the youngest, he got the dirtiest stalls, the oldest rake, the worn shovel with splinters on the handle. There were usually between thirty and forty horses on the farm, and the stench of the stalls was rank and oppressive. The boys worked with towels tied over their mouths and noses to filter the foul air, but that only helped a little; the daily waste of three dozen healthy horses was a formidable obstacle to overcome.

Billy hated his life. He hated the days in school because he knew that they would end all too soon and then it would be off 191 to the goddamned stinking stables. All he could think about sometimes in school was what was waiting for him *after* school. His grades suffered for it. He could not concentrate on his classroom studies, he dreaded the hours after school so. He brought home failing grades, which incensed Mrs. Hudson.

"What's the matter with you?" she asked him. "Your head empty? Come here, let me see—"

She held him next to the wall and bounced his head against it.

"Sounds all right to me. Don't sound empty. Must be a brain in there somewheres."

She bounced his head again. And again. It began to hurt.

"This is what happens to kids who don't use their heads for schoolwork," she pointed out. "Their heads get used for something else, like testing walls."

The woman bounced his head against the wall several more times, and stopped only when he began crying. After that, whenever he brought home a poor grade in anything, which he began to do more and more frequently, she bounced his head against the wall. And gradually she began to do it for his every indiscretion: being late, not cleaning his plate, not making his bed properly. Bouncing his head against the wall became *his* punishment. Perhaps Marge Hudson settled on that punishment for him because she instinctively sensed that he disliked it so. She knew Billy could take the strap without shedding a tear; room restriction meant nothing to him; and other forms of punishment rarely fazed him. But that head-bouncing— Billy hated it with a passion.

Twice he ran away from the Hudson home. Both times the police picked him up and brought him back. Both times he told the police and the Hudsons that he did not want to live there any longer. "I want to live with my real mother," Billy said.

"He can't live with his own mother, officer," Mr. Hudson told the police. "The welfare worker told us that she is morally unfit as a mother and not suitable to have custody of any of her children. The boy is a ward of the court, and the child welfare department has put him here to live."

"You'll have to stay here, boy," the policeman told Billy. "Instead of running away, you ought to thank your lucky stars that you've got a nice place like this to live. Now you stay home and keep out of trouble."

Eventually his conduct became such that Welfare had to remove him from the Hudsons' and find someplace else for him to live. As he was leaving, he said to Mr. and Mrs. Hudson, "I know you're really gonna miss me. It's gonna cost you seven-fifty a week until you can get another kid to take over my job at the horse farm."

The Hudsons just shook their heads resignedly as he left.

A succession of foster homes followed. Some were bad and some were worse. In none of them did Billy really feel that he fit. Like Carl, perhaps like the other Issacs children who had been distributed by the state, Billy always felt like an outsider. He grew from a nervous, crying five-year-old displaced kid, to a tense, hostile thirteen-year-old loner. More and more as the years went by, Billy withdrew into himself; thinking his own thoughts, keeping his own counsel, establishing his own values. Day by day, month by month, he went through life never having contact with anyone that he could honestly say loved him. There were those now and again who *liked* him; but no one, nowhere, who loved him. As he approached his teens, without realizing it, he had grown hollow inside: something was missing from his makeup. He was rowing through life with one oar not all the way in the water. He never heard the word "love." Never.

The one good thing that came out of all those years was Kelly Nash. She lived in the neighborhood of one of the later foster homes they put him in. His and Kelly's was one of those painfully sweet young loves that strikes the uncharted emotions of the adolescent. They had only to lock eyes with each other to know that fate had meant them to be. They seemed so right for one another: Billy a foster kid with no real family, Kelly living with her divorced mother who did not have a lot of time for her. Both fourteen, they came together with a mutual hunger that was almost frightening in its intensity. For the time that Billy lived in the area, they went steady. When he was sent to another neighborhood, he managed to keep in regular touch, calling her on school days, arranging to meet her on weekends. He met her mother and Mrs. Nash seemed to like him. He was invited to dinner now and then, or to spend an evening eating popcorn and watching TV. Billy thought Kelly's little house was the warmest, most comfortable and friendly place he had ever been in; never once did he feel out of place there. He only realized much later that his sense of well-being came from the innocent, selfless love that the fourteen-year-old girl gave him.

With Kelly in his thoughts a lot, Billy actually began for the 193 first time to think about his future. He started paying more attention in school, taking an interest in things that he previously had ignored; and he began to speculate on what he might do with his life when he became a man. He had always been naturally good at freehand drawing; he could copy almost anything, and even create figures and original scenes right out of his mind. He began to apply himself to artistic endeavors at school, volunteering to paint signs for various clubs, or help decorate the gym, or design scenery for school plays in the assembly hall. His mind, for the first time, was moving into the realm of creative thought, instead of simply lying stagnant in a bed of unfortunate circumstances. And Billy felt good about it. About himself. About his future.

Then one day Carl showed up.

"Hey, bro!"

Billy, on his way to school, whirled around at the sound of the voice. He knew instinctively that it was Carl.

"Junior. Hey, man."

"Where you going, bro?" Carl asked with a wide smile.

"School." Billy stepped into the doorway where Carl was standing. "What are you doing here?"

"I'm on my way to see Mom. Thought you might like to come."

"How'd you know I was here?"

"A kid transferred from your school to my school last week. When he heard my name in class, he told me there was an Issacs in the school he just came from. I'm hooking today to go see Mom."

"Where is she?"

"Her and Ruth and Ruth's old man lives over in Parkville. We can hitch. Want to come with?"

"Sure, why not?"

The two brothers stepped out of the doorway and went off down the street together.

Billy had mixed emotions that morning. He was not sure whether he agreed to go with Carl because he really wanted to see his mother, or simply because he wanted to spend some time with his brother. Like Carl, Billy had pretty much resigned himself to the fact that their mother did not want him. Once, between foster homes, he had done exactly the same thing Carl had once done: gone to his mother with a naive but very serious plan for them to live together; a plan that, as she had done with Carl, his mother rejected outright. So on the day that Carl intercepted him on the way to school, he was not deluding himself that going to see his mother would make any difference in his circumstances; he was not even sure that he wanted to see her because he didn't miss her at all, not any longer. What he did know was that he wanted to be with Carl, spend some time with this brother of his who was so close to him in the sequence of their siblings: Carl was the third Issacs child born, Billy the fifth. They had seen each other from time to time over the years, but had never really gotten to know each other. There had never seemed to be time. Today, perhaps, there would be.

Billy and Carl had a lot to talk about. So much had happened to them since that day the welfare people had come and taken them out of school, and divided them up like so much firewood: one stick for this family, two sticks for that family. Each of them had been on the foster home merry-go-round for a number of years now, and they eagerly compared notes on the families they had lived with, the schools they had gone to, the people they knew.

"Shit," Carl bragged, "when I don't like where they send me to live, I just run away and let 'em catch me and put me in training school."

"You really been to training school?" Billy asked in awe. Among adolescents, the Maryland training school had a reputation right up there with Alcatraz and Devil's Island.

"Hell, yeah! Been there twice." Carl laughed. "With my attitude, I'll probably be there twice more." He said it in jest, having no idea how right he actually was. Between the ages of nine and seventeen, Carl would be in and out of training school six times.

The brothers hitched a ride on a salvage truck that day that took them halfway to Parkville. They walked the rest of the way, each of them seeming to enjoy the other's company. Billy told Carl about Kelly, and how crazy he was about her; and Carl told Billy about Jane and how their passion for each other had got him sent to training school for the second time.

"But that's all in the past, bro," he said with a worldliness that impressed Billy. "I got me a new woman now. Her name's Tish and she's got an apartment with a couple other girls. Man, she's crazy about me. Hey, want me to take you over there to meet her after we visit Mom?"

"Sure," Billy said eagerly, "I'd like that." He was touched   195 that Carl thought enough of him to want to introduce him to his girl friend. He decided to try and figure a way for Carl to meet Kelly. Maybe, he thought, the four of them could meet at a movie or something. Wouldn't that be great? Him and his big brother double-dating. Just like regular kids in ordinary families. How about that?

For the rest of their hike to Parkville, the brothers talked about other members of their family, on the Coleman as well as the Issacs side. They knew that Jimmy Coleman, the eldest of his clan, had gone off to North Carolina or somewhere to work as a carpenter. The three Coleman girls—Ruth, Lois, and Ann—were all still around the Baltimore area, all married now; Ruth, of course, had their mother living with her. As for Wayne, the last of the Colemans, neither of them knew for sure where he was.

"I heard he got sent to prison," Carl said. "For pulling a burglary."

"Prison," Billy said solemnly. "Guy."

Their own older brother Roy they knew had joined the Army and gone away. Hazel, who had been with them the day the welfare people took them out of school, had married and moved to the other end of the state. Robert, the brother between Carl and Billy, was in a foster home somewhere, as were George and Wanda, the two youngest Issacs children.

"Christ, we're really spread out, ain't we?" Billy said with a trace of bitterness.

"Yeah. Like a bunch of goddamned strangers."

"Brothers and sisters that don't really know each other. That ain't right, you know."

"Maybe it ain't right," Carl said pragmatically, "but that's the way it is, kid. That's fucking life."

It was noon by the time they found the house that their mother lived in with Ruth and her husband. To their surprise, no one was home. That was unusual because their mother habitually worked night waitress jobs so she could sleep during the day when the house was quiet.

"Let's see if we can get in," Carl said. "Maybe she's just sleeping off a drunk. Come on, let's check the windows."

"Maybe we better not," Billy said. "It ain't our house, you know."

"Hell, it's our *family's* house," Carl said adamantly. "Come on."

They found a kitchen window unlocked and climbed in. A quick check of the house told them that no one was home.

"Let's go and come back later," Billy said.

"Why should we? We're here, let's stay. Let's see what they've got to eat."

In the kitchen they drank some milk and ate a box of powdered doughnuts they found in the refrigerator. Then Billy said, "Come on, we better go now, Junior."

"Let's look around first," Carl said. "See if there's anything to swipe. I could use a couple packs of smokes."

Before Billy could protest, Carl had left the kitchen and started prowling the house. Billy nervously followed him.

"This looks like Mom's room," Carl said, looking in one of the bedrooms. "Sure it is, there's one of her wigs." They both knew that their mother wore red wigs; for some reason, she had lost most of her hair.

When Carl started looking through his mother's dresser drawers, Billy became increasingly more nervous. "Jesus, Junior—"

"Relax," Carl said. "Nobody knows we're here. Look around, see if she's got any money stuck away."

Billy looked around, but he was careful not to touch anything that belonged to his mother. She was a large, strong woman; Billy knew if she found out they'd prowled her bedroom, she'd find them and beat hell out of them.

Carl found a carton of cigarettes and took two packs. He examined some costume jewelry from one drawer, decided it was junk, and put it back. In another drawer, he searched through her underwear.

"Jesus, Junior," Billy said in disgust. He turned and started to leave the room.

"Holy Christ!" Carl exclaimed.

Billy turned and saw his brother staring at a roll of currency.

"It was rolled up in one of her bras," Carl said. He began to count it.

"Junior, you better put that back, man!"

"Shit, there's six hundred fucking dollars here!"

Billy's mouth dropped open. His mother was supposed to be poor. Six hundred dollars was a lot of money.

But Billy's fear overcame his surprise. "Junior, Mom'll kill you if you take that money—"

"How the hell's she gonna know?" Carl demanded. He whirled and held the money up close to Billy's face. "Look at this, man! She's too goddamned bad off to take care of her own kids, but she's got money like this stashed away for herself! Let 197 me ask you something, Billy: has she ever once sent you a fucking dollar of spending money since you been in foster homes? Has she?"

"No," Billy admitted, shrugging self-consciously.

"Well, me neither, man! I was in the fucking reform school and I never got a fucking dollar for smokes or candy or any fucking thing!" Carl took a deep breath and got control of himself. "We're taking the money, Billy," he said evenly. "We got it coming."

Carl walked out of the bedroom, stuffing the roll of bills in his pocket.

Billy followed his brother back out the window. They hurried away from the house, Carl all the while muttering a stream of invectives about their mother, as his injured young psyche dredged up everything bad that had happened to him over the years, and blamed her for it.

"The fucking whore! Throwing us all out into the god-damned street like so much fucking garbage! We're her *kids,* Billy!" Tears streamed out of his eyes, streaked his cheeks. "Her fucking *kids!* She's supposed to love us!"

"Sure, she is," Billy agreed, hurrying alongside him. "But our old man was supposed to love us too, wasn't he? Why blame it all on Mom?"

"Our old man ain't here, Billy. And she *is.* She could at least *try* to love us, couldn't she? Shit, Billy, ain't we human? Ain't we alive? Ain't *somebody* supposed to love us?"

Billy started crying then too. Somebody *was* supposed to love them; Billy instinctively knew that. He put an arm around Carl's shoulders as he walked along with him, both of them crying.

Taking a taxi away from Parkville, they went back to where they had started that morning. At a nearby shopping mall, they went on a spending spree. Carl bought some new clothes. Billy bought a pair of boots. Carl bought a few things for Tish. "Don't you want to buy a present for your girl?" he asked.

"Uh, maybe later," Billy said. He knew he would not be able to bring himself to buy anything for Kelly with stolen money, taken from his mother or anyone else. But he could not tell Carl that, since Carl had already spent part of the money on Tish.

When they got tired of spending their mother's money, Carl took Billy to Tish's apartment. Neither Tish nor her roommates were home, but Carl had a key. They went in, had something to eat again, and then Billy started falling asleep on the couch. He was dead tired. Everything had caught up with him: all the walking that morning, the tension of prowling his mother's bedroom, the theft of her money, their shopping spree. He suddenly felt as if he were going to drop from exhaustion.

"Come on," Carl said, helping him into Tish's bedroom. "Lie down on the bed and take a nap. I'll wake you up when Tish gets home."

Billy went to sleep like he'd been drugged.

The next thing he knew, someone was shaking him. He opened his eyes and looked up. It was a policeman.

On his way to jail, he found out what had happened. His mother had returned home, seen the milk glass and doughnut box, discovered her money missing, and concluded that some of her kids had paid her a visit. She reported the theft and her conclusion to the police. A quick check with the various foster homes, through the welfare department, told them that both Carl and Billy had been absent from school that day. It was easy enough to trace Carl to his girl friend's apartment. When they checked there, however, they found not Carl but the sleeping Billy. Carl had disappeared. Billy was left holding the bag.

That bag got him sent to the Bay Village reformatory for six months.

Kelly wrote to him while he was at Bay Village, but her mother would not let her visit him. Billy was miserable the whole time he was there. Bay Village was not as tough a place as the state training school, but it was still custody: still rigid rules and regulations that he had to observe and obey. The worst thing about it, as far as Billy was concerned, was being away from Kelly. Not a day passed that he did not curse his stupidity for going with Carl that day; curse Carl for coming around to tempt him; curse his mother for leaving her god-damned money in the dresser drawer; curse life for the consistent bad breaks it seemed to deliver his way.

Aside from missing Kelly, Billy adjusted pretty well to the institution. The boys there were not as hardened and street-wise as the ones Carl had faced in training school. They were younger, most of them not yet interested in sex, nearly all of them simple runaways, shoplifters, hubcap thieves: low-grade delinquents that the state had decided did not rate doing hard   199 time in training school. In his letters to Kelly, Billy assured her that the place was not so bad, and he promised to work as hard as he could, to behave himself, and to be ready in six months to get out and face life as a better person than when he left.

Billy meant it too. He had a burning hunger for a better life, and desperately wanted to find a path that would lead to one. He had thought he was on that path, in fact had *known* he was, until the day Carl came along and led him away from it. Not that he blamed Carl. Not really. He readily cursed Carl, but in his mind and heart he knew that no one was to blame but himself. Carl was Carl: high strung, hyper, nervous, cunning, vindictive. Billy *knew* better than to get mixed up in anything Carl did. He had simply faltered that day; given in to the blood tie between them. And it had cost him six months away from Kelly.

Billy kept his word and at the end of six months was ready for release with a spotless record behind him. However, there was the problem of his future.

"We're going to try to arrange for you to live with your mother, Billy," the welfare people told him.

But that had not worked. His mother did not want him around. He was a delinquent, a thief, too much trouble.

"We'll try to find you a suitable foster home," they told him then.

But that did not work either. There was no foster home available for his age, sex, and background.

Billy waited.

Finally: "There's nothing we can do at the moment. We've got you on a waiting list. A foster home will turn up eventually. In the meantime, you can't stay at Bay Village; it's just for short-term commitments. We're transferring you to the Victor Cullen Home. You'll like it there."

Billy let them transfer him to the new reform school.

Then he escaped.

23

Billy could tell that Kelly was nervous the instant she entered the Quality Inn coffee shop. He smiled and waved to her from the back booth. Nervously she smiled back and hurried toward him, clutching her schoolbooks to her bosom.

"Hi," he said as she slid in across from him. "Remember me?"

"Hi. Oh, do I! You look just the same, only older."

He took her hand across the table. "You look just the same, only not older."

Her face turned pink, not quite a blush. "Guy, I've missed seeing you, Billy."

"Sorry I can't tell you the same thing—'cause I've *been* seeing you. About once a week when I couldn't stand it any longer, I'd go over to the laundromat on the corner and watch you as you walked to school."

"Oh, you rat! That wasn't fair!"

Billy smiled. "Listen, one thing I've learned in the past year: don't look for fair in life. Chances are you won't find it." He squeezed her hand. "Want a Coke or something?"

"A Coke would be fine."

Billy waved over to the counter. "Daisy, could we have two Cokes over here, please?"

"Daisy? You know her?"

"I know everybody around here. This is where I work."

"Here? The Quality Inn?"

"Yep," he said with a touch of pride. "I'm the maintenance man. I take care of all the grounds, the parking lot, the pool area—hey, you can come over here and go swimming anytime you want to. I cleared it with Mr. Shenk, my boss."

"Well, for goodness sakes, Billy." It was obvious that she was impressed. "How long have you worked here?"

"Six months." He lowered his voice. "Remember the first time I called you after I escaped? I got the job that day." 201

She shook her head incredulously. "Billy, I'm so proud of you."

Daisy brought the two Cokes. Billy reached for his wallet but she waved him off. "On the house, Billy."

"Thanks, Daisy." When Daisy left, Billy took a small passbook out of his shirt pocket and showed it to Kelly. "I've got a bank account too. Look at this: three hundred dollars saved."

"Billy, my goodness—"

"And look at this—" He showed her a student ID card from the downtown night high school. "I enrolled when the new semester started. I'm taking regular high school classes plus an extra art class."

"Billy, I can't believe this is really you. I mean, this is—is— well, *great!*"

"I knew you'd be surprised. That's why I waited so long to call you to meet me. I wanted everything to be just right. Listen, the cops aren't still looking for me around school, are they?"

"No, not for a long time."

"I didn't think they would be. They were looking for me at the last three schools I went to, but they haven't been around the other two for a long time either. I knew it would blow over. Cops ain't gonna devote a lot of time looking for some reform school runaway unless he's making trouble—and I ain't making trouble. I work here under my own name, I go to school downtown under my own name; nobody bothers me, I don't bother nobody."

Kelly squeezed his hand this time. "Oh, Billy, I'm so glad to see you again. I'm so happy that everything is all right with you. I was afraid you might end up—well, all bitter and mean, you know?"

"Not me," he said proudly. "I don't let 'em get me down, honey. I can make it on my own in spite of the welfare people and the cops and my mom and everybody else. I don't need nobody. Except maybe you."

"Maybe you don't even need me anymore," Kelly said, looking away.

"If I didn't," Billy told her quietly, "I wouldn't have hung around Baltimore after I escaped. I would have run off to Florida or California or somewhere. I stayed here because of you. Remember what I told you that time I called? Remember I asked if you'd run away with me, and you said you would."

202   "I remember."

"Do you still feel that way? Will you run away with me?"

"Yes. I'll do anything you want me to, Billy."

Billy nodded determinedly. "That's all I needed to know."

Later, Billy walked Kelly part of the way home. They held hands, their shoulders brushing. Billy carried her books in his other hand. As they walked along, Billy noticed Kelly's expression become very pensive.

"What's the matter?" he asked.

She forced a smile. "Oh—nothing really."

"Come on. I can tell something's wrong. What is it?"

"Okay, but don't get mad now. I was just wondering if running away is really the best thing for us to do. I mean, look at us, Billy: we're just fifteen years old. I know we both *look* a little older, but we're not. If we run away together, how long will it take before we get caught?"

Billy shrugged. "Maybe we'll luck out and *not* get caught."

Kelly shook her head. "Eventually we'll get caught, Billy. If we were both eighteen, it would be different; nobody would pay much attention to us. But two fifteen year olds are going to be pretty easy to find."

"What if there's nobody looking for us?"

"There would be. My mother would see to that. She wouldn't give the police a minute's rest until I was found."

Billy stopped and faced her. "Are you saying you won't run away with me?"

"I'm saying I think we ought to talk about it some more. We ought to think it over and see if there's a better way for us." She slipped her arms around his waist. "Look, we want to be together; that's what's most important to us. I don't think we should do something that will just let us be together for a little while. I'd like for us to plan ahead and see if we can't work out something for ourselves that will last. Please don't be mad at me, Billy—"

"I'm not," he said quickly. "Really, I'm not. Come on, let's walk some more."

They continued on for a while, not holding hands now, Billy deep in thought, Kelly feeling increasingly nervous about what she had just said. But she had to tell him; she had to be honest with him. She could only hope now that he would accept her honesty.

He did.

"What you said makes a lot of sense," he told her at last. "I 203 want a decent life for us. Being runaways ain't no way to start one."

"Oh, Billy, I just knew you'd understand!" she said happily, taking his hand again and holding it tightly.

"Only thing is," he said, "where does that leave us now? What do we do next?"

"Let's just see each other as often as we can. Let's both think about it, and talk about it when we're together. Oh, Billy, I just *know* we'll find a better way for ourselves."

"Sure, we will," he said.

His tone was not nearly as confident as hers.

They worked on their problem for two months, seeing each other whenever they could. Kelly came by the Quality Inn every day after school, but just for a few minutes: long enough for a Coke, or for Billy to take his afternoon break and walk her part of the way home. Now and then Kelly would say she was going to the library on a weeknight and visit him in his room. They would go to bed together and for an hour or so forget about the outside world and their problems. On Saturday nights, Billy would meet her at a movie somewhere, usually in another neighborhood because he still could not chance being seen by any former schoolmates who might accidentally or intentionally inform on him.

Always they talked about what to do with their future, trying with youthful eagerness to weigh all the factors involved. Kelly put great weight on the fact that Billy had a good job, was making it on his own, and was going to night high school. "How many other fifteen year olds could have made it like you have?" she said almost challengingly. "Not many, I'll tell you that. In fact, *none* that I can name. Most of the guys your age that I go to school with are just overgrown babies with big mouths. They *think* they're hot stuff, but if any of them had to go through what you've gone through, they'd go running home to mommy looking for sugar-titty."

"Such language," Billy chided. "And all this time I thought you were a nice girl."

Despite her praise for him, and the high regard in which she held his accomplishments of the previous six months, and de3 spite the fact that they endlessly discussed their limited options for the future, they neither jointly nor individually conceived any plan that they thought suitable for themselves. The constant weakness in every scheme they thought of was their age. Being fifteen years old undermined the foundation of every idea they came up with. And it was a problem that was only being resolved at the maddening pace of one day at a time.

Finally, in utter desperation and despair, and because there was no one else to whom they could turn, Kelly went to her mother. When she told Billy, he was aghast.

"You *what?* Kelly, are you crazy? Are you trying to get me sent back to reform school?"

"Listen to me," she insisted. "My mother is *not* going to turn you in. She's promised me. She likes you, Billy, she always has. She felt very sorry for you when you got in trouble with Carl, sorry for you when they sent you to reform school the first time; and she thought it was very unfair that you were being sent to another reform school just because there was no place else for you to go. My mother's on your side, Billy, please believe that."

"I ain't *never* had a grown-up on my side," Billy replied dubiously. "Does your mother know that you've been sneaking out to meet me?"

"Yes, she does."

"And she's not mad about it?"

"No, she's not. She wasn't overjoyed about it, but when she heard the whole story, she was just glad we hadn't done anything crazy—like running off together, or me getting pregnant." Kelly looked down at her own hands, which were fidgeting nervously. "Mom wants me to bring you to the house so she can talk to us."

"Suppose you're wrong about the way she feels, Kel?" said Billy. "If you are, it could be the end for us, you know. She could have the cops waiting to grab me when I show up."

"My mother wouldn't do a thing like that, Billy," Kelly said confidently. "She's not that kind of person."

"I hope not," Billy said quietly, as much to himself as to her.

Mrs. Nash made iced tea for them and they sat at the kitchen table to talk. When they first came into the house, as her mother led them into the kitchen, Kelly had turned and given Billy a snippy I-told-you-so look, and quickly whispered, "See any cops, smart guy?" Billy started to slap her on the ass, but he was afraid her mother would see him.

"Well, Billy," Mrs. Nash said when they were seated, "you're certainly looking well. Nice tan, neat haircut, clean clothes. I guess I was expecting you to look shabbier."

"No, ma'am," he said. "I have to stay neat because I'm 205

around the guests at the motel a lot. Mr. Shenk, my boss, says we always have to make a good impression on the guests so they'll stay at other Quality Inns when they travel."

"Kelly tells me you've worked at the motel for eight months."

"Yes, ma'am. I got the job on the third day after I escaped."

"Does this Mr. Shenk know you ran away from reform school?"

"No, ma'am. He thinks I'm seventeen and my parents are dead and I'm on my own. I don't want him to know anything about the other. As long as he don't know, he can't get in no trouble. I wouldn't want to ever cause him no trouble; he's been too good to me."

"How much does Mr. Shenk pay you?"

Billy told her what he earned and what his duties around the motel were; and he explained his living arrangement where he slept in the supply room. "It's really like having a regular motel room, except that half of it is filled with shelves full of bed linen and toilet paper and light bulbs. Best thing about it is I don't have to pay no rent."

Mrs. Nash questioned him about his night school classes: what he was studying and what his grades were. He told her about the art classes he was taking, how well he seemed to be doing in them, and how much he liked them.

"Yes, Kelly mentioned that you had a natural ability to draw. Do you think you'd like to make a career for yourself in some field of art?"

Billy shrugged. "I don't know that much about it yet, Mrs. Nash. And I don't really know what I want to do with my life. I just know that I want to stay out of trouble and I want to have a good life, whatever I do." He glanced away as if embarrassed. "I'm tired of living like I wasn't supposed to be born. I got a right to be in this world same as anybody else. I didn't ask to be born, but now that I'm here I want to be happy and enjoy life like other people do. I got just as much right to happiness as anybody else. That's the way I feel."

There was silence at the table for a moment. Kelly's eyes watered but she did not allow herself to cry. Mrs. Nash studied Billy closely, glancing over at her daughter now and then to weigh Kelly's reaction to Billy's words. It was clear to her that the two young people cared very deeply for one another. Their exchange of looks, their quick touches, their occasional secret whispers told her that.

206

Of course it would have been nice if Kelly had become involved with the captain of the school tennis team or the son of a local banker who was destined to go to Yale, instead of a scruffy reform school escapee who apparently came from one of those white trash families that did nothing but produce generation after generation of misfits. Thank God this kid Billy at least had aspirations of climbing up out of the family sewer. Things *could* be worse, she decided.

"Billy, I'm very impressed with what you've been able to accomplish in the past eight months," she told him. "I'd like to help you. At the same time, I want to be completely honest with you and tell you that whatever help I give you, I'll be doing it for Kelly. I don't want to lose my daughter. I don't want to put her in a position where she feels forced to do something foolish, like running away or getting into trouble of one kind or another. Do you understand what I'm saying?"

"Yes, ma'am. I don't want Kelly hurt either, Mrs. Nash. I ain't going to insult you by saying that I love her as much as you do. You're her mother and you've loved her a long time, but I want you to know that I *do* love her too."

"I can tell that, Billy. And I hope that you *do* love her as much as I do. If that's the case, then neither one of us will hurt her. Now then, I'd like to make a deal with you two. Will you listen to my proposition with open minds?"

"Of course we will, Mother," said Kelly.

Billy shrugged. "Sure."

"All right," Mrs. Nash said. "How would you like to move in with us, Billy?"

Billy and Kelly looked incredulously at each other. Then Billy said, "Uh, what do you mean exactly?"

"I mean move in with Kelly and me. Come and live with us in our home, as part of our family—small though it is."

Billy suddenly felt out of sync. "Well, I—I don't know, Mrs. Nash—"

"Let me explain it a little. There's an extra bedroom here that Kelly and I can fix up for you. You can come live here, have your meals with us, everything. At the same time, you could keep your job at the motel and continue with your night school. You and Kelly could have all the time together you wanted without her having to sneak off to meet you somewhere. And the two of you then wouldn't have to consider doing anything foolish like running away. You'd have a place to live at least until you were both old enough to go out on 207 your own. Kelly could finish regular high school; maybe you, Billy, could get a diploma at night school. The whole point is that you two wouldn't have to rush into anything; you wouldn't be pressed with any urgent decisions. The arrangement would give you the one thing you seem to need so desperately in your relationship: time." Mrs. Nash sat back and smiled. "Well," she asked, looking from one to the other, "what do you think?"

"Oh, Mother, I think it's a wonderful idea!" Kelly said exuberantly before Billy could even react. She grabbed his hand and squeezed it. "Billy, don't you think it's a super idea!"

"Sure sounds nice, all right," Billy said. He wanted to be as enthusiastic about the offer as Kelly was, but his built-in defense mechanism would not let him. Instinctively he did not trust adults; they had always hurt him one way or another. This offer of Mrs. Nash's *seemed* sincere enough—but Billy had been fooled before. Past experience had taught him to move cautiously with adults.

"Uh, Mrs. Nash, I wouldn't feel right about living here unless I could pay my own way. I couldn't have you supporting me."

"All right. Why don't we do this: figure out how much you've been spending every week for your meals in the coffee shop or wherever, and you can contribute that much to the household for room and board. Does that sound fair?"

"Well, yes ma'am, it does."

"Is anything else bothering you?"

"Uh, no ma'am, not that I can think of."

"What about you, dear?" she asked her daughter.

"Guy, no! I think it's fabulous!"

"All right. Let's establish a couple of ground rules then. First of all, understand that it is not my intent that you two should start living as husband and wife. You'll each have your own bedroom and I'll expect you to sleep in it. While you'll certainly have considerably more time together, most of it will be when I am around. I'm going to expect both of you to conduct yourselves like proper young people should.

"The second thing is what we'll tell the neighbors. We're really not that close to any of them, but there's no way to keep them from knowing you're here. Fortunately, we live on the outer edge of Kelly's school district, so there aren't any nearby families that have kids who would know you. We'll just say you're a nephew of mine who's come here to work to earn money for college. What with your job during the day and school several nights a week, you really won't be around all that much. As long as Kelly doesn't bring any friends home and, Billy, you keep a low profile in the neighborhood, I don't think we'll have any problems at all. Well, how does it sound?"

It sounded like a dream come true to Kelly, and to Billy like it might, just might, be the one break in his life that could turn things around for him, give him a chance, a shot at living the way other people lived. Billy still had some latent reservations based mainly on his inherent distrust of adults; but because he cared so deeply for Kelly, and because he felt instinctively that Mrs. Nash would do nothing deceitful where her daughter was concerned, he made up his mind to throw himself wholeheartedly into the new arrangement. He vowed to do his part to make it work, one hundred percent: he would follow Mrs. Nash's rules right down the line, do absolutely nothing to arouse her ire; he would, in fact, be like a son to her, if she permitted him to.

Billy moved into the Nash home and into his new living arrangement with the same determination that had driven him to succeed at his new job and at night school; and with a high expectation that the move was a definite, positive step upward and forward for him. To his delight, everything worked out beautifully. He fit in with Kelly and Mrs. Nash as if they were his real, blood family; and he found that they accepted him almost as if he had always been there. He had expected that acceptance from Kelly—she loved him—but he had not been too confident about Mrs. Nash. He was pleased that much more then, when, after the first week, she actually began to show affection toward him; kissing him goodnight on the cheek, ironing his shirts, being sure to buy his favorite foods when she did the marketing. She acted like a real mom to him, and Billy was quietly moved by it.

Billy would later speculate how his young life would have turned out had he been able to stay on in the Nash household and grow to maturity in that environment of caring and giving. He was sure that he would have grown to be a respectable, responsible, and successful member of the community; probably married Kelly and given Mrs. Nash grandchildren to dote on; become a good commercial artist, maybe with his own studio . . .

209

Dreams. Fantasies. The hopes of the hopeless.

Billy never had a chance. He was a born loser, with never a prayer of getting away from who he was and what he was.

The past always caught up with him.

Carl always came around.

24

When Kelly Nash answered the doorbell that Sunday night, she knew at once who the smiling, nice-looking young man on the porch was.

"Is Billy Issacs here?" he asked.

"Who are you?" she asked back, though she was sure she already knew.

"I'm Carl. His brother."

"Would you like to come in?"

"I'll just wait out on the porch, thanks," Carl said, still smiling. "Just tell him I'm here."

A minute later, Billy came out. "How'd you find me, Junior?" he asked, without greeting his brother.

"Mom told me you were here."

Sure, Billy thought. He might have known. A couple of months earlier he had impulsively gone to visit his mother and Ruth, just to let them know he was alive and well. He had felt obligated to tell them where he was living; after all, if anything ever happened to any member of his family, he would want to be notified. He realized now that he should have told them that he did not want anyone else to know where he was, but it simply had not occurred to him. Now, too late to do anything about it, Carl had shown up.

"Hey, bro," Carl said, still smiling, "you're not still pissed at me about stealing the old lady's money, are you? I mean, *she* got over it, man, and it was her money." He slung an arm around Billy's shoulder. "Come on, Billy. Brothers ain't supposed to carry grudges. Hey, I took a chance even coming to see you. I'm on the run, bro."

"What do you mean?"

"I mean I'm wanted, man. I escaped from Poplar Hill."

"No shit?"

"No shit. Me and two other boys. They're waiting in an alley about a block from here. Come on down and meet them."

Billy shook his head. "I don't want to meet anybody."

"One of them's your brother Wayne," Carl said quietly.

"Wayne?"

"That's right."

Billy swallowed dryly. "Jesus. I don't even hardly remember him."

"He remembers you. Come on down and see him. He wants to see you. He's been in prison a long time. This may be the only chance you'll ever have to meet him; he's on the lam too. Come on."

"Okay. Wait a minute."

Billy went back into the house. Mrs. Nash was out playing Sunday night bridge. Kelly was watching television.

"Listen, Kel, I'm going with my brother for a few minutes. Just to see another brother of mine I haven't seen in years. I'll be right back, okay?"

Kelly shrugged. "Sure, okay."

Billy knew from the expression on her face that she did not approve. But he went anyway. It would just be for a few minutes.

As Billy and Carl walked quickly down the dark street, Billy was pleased to see that he was now as tall as his older brother. As a matter of fact, when he stood up straight with his shoulders back, he was even taller, because Carl had a tendency to slouch. Billy concentrated on walking tall; he felt it necessary to impress on Carl that he wasn't a kid any longer.

In the alley, two men waited next to a fairly late-model car. One man, Billy saw, was black. The other was his half brother Wayne Coleman, whom he was certain he would never have recognized if they had passed each other on the street.

"Hey, Wayne, look who I got here," Carl said as they walked up.

Billy and Wayne faced each other for an awkward moment, much as Carl and Wayne had done when they met in Poplar Hill. Then, because Billy was really a kid and not a man, Wayne reached out and pulled his brother to him in a hug.

"Hey, little bro, how are you?"

"I'm good, Wayne. How are you?"

Wayne grinned. "Oh, aside from being a fugitive from fucking justice, I guess I'm making it okay. Did Junior tell you we need some help?"

212

"No," Billy replied, glancing suspiciously at Carl.

"I wanted him to come down and see you first," Carl said. He draped an arm around Billy's shoulders again. "We need some clothes, bro. We got to get out of these prison denims. Can you spare us a few shirts and things?"

"Yeah, I guess so," Billy said. He could not say no to his brothers when they were on the run from the law.

"Hey, good deal," said Wayne. "Listen, Billy, I want you to meet a good friend of mine. This here is George Dungee. He escaped with us."

Billy shook hands with George. He noticed in the dim light that George's face seemed to be twisted in a grimace, as if he were in pain.

"Is something wrong?" he asked.

"Lost my glasses, man," George said. "Can't see so good without them."

"Yeah, hey, can you get us a flashlight?" Wayne asked. "We got to find those glasses for him before we leave. They're around here somewheres; we just ain't been able to find them in the dark."

"Yeah, I'll get you a flashlight," Billy said.

When Billy returned to the house and went into his bedroom, Kelly followed him. Her eyes got wide when she saw him taking clothes out of his dresser drawers. He stopped and put his arms around her.

"Listen to me," he said quietly. "I'm going to give my two brothers some of my clothes. They've escaped from prison and they're trying to get away—"

"Billy, you shouldn't get involved in that," she said sternly.

"They're my brothers, Kelly. I have to get involved."

"You're going to risk losing everything you've been working for," she warned.

"No, I'm not. I know what I'm doing, honey. I know what I *have* to do." He patted her cheek. "It'll be all right, I promise. Listen, get me the flashlight, will you? A guy that's with them lost his glasses and needs to look for them."

After telling Kelly that he would not be gone long, Billy took the flashlight and three sets of clothes back to the car in the alley. Wayne immediately took the flashlight and searched for George's glasses. He found them in some weeds along an alley fence. "Hang onto the goddamn things now, will you?" he said as he handed the glasses to the black man.

"I will, Wayne," George said contritely."I promise."

The three escapees changed clothes there in the alley and threw their prison denims into a convenient trash can.

"Hey, little bro," Wayne said to Billy, "we're going to go see the old lady and Ruth for a while. Want to come along?"

"I better not," Billy said. "I told my girl I wouldn't be gone long."

"Well, you won't be," Carl said. "You know the old lady can't stand having any of her kids around for any length of time. She probably won't let us stay more'n half an hour at most."

"We wouldn't stay too long anyways," Wayne said. "We got to get the hell out of this area, head south or somewheres."

"Come on and ride around with us a little bit anyway," Carl prompted. "Hell, we might never see each other again after tonight."

Billy got in the car, sitting with Carl in the front seat, while Wayne and George shared the back seat. Billy sat turned partway around in the seat so he could talk to Wayne. His older half brother asked him about his girl, his job, his night school, seeming to be genuinely interested in how Billy was doing and what kind of future he was planning for himself.

"Goddamn if you ain't turning out to be a smart fucking kid," Wayne praised. He reached up and slapped Carl on the shoulder. "Shit, Junior, ain't it gonna be something if one of the family turns out to *be* somebody?"

"Sure enough," Carl replied without enthusiasm. Billy studied Carl for a moment, as best he could in the gray alley light. He could have been wrong, but Billy thought he detected a hint of jealousy in Carl's tone. He wondered why. Maybe, he decided, if Junior can't make anything out of his own life, he doesn't want nobody else to either. If Junior goes down the toilet, then everybody should go down the toilet.

They drove around for an hour, then Carl said, "How 'bout going to see the old lady now, Wayne? Billy, you might as well come with us; we're halfway there already."

"Yeah, give the old lady a treat," Wayne said. "Ain't often she gets to see three of us together."

"Okay, I guess," Billy said. Kelly would understand.

Carl drove to Parkville and pulled into the gravel drive of the little house where their mother lived with Ruth and her husband. The lights were on in the living room and they could see Ruth and their mother watching TV.

"We ain't staying but a few minutes now," Wayne said.
"The cops'll be checking this place out before long. Georgie,

you stay in the car. Keep your eyes open. If you see any cop cars, give us a short blast on the horn."

The three brothers walked in unannounced, surprising their mother and older sister.

"My god, I don't believe this," Ruth said.

"Believe it," their mother said wryly. "Bad luck always comes in threes."

"Jesus, ain't anybody glad to see us?" Carl asked indignantly.

Ruth looked angrily at Billy. "What are you doing with them, Billy?" she snapped. "You're doing all right for yourself, you're on the right road; what the devil are you messing it up for by running with them?"

"Just a minute now, we are the kid's brothers, you know," Wayne interjected. "It ain't like we're trying to lead him astray."

"Shut your mouth, you," their mother snapped at Wayne. "You ain't got the sense God gave a goat. Nor you either," she spat at Carl. She turned to Billy. "I thought there was some hope for you, boy. I thought you was on the right track. What in hell are you running with them two for?"

" 'Them two!' " Carl said irately. "Hell, we're your sons too, you know!"

"Shut up, Junior!" their mother said. "You're no good. You been no good since the day you were borned. If I'd had any sense, I'd have drowned you and sold the milk." She turned back to Billy. "I asked you a question, boy: why are you running with them two?"

Billy shrugged helplessly. "I ain't really running with nobody, Mom; I just came by with 'em to see you and Ruth—"

"The cops has already been here looking for them," their mother said. "The fools broke out of prison."

"We're fools, all right," Carl said, "but not for breaking out of prison. We're fools for thinking we'd be welcome around here."

Their mother looked knowingly at him. "You didn't come here looking for no welcome. Most likely, you came wanting money."

"We didn't neither," Wayne protested. "We really just come to say goodbye, 'cause we're leaving these parts and ain't never planning to come back. Hell, if we was looking for money, do you think we'd come *here?* You ain't never got any."

Their mother grunted derisively. "Oh, no? Why don't you ask Junior; he might tell you differently?"

Wayne frowned. "What's she mean, Junior?"

"Nothing," Carl said, embarrassed. "She's crazy. Don't pay no attention to her. Come on, let's get the hell out of here."

"Yeah, we might's well," Wayne said, sighing quietly. "There ain't nothing here for us. Never has been."

Wayne and Carl headed for the door. Billy meekly followed after them.

"You damn little idiot," their mother said to Billy, "you better get out of their company as quick as you can. You stay with them and you're going to end up in bad, bad trouble. Mark my words now."

"Billy, go on back to that nice home you got, honey," Ruth told him. "You been doing so good for yourself; don't ruin it now."

Billy went on outside without saying anything. He got back in the car with his brothers and George Dungee, and they all drove off.

Billy stayed with the three fugitives all night. They alternated driving around for a while, parking for a while. They stayed mostly on back streets, side streets, along railroad tracks, so as not to encounter any patrol cars. Billy stayed because Wayne and Carl were very upset over the scene at their mother's house, and he did not think it would be right to leave them before they calmed down.

"Shit, that's what we are to her!" Carl ranted. "That's all we've ever been, all of us! Just so much shit!"

"Why the fuck'd she have us if she didn't want us?" Wayne said. "I mean, why keep having one fucking kid after another, year after fucking year like that? It's crazy, man, it's stupid!"

"Maybe she just liked to fuck," George Dungee offered lazily.

Carl turned on him. "Hey, man, this ain't your fucking business!"

"Don't be getting on George's ass," Wayne told Carl.

"Make him shut up about Mom then," Carl said defiantly. "He ain't got no business making a crack like that."

"Awright, I'll tell him to shut up, but don't go climbing on his ass like that, Junior. You climb on his ass, you're climbing on mine, understand?"

Carl stared flatly at his older half brother. "I do now, Wayne."

"Awright, fine." Wayne turned to the black man. "Keep out of it when we're talking about our family, George. Okay?"

"Okay, Wayne," said George. He rested his head back and closed his eyes. It didn't make any difference to him.

All this time, Billy sat and listened, not interfering in the dialogue between Wayne and Carl, not interrupting their tirades; merely interjecting his presence every now and then as, he hoped, a calming influence.

"Here, Wayne, have a cigarette," he would say. Or, "Junior, if you want to park for a while, there's a coal yard about two blocks up that's usually deserted." Or he'd try to turn their minds to other thoughts. "Hey, Wayne, 'member when I was just a little kid an' you an' Roy used to work with Daddy after school? Junior, 'member when Granddad used to come over on Saturdays and you and him would wrestle? 'Member?"

Gradually, over a period of several hours, Billy got both of them calmed down to the point where they forgot about their mother and began to reminisce about the good times they remembered, when they were both very young, before Archie had left and the family had been torn asunder. The two older boys talked about many things that Billy was too young to even remember, so he just sat and listened. It was good to hear family talk that was not strife ridden and angry; talk that made them sound almost like normal, ordinary people. Billy felt a warmth inside just listening to them.

Twice during the night Billy thought about asking Carl to drive him back home. But each time he decided against it. He was enjoying the company of his two brothers—the first time he had been with two of them at once since he was five years old—and, because the thought that they were fugitives never left his mind, he wanted to extend his visit with them as long as possible. Later, when it got to be too late, he told himself that he might as well stay all night then; it would be better than disturbing Kelly and her mother by coming in at two or three in the morning.

So they sat in the dark car and talked and smoked and remembered. Once, around three, they pulled into an all-night drive-in for coffee and pie, which Billy had to pay for since Carl and Wayne had no money.

"I don't see how you guys are gonna make it, starting out broke like this," Billy said.

"We'll make it," Wayne promised. "All's we got to do is rob us some guns someplace; sporting goods store, probably. Then pull a couple of stickups on our way to—where, Junior? Where we heading?"

"Florida," Carl said. It was where he and Sharon had   217

planned to go, where they had wanted to make a new life for themselves. He had spent many hours daydreaming about the sunshine, beaches, and palm trees. Might as well head there as anyplace else, he thought. Florida might still work out for him. "Florida all right with you?" he asked Wayne.

"Hell, yes!" Wayne replied enthusiastically. "I always wanted to see Florida."

When daylight came, Carl drove Billy back to the Nash house. They parked in the alley behind the house.

"You guys wait here for a couple minutes," Billy said. "I've got forty bucks in the house; I'll get it for you."

"No, bro, you don't have to do that," Wayne said. "We'll be okay."

"Hey, it'd be gas and chow money until we can score," Carl said to Wayne.

"Sure. And I don't need it for nothing," Billy said. The money was actually for Kelly's birthday present, but he wanted to see his brothers have the best chance possible of getting away. And he could earn more before Kelly's birthday.

"If you're sure it won't strap you," Wayne said.

"It won't. Wait for me."

Billy took the flashlight he had brought out and hurried up to the back door. He eased into the house as quietly as he could. In his room, as he was getting the money out of a shoe box, Kelly came in, putting on her bathrobe.

"Billy, where've you been?" Her voice had a tremble in it.

"Just with my brothers, hon. Just riding around, talking and stuff. It's okay; nothing's wrong."

"It's not okay, and something is wrong," Kelly said. "The police were here last night."

"What?" Billy's mouth dropped open incredulously. He stared at her for a moment, then shook his head firmly, as if by doing so he could erase her words. "They couldn't have been—"

"They were. About one o'clock."

He wet his lips. "Looking for me?"

She nodded. "You. And your brothers. And some black guy."

Billy sat down on his bed, mouth still agape. Jesus, how the hell did they know where to look? Shaking his head, he said, "I don't get it. How'd they know to come here?"

"Your brothers found you," Kelly reminded him. "Don't you think the police are as smart as they are?"

Carl had found him through their mother. Billy was sure she would not have told the police where to look last night, nor would Ruth; but either of them might have told someone else—a neighbor, a welfare worker—and that person might have tipped the law. Billy looked up at Kelly, remembering her words of several hours earlier: *you're going to risk losing everything you've been working for.*

She had been right.

"Did the cops say when they'd be back?" he asked.

"No. They just left a card with Mom, for her to call if you came back."

"What'd your mom say? About me, I mean?"

Kelly shrugged. "Not much. She's disappointed, for sure. She thinks you let us down."

"Jesus Christ, Kelly, those guys out there are my *brothers!*" he pleaded. "What am I supposed to do: turn my back on them?"

"No, of course not. Turn your back on us, though. My mom and me. We're not as important as your brothers."

"Oh, shit, cut it out."

He shoved the forty dollars into his pocket and started for the door.

"I'm going to give them some money and then they'll be gone," he said. "When I get back, we'll wait for your mom to get up, then try to figure out what I should do. Okay?"

"Yeah, okay," Kelly replied, her tone thoroughly disgusted.

Billy hurried back out to the car and got in.

"The cops were here," he said.

"When?" Carl asked tensely.

"About one."

Wayne leaned forward urgently. "Think they've got the place staked out?"

"I don't think so," said Billy. "They left a card for my girl's mother to call if I showed up."

"Shit. We better get the fuck out, *fast,*" said Carl. "You bring the dough?"

"Yeah." Billy gave him the forty dollars.

"Listen, bro, you better come with us," Carl told him. "You're in deep shit if you stay."

Billy shook his head. "I think Mrs. Nash and Kelly will stick by me. I been out a year now, haven't got in no trouble, been working and going to school. I think I got a good shot at being put on probation, maybe even being put in Mrs. Nash's custody—"

"You're dreaming," Carl told him flatly. "Tell him he's dreaming, Wayne."

219

"Well, hell, Junior, the kid *has* been doing all right. Maybe they'll give him a break."

"You two are really something," Carl said, amazed. "When the fuck did any of us *ever* get a break?" He turned halfway around in the seat so he could see both of them. "Jesus Christ, use your fucking heads!" He jabbed a stiff forefinger at Billy. "You're a fucking ward of the goddamn state; you're a foster home runaway; you're an escapee from the Victor Cullen reformatory; you been a fugitive for a fucking year; now the cops know where you live, and know you've been out all night with three escapees from Poplar Hill riding around in a stolen car—"

Billy's mouth dropped again. "Stolen car?"

"Well, sl.it, yes! 'Course it's stole. Jesus Christ, Billy, did you think we went out and bought the motherfucker on time payments or something? What the fuck, man."

Of course. It had to be stolen. Billy had simply not given any thought to where it came from. Sometimes things happened too fast for his fifteen-year-old mind.

"Let me tell you something, bro," Carl continued in a now cold, even tone. "You wanna know what's going to happen if you stick around here? They gonna get you not only for your own escape, but for helping us with ours, too. For giving us clothes and money. And if they catch you in your girl friend's house, they'll probably get her and her old lady for harboring an escapee. Shit, Billy, there ain't no way you can win. What surprises me is that you ain't figured it out for yourself yet."

Billy turned forward in the seat and stared out the windshield at the quiet, still, early-morning alley. Jesus, what a mess he'd made of everything. He felt tears well up in his eyes—not for himself alone, but for him and Kelly together. He knew he had to protect Kelly and her mother, no matter what. There was no other course open to him.

"Get going," he said to Carl, making no move to get out of the car.

"All right!" Carl said with delight.

He started the car and drove out of the valley, heading for Florida.

And Georgia.

Interlude:
THE ALDAY FAMILY
25

Jimmy sat down across the supper table from Ned. They were in the kitchen; Ernestine was still at the stove. Jimmy noticed that his father's face looked strained.

"Has the pain been bad today, Daddy?" he asked quietly.

Ned's jaw clenched and he pursed his lips briefly. Then, without actually answering the question, he said, "A man who can't take pain ain't much of a man."

It was the pain of severe arthritis that constantly laced the older man's body, sometimes bad, other times not so bad. The thing that worried Ned was that he expected the day would come when it would *always* be bad. That was the only dread he had in life. Aside from that, the business of being an arthritic was mostly an irritant that slowed him down and occasionally brought him to a halt. When that happened, he could not do his share of the farm's physical labor. That galled him: sometimes—like the arthritis itself—more than others. He had gradually begun to accept it, to live with it with a modicum of resignation, but it was something he really had to work at.

"Daddy, it might make you feel better if you was to come to prayer meeting with us," Jimmy said. He kept his tone conversational, so that it would not sound as if he were nagging his father.

"Don't see how," Ned replied, just as neutrally. "I can't believe the good Lord would give me arthritis just to get me to go to church to get relief from the misery." He smiled at his youngest. "God don't work thataway, son."

"Yessir," Jimmy acknowledged contritely..

Ned still had not been saved. It worried him sometimes, not for himself because he had long ago made his peace with formal religion; but for Ernestine, who had given her life to him, and whom he knew grieved over his unsaved soul. He would have given a lot if he could have been able to satisfy Ernestine and his own conscience at the same time; but the fact of the matter, as he had patiently explained to Jimmy one time, was that he had simply never received the call.

"But Brother Hill is always after you to come forward," Jimmy protested.

"That," Ned had pointed out, "is *encouragement;* it is *not* a call from Jesus."

"On the day when me and Jerry and Shugie was ordained deacons, didn't you feel no call at all?" Jimmy asked. Ned shook his head.

"None a'tall. A whole lot of pride—but no call. I wish I had, boy. Nothing would have pleasured me more. But it just wasn't there."

Jimmy remembered that day well. Ned had attended the services at Spring Creek Baptist Church, and Reverend Fred Hill had knelt at his pew and tried every way he knew to get Ned to come forward and accept Jesus Christ as his savior. But Ned had not done it. To his precise mind, Brother Hill's pleading simply was not a call—and that was that.

What most people did not know about Ned Alday was that he had regular dialogue with God. He spoke to his savior often—in the woods, under the sky of the open fields, in his home at night after all his loved ones were asleep. Ned *knew* God; he had known Him for years. If God had wanted Ned to be like everyone else, to pray like everyone else, to come forward like everyone else, why, Ned was certain God would have made His wishes absolutely clear.

"If a call ever comes," he told Jimmy, "a *real* call, I'll hear it, boy. But the way I figure it, God must kind of like Him and my's informal little chats in the fields and the woods and the dark of night. Maybe God ain't called me 'cause He likes me just the way I am."

Looking at his father, listening to him, it was easy for Jimmy to believe him. The way Jimmy saw it, how could the Lord *not* like Ned Alday?

Even so, Jimmy's worry was not completely assuaged.

After supper, Jimmy drove over to his Uncle Aubrey's house, a few miles away. Aubrey, the younger brother who had once lived with Ned and Ernestine, and who had married the pretty little practical nurse named Inez, made his home along a back country road where two other Alday brothers also lived: Paul,

222

and the youngest of the four, Everett, whom everyone called Bud. Parking in the front yard, Jimmy went over to the side patio where his uncle was rocking.

"Hey, Uncle Aubrey."

"Hey there, Jimmy." Aubrey turned his head toward the open kitchen window. "Inez, honey, bring Jimmy a glass of that iced tea." Aubrey sipped at his own tea while he studied the serious expression on his nephew's face.

Aubrey was fifty-eight now, but age had not slowed him down a bit. The one-time renowned bird-dog trainer still worked the land almost as vigorously as he had in his youth. Every day he was out in the fields with Ned and Ned's boys; and unlike Ned he seemed to get stronger and sturdier of limb as he got older.

Aubrey and Inez had two sons of their own, one grown, Benny, and one still a pup, Curtis. Benny worked at the nearby paper mill with Aubrey's younger brother Bud, and a cousin, Andy, son of the other nearby brother, Paul. There were also four daughters in Aubrey and Inez's branch of the Alday family, all of them grown, all married but living no farther from their parents than Tallahassee, sixty miles away. There were twelve grandchildren.

After Inez had brought Jimmy's tea and gone back inside, Aubrey stopped rocking and said, "What's troubling you, boy?"

"It's Daddy and the church," Jimmy admitted quietly. "I just haven't been able to reconcile myself with the fact that he won't come forward." Jimmy looked at his uncle almost desperately. "Uncle Aubrey, you came forward a few years ago. Late in life, like Daddy is. What made you do it?"

Aubrey suppressed a slight grin. "Tell me, boy, ain't you never heard nobody say why I did it?"

Jimmy blushed and avoided his uncle's direct gaze.

"Come on now, tell me about it," Aubrey prompted. "I ain't gonna get mad. I've heard it myself a time or two."

"Well, sir," Jimmy said, "I did kind of hear once that you joined the church 'cause you felt guilty about being a member in good standing in the Salem Masonic Lodge for more'n twenty years without even belonging to your own church. But I never believed it, Uncle Aubrey," he added quickly.

Aubrey chuckled quietly. "*You* might not believe it, but lots of folks does. But it don't bother me; I don't pay no mind to   223 such talk. Let me tell you something, Jimmy: I been a God-fearing man all my grown-up life. On Sundays when your Aunt Inez took the kids off to church, I used to go out to the barn and kneel there by myself to do my praying to God. I always figured that sooner or later I'd hear a call to go forward and give myself publicly to Jesus. That call, that inner desire, came in 1966 when I was fifty-one years old. Some folks talked about how it wasn't nothing but a guilty conscience that drove me to it; but lots more looked up to me for heeding a call at that age. It wasn't an easy thing to do."

"Do you think Daddy will ever get a call, Uncle Aubrey?" Jimmy asked anxiously. "And do you think he'll heed it if he does?"

"Oh, he'll heed it, all right," Aubrey said confidently. "Ned's an honest man, and honest men don't play games with the Lord. As to whether he'll ever *get* the call or not, why, I can't say." Aubrey leaned forward to where he could put a hand on his nephew's knee. "Listen to me, boy: if you're worried that your daddy might not get to heaven, you can just stop right now. Your daddy is a good man, son, and good men always go to heaven. Hear me?"

"Yessir, Uncle Aubrey. I hear."

Jimmy felt a little better after having the talk with Aubrey, but he still was not convinced that Ned did not need to be saved. Jimmy did not know exactly why the subject of death, Ned's death in particular, had been on his mind so much of late. His daddy was in poor health, true, but that was not it, not all of it. There was something else, something nebulous, on which his mind could not quite focus. It was vague yet frightening.

Jimmy was glad he had talked over the matter with Aubrey; he only wished he had some better assurance of Ned's fate than Aubrey's conviction that "good men" always went to heaven. In Jimmy's newly embraced religion, it was generally accepted that one *had* to be saved to get to heaven. Jimmy could only hope that if Ned could not somehow be prodded into baptism, when his time came, God would make an exception.

Because his daddy *was* a good man.

Since the first of the year, Jimmy had been seriously contemplating marriage. Not marriage to anyone in particular,

224

although he did have two girls in mind whom he had been dating, and between whom he would probably choose—but for now his thoughts were on marriage in *general*. With his mind on this subject, Jimmy liked to walk down the road a quarter of a mile from Ned's house and visit with Jerry and Mary. Most particularly Mary. Jimmy considered her an ideal wife and he liked to study her, watch the little things she did with her hands, watch how she tidied and straightened, how she patted her hair, how she moved and spoke. Whether he was aware of it or not, Jimmy was measuring his own prospective fiancée against everything he liked about Mary. Jerry, he had long since decided, was one lucky man—even if they didn't have a baby yet.

Jerry and Mary had been married going on three years that spring of 1973. Jerry, of course, still worked the land with his daddy, brothers, and uncle. Mary had given up her job at the bank in Bainbridge and gone to work in the office of the Seminole County Family and Children Services Bureau. She had taken the job so that she could be closer to home and not have to drive so far. Home—the big green-and-white trailer up on blocks—was very important to Mary. She kept it immaculate at all times, in case unexpected company—like Jimmy— dropped by, which frequently happened. The Aldays, she had learned early on, were "visiting" folks: they liked to come visit, liked to have people come visit them.

One of the main things about his sister-in-law that impressed Jimmy was the fact that she kept up not only the inside of their home but the outside as well. With Jerry's help she had cultivated a small lawn in front of the trailer, facing the road, and all around the front and sides she had planted and was raising petunias, blackeyed susans, and other colorful garden flowers. Next to her family and her home, Mary loved growing flowers more than anything in the world.

"How'd you learn so much about flower growing?" Jimmy asked her one day when he was helping her weed.

"I don't know, Jimmy," she replied. "I never was really aware of actually *learning;* I just kind of grew up with flowers; my mother had lots of them and I used to help her. I guess I must have learned it then without even realizing it."

"I admire girls that know lots about flowers and things," Jimmy had said.

Mary smiled impishly at him. "You surely have taken an   225 interest in domesticated matters of late. Who's the lucky girl going to be?"

"I'll let you know as soon as I find out myself," he replied with a half-shy smile. He had not told anyone yet that he had narrowed the field of eligibles down to two.

Jimmy Alday definitely planned to be married before the summer of 1973 was over.

26

As much as Jimmy admired Jerry's wife Mary, the young man was also acutely aware that he had a second sister-in-law: Shugie's wife Barbara.

Shugie and Barb lived in their own large mobile home, which was set off to the side of Ned's big front yard. Married six months longer than Jerry and Mary, they did not have any children yet either. Shugie, like his brothers, worked the land; Barbara still had a job uptown in Donalsonville. She had left the Thomas Five and Ten and gone to work for a while at Piggly Wiggly Market but, tiring of that, she had subsequently taken a job for a man named Bill Woods, who owned several small businesses in town. She kept books for him and was in charge of his cash receipts.

Jimmy realized that although he could not find as much to admire about Barbara as he could about Mary, it was by no means Barbara's fault. Most of what Jimmy admired in Mary evolved from her ability as a homemaker. And in Barb's case there simply was not as much to do around her mobile home as there was around Mary's. Barb's trailer, being in front and to the side of Ned's house, already had a lawn and flowers. All Barb had to do at home, really, was to keep the inside tidy—and Jimmy knew that was no job at all. Shugie was almost as neat and fussy about things as their older brother Jerry. Barb had told Jimmy one day how close to perfection she considered her husband.

"Shugie's only got one bad habit in the world," she said, "and that's his smoking. Take away his cigarettes and he'd be as perfect as any man could be." She had eyed Jimmy curiously then. "How come you don't smoke, Jimmy? With both your older brothers doing it?"

Jimmy had shrugged. "I don't have the time for that kind of stuff," he said self-consciously.

Barb sometimes made him a little uncomfortable. She had a habit of analyzing things. Like the smoking: if two did it, why didn't the third? She was a lot more curious than any woman he had ever known, and a lot smarter too. Watching quiz shows on television, she could usually answer the questions quicker than the contestants. Jimmy *wanted* to like Barbara as much as he did Mary, but something inside himself would not permit it. He guessed the truth of the matter was that Barbara was just a little too smart, too aggressive, perhaps too self-confident to suit him. He liked for a woman to have self-confidence, but only in things like growing petunias.

Sitting on the front porch one night, Ned waxed philosophically about the last two children he and Ernestine had at home; Jimmy, and the baby of the family, Faye, who was seventeen and a senior at Seminole County High School where she was due to graduate the middle of May.

"I'm bettin' now that Faye marries and leaves home before Jimmy does," Ned decided. He heard Ernestine sigh.

"Lordy, are we on *that* again?"

"What's your feeling on it?"

"Oh, Ned, I don't know. Goodness."

"Have you heard anything of late about Jimmy being serious about some little ol' gal up in Donalsonville?"

So that was it. He'd heard a rumor and he was worried that Jimmy's departure from the fold might be imminent.

"I haven't heard anything that would set me to worrying," she replied noncommittally.

Ned fell silent for a few minutes, smoking his pipe, massaging his arthritic elbows and knees. Maybe Jimmy was going to fool him the way Jerry had. He recalled several years back when he had not given the older boy much of a shot at marriage, and then Jerry had done a complete turnabout and brought Mary Campbell home. And what a catch she had been; Ned thought her faultless. Lord, if Jimmy could do as well—

If Jimmy *did* come up with some marriage plans this summer, Ned already had two or three spots picked out that Jimmy could have his choice of to put a new mobile home on. All of them within walking distance of Ned and Ernestine's house.

"Jimmy *has* settled down pretty much in the past few 228 months," Ned mused aloud. "I can't remember when the last time was he run off into the woods to cook hisself a wild break-fast. And he don't hardly ever talk about foolishness anymore. Remember how when he was younger he wanted to learn to fly?"

"I remember."

"Nowadays he just seems to concentrate on work. He's the best worker of the lot, you know. Outworks Jerry and Shugie and Aubrey *and* me. 'Course, outworking me's no chore any-more."

"Hush that talk. You do your share."

Ned sighed an almost wistful sigh. "You know," he said qui-etly, "Jimmy's good company to an old man laid up with arthritis."

Ned puffed contentedly on his pipe.

With family tradition and perpetuity so much on his mind that spring of 1973, Jimmy frequently initiated conversations, particularly with Ned, about the size and scope of the Alday clan.

"How many of us you figure there are in Seminole County, Daddy?"

"Hard to say, son. A right smart number, though. There's our branch of the family, your Uncle Aubrey's, your Uncle Paul's, your Uncle Bud's—probably got thirty or forty with just those branches; then add on all the kids in the next gener-ation—you'd have a goodly number, all right."

"What about Aunt Inez and them?"

"Well, legally your aunts shouldn't be counted, not if you're just considering the Alday name. When they get married, why, they're leaving the Aldays and joining another family. It's like your mother done; she was once a Johnson—but she can't rightly be called a member of the Johnson family after all these years with me, and after giving birth to nine Alday children."

"I reckon not," Jimmy said, grinning. "She probably don't even remember she ever was a Johnson."

"Oh, yes, she does," Ned quickly corrected him. "Our kind don't forget their stock, son. We don't forget who we come from, where we come from. Most people of the land are like that; it's the land, I reckon, that *makes* us like that—because it's the land that binds us together. Folks that don't own land, why, some of 'em ain't no better'n gypsies: they move here, move there, wander from place to place, set a spell, then   229 wander some more. Why, there's kids that grow up and never know their family no fu'ther back than their granddaddies. You and your brothers *already* go back one generation beyond that; and *your* children will know who came before them for *five* generations. Then six, then seven. As long's there's Aldays working this land, they'll know who they come from—and they won't never forget it."

The book, Jimmy must have thought when Ned talked to him like that. The history of the Aldays: it was a thing he *had* to do. Someday. When the time was there.

In the meantime, when he carried his other plans through to fruition, when he picked a girl and got married, when he fathered that grandbaby boy, there was something he could do, and *would* do, right then.

He would name that baby Ned.

4

MAY 14, 1973

27

They were in their third stolen vehicle. They had stolen a car in Maryland, abandoned it, then stolen a pickup truck in Pennsylvania. Abandoning that, they had stolen a second car, also in Pennsylvania. They still had the second car, a green 1968 Chevrolet Chevelle Supersport.

Carl was driving, as usual. Billy was riding beside him. Wayne and George Dungee were in the back.

"That ol' ocean sure was something," Wayne said.

They had driven down the length of the eastern seaboard to Florida so Wayne could see the ocean. At any point along the way, they could have turned off Interstate 95, headed east a hundred miles or less, and seen the ocean along the shores of Virginia or North Carolina, South Carolina or Georgia. But for some reason their tunnel mentality did not offer them that choice. They—or rather Carl—had decided that they were going to Florida so that Wayne could see the ocean; and as far as any of them were concerned, Florida was the only place where the ocean was *at*.

Carl, of course, had his own reason for wanting to drive down to Florida. That was where he and Sharon had planned to start their new life. Get a little house near the beach. Get jobs and work for a living. Maybe have kids. Get a dog. Live like regular people.

Shit.

Might as well have tried to throw a rope ladder to the moon, Carl would think years later.

"Yeah, boy, that ol' ocean was sure something," Wayne rambled. "Wasn't that ol' ocean something, Georgie?"

Dungee smiled his lazy smile. "Sure 'nough. Something."

They had spent the night in a motel at Flagler Beach, then started back north that morning. In Jacksonville, they had turned west on Interstate 10, along Florida's panhandle.

233

"Where we going now?" Billy asked after they had been driving a couple of hours.

"Looking for some money, what else?" Carl said wryly. "Seems like we spend it faster'n we can steal it."

"What you got planned this time, bro?" Wayne asked from the back seat.

Carl shrugged his shoulders. "Same old thing, I guess. Hit the back roads, find us a little country store, maybe two or three of them, and take what we can get."

"Sounds good to me," Wayne said, as if approving Carl's plan.

Sure, Carl thought. Any fucking thing sounds good to you. Long as you don't have to do no heavy thinking. A sly smile came over Carl's face. "Say, bro, what'd you think of that old ocean, huh?" he asked deliberately.

Wayne smiled widely and slapped his knee. "Man, that old ocean was sure something else!"

Asshole, Carl thought.

Carl stayed on the interstate for a couple of hours, driving idly along. When he got tired of it, he turned off on a state road, Route 19, and headed north.

Route 19 took them into Georgia.

In Seminole County, the Alday men were tending to the business of the land.

Jerry was in one section, working alone, planting corn. Jimmy was on a tractor in another section, across the highway, discing the land, preparing it for the next crop. Shugie and his Uncle Aubrey had hitched a flatbed trailer to one of the pickup trucks and gone into Donalsonville to get a tractor they had in for repair. Ned had been home all morning nursing his arthritis.

Jerry planted corn mechanically, without even thinking about what he was doing. He had planted so much of it over the years that he was certain he could have done it with his eyes shut. It was good that he was so proficient at it, however, because he had a lot of things on his mind, and solitary field work was a good time to think about them. One of the things troubling him this day was what to do about the Seminole County Democratic executive committee. As things stood, it was a pretty lean committee: he was the only member left; the other four had resigned. Now it was up to him to see if he could find four more good Democrats to replace them. Preferably four who would not up and quit between elections when things got slow. Between elections was a very important time; that was when you could get some of the hard-core middle-of-the-roaders to swing over.

While he was mulling over names of men he might ask to serve, Jerry thought also of the new pickup truck he had helped select the previous Saturday to be presented to B.B. "Fess" Baker, his old agriculture teacher, by the Young Farmers Club. Jerry was president of Young Farmers; the truck was being given to Mr. Baker in appreciation of the thirty-four years of farming instruction he had given to the young men of Seminole County. Picking out that truck for Fess Baker had been one of the happiest experiences of Jerry's life; presenting it would be another.

But the thing that was most on Jerry Alday's mind this day was the secret trip to California. All his life he had wanted to see California; now he was actually making plans to do just that. It was to be a big surprise for Mary: two weeks in sunny California. Trips to Hollywood and Disneyland. A tour of movie stars' homes. The Pacific Ocean. Mary was going to be the most surprised girl in the whole county when he told her about it.

Jerry paused in his work and lighted a cigarette. He was about out of corn seed. In a little while, he would have to go up to his daddy's house and get some.

When Carl got into Georgia, he began to drive the back roads looking for a suitable robbery target. Out of Thomasville he drove Route 319 back south toward the Florida line, then turned onto a state road, Route 93, north again. He continued like that for more than two hours, zigzagging up and down, north and south: down Route 111, up Route 179, down Route 262, up Route 27. At one point they ran low on gas and Carl pulled into a station. They bought five dollars worth, spending half of their last ten dollars. Then they drove on. At another point, Wayne told Carl to stop at a package store. He took the remaining five dollars and bought a dozen cans of beer with it. He, Carl, and George began drinking beer as they continued driving. Billy was asleep again; he had been dozing on and off most of the afternoon.

Finally Carl found a country store that suited him, just   235 south of Cairo, Georgia. "I'll keep the motor running," he said to Wayne. "You and him," he nodded at Dungee, "go in and take it."

Wayne and George each put pistols under their shirts and entered the store. A few moments later they came out, walking briskly, and got into the car. Carl burned rubber getting back onto the road and sped away, the accelerator all the way to the floor. Wayne waited until the speedometer needle touched eighty; then he grinned at George and calmly said to Carl, "What you driving so fast for, bro? We ain't done nothing."

Carl glanced at him, frowning. "You didn't take that joint?"

Wayne shook his head. "The owner had a shotgun laying right under the cash register keys."

Cursing under his breath, Carl slowed. He looked at the needle on the gas gauge. Less than a quarter of a tank left.

They had to score soon.

The last thing Aubrey Alday had said to his wife that day was that he might be late coming home for supper. "We've got that one tractor laid up for repairs in Donalsonville, that me and Shugie are going uptown to get. Jerry'll be out planting corn by hisself while we're gone. When we get back, depending on how much he's been able to get done, we just might have to finish it up by tractor light tonight. Anyhow, don't worry none if I'm late."

Not that Inez would have worried. She knew her husband. At times during their married life back in their younger days when things were tight, Aubrey would sometimes stay out half the night running hounds to train them. He had never been a man to quit work just because the sun went down. Like the rest of the Alday clan, he quit only when the job was done for the day.

Aubrey and Shugie hauled the repaired tractor back from town that afternoon. They unloaded it in one of the fields about two miles from Ned's house. Then they decided it might be a good idea to feed the family's hogs before getting to the corn planting. They set off to do that.

Ned himself, meanwhile, had calculated that Jerry would be running out of corn seed soon. Taking his jeep, he threw some sacks of seed into the back and drove out to the field where 236 Jerry was planting. On the way, he saw Jimmy far across another field, on a tractor, discing. He waved, but Jimmy was too far away to see him.

Uptown in Donalsonville, Jerry's wife Mary was at work at the Family Services office. She wanted to talk to Shugie's wife Barbara for a minute, but was not sure where to call. Mr. Woods, whom Barb worked for, owned three businesses there in town, and Barb was liable to be at any of them. Mary finally decided to try the doughnut shop first. Her guess was right; Barb was there.

"Hi," Mary said. "Listen, do you want to come by my house right after work and get some flowers? I've got some real pretty zinnias and marigolds that I want to cut back."

"I sure do," Barbara said. "I was just thinking about asking you if it wasn't time to thin them out again. You think the men will be working late?"

"Wouldn't surprise me any. But whether they do or not, stop by anyhow. It'll only take us a minute to cut the flowers."

"All right, hon. I'll see you right after work," Barb said.

Hanging up the phone, Barbara thought about how pretty Jerry and Mary's house trailer looked with all the flowers growing around it.

Others were looking at Jerry and Mary's house trailer right then, but they were not thinking how pretty it looked.

Carl had just driven by and twisted his neck around to look back at the place after they passed it. He slowed down. "There ain't no cars around there," he said.

"Yeah," Wayne said. He licked his lips. "Turn around and pull up to it. We'll burglarize the son-of-a-bitch and be gone in five minutes."

"Right," Carl said. They needed gas money badly.

Carl maneuvered the Chevrolet around on the narrow road and drove slowly back to the clearing. He guided the car into the driveway that led around behind the trailer and stopped, leaving the engine running. For a moment they just sat there, looking around. Everything was still, quiet. Back around front, a light breeze rustled the leaves of a single hackberry tree. Beyond the clearing in back, the fields were bright green with new corn stalks. There was no sound of anyone about.

"Go knock on the door," Carl said to Wayne. "See if anybody's there."

Wayne went up the three steps to the back door and knocked. There was no response. He looked down at Carl for further instructions.

"Check the door," Carl said impatiently from the car.

Wayne turned the knob and the door opened. He looked back at Carl and grinned.

"All right!" Carl said. "Billy, you come with me," he ordered. "You," he said to George, "get up here under the wheel and keep your foot on the gas to keep the motor running."

Carl and Billy went up the steps to where Wayne waited by the open kitchen door. Carl went in first, then Wayne, then Billy.

"You and me'll search the place," Carl said to Wayne. "Look for money, jewelry, anything. Billy, you keep watch out the front window in case anybody comes."

On a pair of swinging cafe doors, Carl found a gunbelt and holster that belonged to Jerry Alday. It was a black leather rig with cartridges in bullet loops all the way around the belt. The pistol in the holster had a pearl handle. "Neat," Carl said to himself. He buckled the belt around his waist and tied down the holster to his thigh with a rawhide thong.

In one of the two bedrooms, Carl found a porcelain piggy bank on the dresser. He picked it up; it was heavy. Jerry and Mary Alday saved silver dollars; they had seventy-one of them in the bank.

"Carl!" Billy hissed from outside the door. "Here comes a jeep!"

Carl dashed into the living room and looked out a window in time to see a blue jeep with two men in it drive up to the trailer from the road. Wiping his mouth on the back of his hand, Carl whirled and stared first at Billy, then at Wayne, who had come out of the other bedroom. He kept looking from Billy to Wayne, Wayne to Billy.

"We've got to get out of here!" he finally blurted. "Out the back!"

The three of them ran to the back door, but when they got there it was too late; the jeep was already coming around the trailer and pulling up to park.

"Out the front door!" Carl said.

They hurried back to the front of the trailer, their eyes wide, faces frightened, their animal urge to run taking over. At the front door, however, they found that they had no place to go; their car was out back.

"Wait a minute," Wayne said. "Hold it. We can't go running up the fucking highway on foot."

"We got to get out of here!" Carl repeated urgently.

"Were gonna have to take care of them two first," Wayne said. He was feeling in control.

"Jesus, Wayne, they're gonna catch us here!" Carl almost whined.

"Not if we catch them first. Come on, let's get 'em!" Wayne headed for the kitchen door. Carl, swallowing dryly, hesitating a moment, finally followed, as did Billy.

The three brothers hurried down the back steps before either of the jeep's occupants could get out. Jerry Alday was behind the wheel. His father Ned was in the passenger seat beside him. They had just come in from the field where Ned had taken Jerry some more corn seed. The two men exchanged quick glances.

"Who are they, son?" Ned asked quickly.

Jerry's eyes flicked from one to another of the strangers. "I don't know, Daddy. But they've got guns, all of them—"

At that moment, Carl burst past Wayne to get to the jeep first. It was essential, he felt deep down inside his nervousness, for him to resume command as quickly as possible.

"Shut up, you!" Carl snapped at Jerry Alday. "No talking!" Carl's hands, one of them pointing the gun, were trembling.

"Careful of that gun," Ned said urgently, raising a hand as if to ward off an accidental bullet.

"I said shut up!" Carl barked, jerking the gun barrel from one to the other. "Get the fuck out of that jeep! Make any funny moves and I'll fucking kill you!"

Wayne and Billy exchanged quick glances. Ol' Junior sure liked to put on a show. At this point, Billy was feeling a little nervous too, but not nearly as much as Carl. Billy looked at Wayne again; his older half brother appeared to be the calmest of all.

"Come on, come on, hurry your ass up!" Carl ordered. He stepped over close to Ned. "You old son-of-a-bitch, you don't think I'll use this, do you? You try anything and you'll fucking see! Move, goddamn it!"

Jerry slid out from behind the wheel. Ned, struggling with his arthritis, had to force himself out. Carl and his brothers herded them toward the trailer. On the way, Carl gestured for George Dungee to also come inside, in case the two men tried to give them any trouble The nigger fuck-boy might not 239 be much help, but he would be better than no help at all.

"Billy," Carl said, "get on inside ahead of us and watch out that front window again."

Carl wiped a perspiring upper lip with his forefinger. Goddamn, he thought. A simple robbery had suddenly turned into a technical kidnapping. They had to get the hell out of there—and quick.

"Come on, move, goddamn you!" he said, pushing Jerry into his daddy's back as Ned painfully negotiated the three steps up to the door.

Once inside, standing at the kitchen table, Carl waved the gun back and forth again. "Empty your pockets on the table," he ordered.

Jerry and Ned did so: wallets, pocket knives, loose change, Jerry's cigarette lighter.

"Take off that ring," Carl told Jerry. It was a horseshoe-shaped ring with a single diamond in the center and smaller stones, chips actually, around the curve of the horseshoe. Jerry took it off and put it on the table. Wayne stepped over and immediately picked it up before Carl could. Carl frowned but Wayne ignored him.

"What's a hick like you doing with a nice ring like this?" Wayne asked, and put it in his pocket without waiting for an answer.

"All right, get over there in the corner and sit on the floor," Carl said, waving the gun toward the corner he meant.

Ned and Jerry moved into the corner. Ned, still fighting his arthritis, could not get down onto the floor by himself. Jerry got up to help him.

"What the hell you think you're doing?" Carl demanded.

"He's my daddy and he can't move good," Jerry said. "I have to help him." It was the first thing either of the Aldays had said since being forced out of the jeep. Jerry held one of Ned's arms and Ned braced his other hand on the seat of a chair, and in that fashion he was able to lower himself to the floor.

"You two live here?" Carl asked.

"I do," Jerry said. "My daddy lives up the road a piece."

Carl motioned Wayne over by the refrigerator, out of range of hearing of the captives. "What do we do now?" he asked his older half brother. "Tie them up?"

"Fuck that," Wayne said, trying to sound hard. "Let's blow 'em away." Wayne was feeling the importance of authority for the first time. And why not? Hadn't Carl frozen at the living

240

room window when they saw the jeep pulling in? It had been Wayne who had initiated the action of taking the two men. And wasn't Carl now asking him, Wayne, what to do with their prisoners? Maybe Carl was at last beginning to recognize that Wayne could lead as well as he could. "I vote we blow the fuckers away," Wayne reiterated.

"We got no reason to blow 'em away," Carl said. "Let's just tie the bastards up good."

"No! Shit, no! We leave 'em alive, they'll put the finger on us someday. We got to do 'em, bro."

Carl wet his lips. He had not counted on any killing. "Look, Wayne, we come here to get a few bucks. We got it. Let's tie these guys up and split—"

Wayne turned his head a little and looked sideways at Carl. "Ain't chicken, are you, bro? Scared of a little gunplay?"

"Fuck you, Wayne. I ain't scared of nothing you ain't scared of."

"Then let's blow 'em away."

Carl glanced over at Ned and Jerry Alday. Hell, they hadn't done nothing to deserve getting wasted. A couple more minutes and he and the others would have missed them entirely. Now to just decide to kill them? It didn't make sense.

"They can identify us, bro," Wayne prompted. "We've *got* to do them. If you can't cut it, I'll get George to help me."

"Hey," Carl said, flashing anger, "I can do *anything* your nigger fuck-boy can do!"

"All right then," Wayne said, smiling.

Carl took a deep breath. "We'll blow 'em away," he said.

"Hey, mister," Jerry Alday called from the corner. Carl and Wayne went over to him. "I don't know what you're here for, mister," Jerry said. "I got a piggy bank in there with about seventy silver dollars in it. My wallet's got about ten dollars in it. My daddy's has got five or six dollars in it. I wish you'd just take the money and leave before my wife gets home."

Carl and Wayne exchanged a quick, interested look. The blood drained from Jerry Alday's face. The sick expression that came over him told Carl and Wayne that he realized he had made a horrible mistake mentioning his wife. Quickly he tried to rectify it.

"She won't have no money. I mean, no more'n one or two dollars for going to work—" His words trailed off weakly. He saw it was no use. Tears came to his eyes and he tried to blink them back. "Why don't you go?" he pleaded. "Please, just go." 241

"We're going, all right," Carl told him. "But we got something to do first. You know we're escaped convicts, don't you? Well, we are. Now, I ain't going to stand here and give you no sermon about how you ought to keep your doors locked, and how you ought to help guys like us that gets off on the wrong foot, help us when we're in prison, that kind of thing. I ain't gonna tell you none of that 'cause it's too late. Too late for you, too late for me." He turned to Wayne. "Which one do you want?"

"That one," Wayne said, pointing at Ned.

Figures, Carl thought. The old crippled one. "Swell," he said. "You take Pop, I'll take Buddy." He turned back to the men. "Get up," he ordered.

Jerry got up quickly and helped Ned to his feet.

"All right, move on into that bedroom," Carl ordered Jerry. Ned and Jerry just stood there, hesitating, looking at each other, not sure what to do. "Move it," Carl said, brandishing the pistol. Jerry, hands half raised, moved toward the bedbedroom.

"You too, move," Wayne told Ned. "This way." The elder Alday, slightly bent now from the exertion of getting down onto and up from the floor, walked unsteadily toward the opposite bedroom.

As Carl guided his prisoner into the bedroom where he had found the piggy bank, he noticed for the first time a shotgun standing up in one corner. Jesus, he thought, how in hell did I miss seeing that the first time around? He saw Jerry glance at the weapon. "Just lay down on that bed," he said coldly, keeping the pistol steady.

"There ain't no sense to this, boy," Jerry said.

"Don't you call me 'boy,'" Carl snapped. "Lay down, goddamn it!" Carl was nervous now, feeling wet under the arms. Jerry stretched out on the bed on his back. "The other way, goddamn it!" Carl ordered. "Face down!" Jerry rolled over.

What the hell do I do now? Carl wondered. He had put himself into a bind with Wayne by agreeing to kill these two hicks. It was not the smart thing to do, and Carl knew it; but there did not seem to be any way to back out without looking like he was chicken. Maybe, he thought, Wayne would come to his senses in the other bedroom and decide just to tie them up—

Then he heard a single shot from the other end of the trailer.

Shit.

Too late now, man. As usual.

On the bed, Jerry raised his head and looked toward the door. There was a terrible, frightened frown on his face. "Daddy?" he said, tentatively.

Shit, Carl thought again. He stepped over next to the bed, held the gun barrel mere inches from the back of Jerry's raised head, and fired four times.

Jerry Alday flopped down and lay still. Carl turned and fled the room. He met Wayne in the middle of the trailer. "Did you do it?" he asked, even though he had heard the shot.

"I done it," Wayne confirmed.

Billy and George, both standing by the front windows, exchanged glances, looking frightened.

They all stood like that for a suspended moment, and then they heard a strange, strangling sound coming from the bedroom from which Wayne had just hurried. They all turned to look. What they saw made their eyes widen in horror.

Ned Alday was shuffling toward them, arms outstretched, blood streaming from a single wound on the right side of his face. His eyes were fixed, staring, as he came forward. The fingers of one hand were bloody where he apparently had reached up to touch his wound.

"Jesus Christ!" Carl gasped, blanching. Wayne began to tremble. Billy and George backed away in revulsion. Carl brushed past them all, grabbed Ned by the shoulder, turned him around, and pushed him roughly back into the bedroom. Inside, he flung the elderly, arthritic man face down on the bed. Holding the pistol close to his head, he shot him three times in the back of the skull. Then he stood over him, listening. Ned was still breathing. Carl pulled the trigger again. The gun clicked empty.

"Wayne, get in here with your gun!" Carl snapped.

Wayne hurried in and Carl snatched the pistol from him. He leveled it at the back of Ned's head and shot him three more times.

Ned lay still then and the breathing stopped.

In one bedroom, Ned Alday, age sixty-two, husband to Ernestine for thirty-eight years, father of nine, grandfather of seven. A man of the land. Hunter, trapper, fisherman. Pipe smoker. Mischief maker. Storyteller.

In the other bedroom, Jerry Alday, age thirty-four, husband to Mary for three years. Also a man of the land. Neat, orga- 243

nized, fussy. A particular man, a practical man, but a dreamer too. Civic-minded, an example to the young men of his community. The last word he spoke was "Daddy."
Ned Alday. Dead.
Jerry Alday. Dead.

"There's one of them big green things coming in the driveway!" George Dungee said urgently.

Carl looked out a front window in time to see the end of a green tractor pull around the mobile home.

"Was anybody on it?" he asked, and immediately felt stupid.

"Sure," George said, almost indignantly. "You don't think it driving itself, do you?"

Carl ignored the retort and hurried to the kitchen, where Wayne was already looking out the back door. Jimmy Alday, dressed in coveralls, had parked the green John Deere tractor with which he had been discing the field, and was climbing down. Brushing off his pants legs, he walked toward the trailer.

"He heard the shots!" Carl hissed.

"Don't look like it," Wayne reasoned. "He ain't in any hurry."

"He heard the fucking shots!" Carl reiterated, as if Wayne had not understood him. Wayne shrugged and did not argue the point. What difference did it make anyway? Except that one way Carl was right, and the other way Carl was wrong. And Carl dearly hated to be wrong about anything.

Outside, Jimmy glanced curiously at the unfamiliar car with the Pennsylvania license, then walked up to the back door and knocked. Wayne opened the door, leveled his gun at him, and said, "Come right in."

Jimmy, startled by the gun, took a step back. He locked eyes with Wayne. Then he glanced down at the gun. From it, his eyes shifted quickly back out to the yard. Jerry's jeep was there—but where was Jerry? Inside? Tied up? Being robbed?

Clenching his jaw, Jimmy took another step back, glancing to the right and to the left, seeking some route of escape.

"You won't make it," Wayne said with a leer. He thumbed back the hammer of his revolver.

Still, Jimmy tensed and seemed to crouch, ready to spring. His eyes were riveted on Wayne Coleman's.

"Come in here or I'll kill you," Wayne said, raising the gun so that its muzzle now pointed at Jimmy's face. "Inside—now!"

244   Jimmy came inside. He saw Carl, with several large spots of

blood on his shirt. "What have y'all done?" he asked, his voice fearful.

"What'd you come here for?" Carl asked, his own voice threatening.

"I—I came to see my brother—"

"No, you didn't. You heard shots, didn't you?"

"I didn't hear no shots," Jimmy said.

"You're a fucking liar!"

Wayne stepped forward. "Take off that cap and them sunglasses. Empty your pockets."

Jimmy obeyed but could not get to all of his pockets because of his coveralls.

"All right, take 'em off," Wayne said.

Jimmy took off the coveralls and put the contents of his pockets on the kitchen table. Wayne started examining Jimmy's wallet.

Carl was extremely nervous now, eager to get away from this place, to take off the shirt that was splattered with Ned Alday's blood. He took two cartridges from the belt around his waist and quickly loaded his empty gun. Pointing it at Jimmy, he said, "Move in there to that couch." Jimmy half backed into the living room next to a sofa. "Lie down," Carl said tensely.

Jimmy swallowed dryly. "What—are you going to do?" he asked.

"Lie down!" Carl stormed.

Jimmy lay down on the couch, looking up at Carl.

"Turn your head the other way," Carl said. "Do it!"

Jimmy faced the back of the couch. Carl stepped close, putting the pistol muzzle an inch from his head, and shot him twice. Jimmy's body bucked; his left arm and leg slid off the narrow couch, letting his hand and foot rest on the floor.

Jimmy Alday, twenty-five years old, unmarried. A fourth generation descendant of the Georgia settler Math Alday. A young man of the farmland and the woodland. A young man who cooked wild game over an open flame on the bank of a river, and dreamed of writing a history of his family.

Jimmy Alday. Dead.

"That goddamned tractor's blocking our car," Wayne said, looking out the back door.

"I'll see if I can move the fucker," Carl said. He knew if *he* didn't move it, it wouldn't get moved. Wayne would talk about 245 it for an hour, then probably forget it. "You," he said to George Dungee, "keep watch out the front window. One of these ass-holes has got a wife due home."

Carl hopped off the back porch and hurried to the tractor. He climbed up on the seat and sat there wondering exactly how to operate the thing. He wished now that he had not shot the man on the couch so quickly; he could have made him move the goddamned tractor first.

As he was sitting there, Carl saw a car turn in from the road and come along the driveway toward him. Shit, he thought, and nervously touched the gun on his hip. The gun was now empty but Carl was too rattled to realize that. He tried to keep his face turned away so the driver of the car would not see that he was a stranger.

The car, a blue 1970 Chevrolet Impala with a white top, pulled up behind the stolen Pennsylvania car and parked. The driver got out and Carl saw for the first time that it was a woman. Mary Alday. She looked vaguely familiar to Carl, al-most as if he had seen her somewhere before. She reached back inside the car for her purse and a bag of groceries. Closing the door of her own car, she glanced curiously at Carl, who was staring at her, then started past the stolen car to the trailer.

While Mary Alday was walking past the unfamiliar car blocking her carport, Carl jumped down off the tractor and ran up behind her, gun drawn. He grabbed the back of her blouse, showed her the gun, and said, "Don't turn around, lady. Just walk right on in the trailer."

Mary, startled, tried to pull away from him. Carl tightened his grip on her blouse.

"Lady, I'll kill you right here!" he hissed. "You'd better walk!"

Mary might have been able to pull away and run; Carl was not that big or that strong. Had she known that the gun he held was empty, she probably would have done so, for though sweet she was also spunky, with a bit of a temper when riled. But the sight of the gun, out and in firing position, frightened her. So she did what Carl told her to do.

Inside, Carl found Billy and George Dungee arguing. "That son-of-a-bitch wasn't watching like you told him, Carl," Billy said hotly. "He was looking around the fucking place! It was me that saw the woman drive up, but I couldn't get back there quick enough to warn you."

"I was watching," George protested weakly. "I just turned away for a minute."

"Never mind," Carl said. "We got her, that's all that matters." He took the grocery bag and purse away from Mary and took her by the arm, pulling her close to him. Goddamn, she looked familiar. His glance dropped to her bust. "I'll bet you're nice to have fun with," he said with a leer.

"Quit it!" Mary said, jerking her arm loose. "Leave me alone!"

George Dungee giggled. Carl's eyes narrowed. He slapped Mary across the face. "The next word you say, I'm going to kill you," he threatened. He knocked the bag of groceries off the table, snatched up her purse and emptied its contents onto the table. He rummaged through the spilled contents: a wallet, her keys, what looked like a small vial of perfume, a small packet of tissues.

"You live here?" Carl asked, despite his warning to her not to speak again. "Answer me, goddamn it!"

"Y-yes—" Mary said.

Just then, Billy hurried in from the living room. "There's a pickup truck coming!"

"Goddamn," Carl said tensely. "What the fuck is this, some kind of meeting place?" Mary, next to him, started whimpering. "Shut up!" he snapped at her. "I got enough fucking troubles without listening to you cry!" Stepping over to the back door, he looked out and saw the pickup truck pull up to a stop. There were two men inside. They remained in the truck, talking to each other, looking puzzled or worried, Carl was not sure which. "Watch her," Carl said to Wayne. He turned to Billy. "I'm gonna test you right damn now, Billy. We're going out the front door, one of us is going around each end of this place, and we're gonna come up on that truck from both sides and throw down on them farmers out there. Now don't you let me down, you hear me? If you do, I'll kill you first before I kill them. You understand me?"

Carl was glaring coldly at Billy, with the same look that he had showed to their victims. His eyes were wild and dangerous. *Jesus Christ,* Billy thought, *he really means it.*

"Come on," Carl said, waving the gun at him, "let's go."

Swallowing dryly, Billy followed him outside. They split up, Billy running up on the passenger side of the truck, Carl on the driver's side. The driver was Shugie Alday; the man with him was his uncle, Aubrey Alday.

"Get out," Carl said to Shugie, pointing his still-empty gun. "You too, out," he said to Aubrey. Billy was covering them with a .38 pistol that *was* loaded.

The brothers herded the two men into the kitchen. Shugie and Aubrey saw Mary, frightened, backed into a corner. Carl moved over next to her and was standing there, wearing a gun-belt and holster like some kid playing cowboy. Aubrey, the long-time western movie fan, shook his head and laughed a short, wry laugh.

"I don't believe this," he said.

"You laughing at me?" Carl demanded angrily.

Aubrey's expression changed and he glared at Carl. Shugie, seeing Carl's face turn red with anger, quickly said, "No, he wasn't laughing at you."

From the living room came a rustling, scraping sound. Mary looked in and saw Jimmy on the couch. His body, still in its death throes, had twitched and jerked several times, causing the toe of his left boot to scrape on the floor. Mary could not see Jimmy's face, so she did not know who he was; she only knew that he appeared to need help.

"T—that man on the sofa is hurt," she said to Aubrey and Shugie.

"Shut up," Carl ordered. He stepped over to Wayne and they held a hurried, whispered conference. Then Carl took Mary by the arm and guided her into the bathroom. "Get in there with her," he said to George. "Make sure she don't come out." George went into the bathroom and Carl shut the door. "All right, you, old man," Carl said to Aubrey, "you like to laugh so much, I'm gonna give you something to laugh about. Get on in that bedroom."

"And you," Wayne said to Shugie, "go on down to that other bedroom." As Shugie moved out of the kitchen, Wayne picked up a towel from the kitchen counter and followed him.

Carl forced Aubrey into the bedroom where he had killed Jerry. "Get on the bed there next to Buddy," he said. Aubrey put a knee on the bed and at that moment both he and Carl heard a single, muffled shot from another part of the trailer. Aubrey turned and started to stand back up, but Carl kicked him in the back and knocked him facedown next to Jerry. Before Aubrey could move again, Carl reached over, aimed at the back of his head, and pulled the trigger.

The empty gun clicked.

Oh, Jesus! Carl thought. He ran from the room, ran up to Billy, and wrenched the .38 from Billy's hand. Running back into the bedroom, he expected to find Aubrey up off the bed by then; but Aubrey had only raised himself up and was staring transfixed at Jerry's blood that was all over his hand and shirt-sleeve.

"Oh, no," Aubrey said, beginning to cry at the sight of Jerry's blood. "Oh, no—please—no—"

With a rush of relief, Carl stepped quickly over to him and shot him once in the back of the head. Aubrey's head dropped to the bed and he lay still.

Carl walked to the center of the trailer, where Billy still stood. "You hear that old bastard beg for mercy?" he asked. It was not until much later, thinking about the scene, that Carl would realize that Aubrey Alday had not been begging for mercy; he had simply been praying aloud that the sight of his dead nephew beside him would somehow not be true.

Wayne came in and joined them. "Everything okay?" Carl asked.

"Okay," Wayne confirmed.

Just to be sure, Carl stepped into the other bedroom for a look. He found Shugie lying facedown across the bottom of the bed, on an angle with his lower legs draped over his dead father's legs. His right ear was torn apart by a gaping red wound.

Aubrey Alday, age fifty-eight, husband to Inez for thirty-five years, father of six, grandfather of twelve. A crack rifle shot, trainer of bird dogs, a Mason, a cook, and a lover of that great American creation, the cowboy movie.

Shugie Alday, age thirty, husband to Barbara for three years. A man of the land. Like his brothers, a deacon of his church. Religious song director. A young man whose real name, Chester, had been almost forgotten. A young man who met his bride-to-be at a Tastee Freeze stand, with a strawberry cone in his hand.

Aubrey Alday. Dead.

Shugie Alday. Dead.

Carl took Mary Alday's car keys and went outside. He unlocked the trunk, found nothing of value, left it open. He searched the inside, the glove compartment; still nothing. Going over to the stolen Pennsylvania car, he opened that trunk, left it open, and reached into the back seat for a can of beer. Popping the can, he took a long swallow. Back inside, he opened the bathroom door and motioned Mary Alday and George Dungee out. He stared at Mary again, wondering who in hell she reminded him of—

Then it came to him. *His mother.* Mary Alday looked like a photograph he had once seen at his grandmother's house: a photograph of his mother when she was a young girl. Jesus.

Carl turned to Billy. "You and George go out there and transfer all our things to the trunk of the woman's car."

He drank another long swallow of beer as he watched his brother and the black man leave. Then he looked at Mary again. She was young, pretty, had a good figure—like his mother must have had once before she became a fucking baby machine. Carl suddenly felt the stirring of desire. He didn't give a goddamn if she *did* look like his mother. That might even make it better.

Carl turned to Wayne. "Go on out, bro. I'll holler when I'm finished."

Wayne grinned lewdly and went outside.

Carl finished the beer and set the can on the counter. He stared flatly at Mary. "Pull them pants off," he ordered.

Mary backed away, terrified. "No, please, don't make me do that—"

Carl's right arm snaked out and he slapped her with a solid blow across the face. "Get them fucking pants off, I said!"

Sobbing, Mary removed her pantsuit slacks. From force of habit, she started to fold them neatly. Carl snatched them out of her hands. "Take them panties off too." She had barely got them off when he snatched them also and threw them on the floor under the table.

Now Carl looked around for a place to have his sex. The two bedrooms were out; two bodies in each, both beds bloodsoaked by now. The living room couch was also out; also bloodsoaked, another body.

Shit, Carl thought, nothing ever goes right. Well, fuck it.

"Get down on the floor," he ordered Mary. She was slow to respond, so he grabbed her shoulder and forced her down. He unbuckled her husband's gunbelt and laid it on the counter; dropped his pants and underwear down around his ankles, and got on top of Mary. She had her eyes closed and was mumbling something, some kind of prayer. Carl ignored it. He pushed her pantsuit top up and pulled her bra up over her breasts. Then, with his body and his hands and his mouth and his maleness, he violated the helpless woman, totally and completely.

While Carl was raping Mary, the door opened and Billy started to come in. When he saw what was happening on the kitchen floor, he retreated and closed the door.

250

"Carl's poking that woman," he told Wayne.

"No shit," Wayne said, feigning surprise. Billy blushed, embarrassed, and went over to where George was standing by the Pennsylvania car.

Several minutes later, Carl opened the trailer door and called, "Wayne—"

Wayne went into the trailer. Billy and George stood looking at each other. George looked as if he were angry about Wayne going into the trailer where the woman was. Billy shrugged at him; he did not know what else to do. The two of them waited what seemed like a very long time. Billy kept hearing sounds: some of them real, from the woods and fields; some of them imagined. Finally Billy went up to the door again and opened it a crack. He saw the same scene on the kitchen floor again, except now it was Wayne, his trousers lowered, down between Mary Alday's naked, spread legs. Billy looked at the woman's contorted face, her tightly closed eyes, her arms stretched out at her sides, hands curled into fists. Billy shivered and looked away.

This is not real, he thought. *None of this is happening.*

Billy did not know how much time passed, but the next thing he knew the trailer door was slammed open and Carl came out, guiding a now-dressed, blindfolded, gagged Mary Alday beside him. Wayne followed. Carl walked the woman over to her own car and put her in the back seat. George Dungee was already in the car, also in the back seat. Having assumed they would be taking that car, he had taken his usual seat to pout about what he knew Wayne was doing to the white woman. Carl stared at him for a moment and started to tell him to get out. Then it occurred to him that George had not done anything yet: he had not killed, he had not raped. Fucking nigger would probably get off if they got caught, he thought.

"Here," he said, pushing Mary onto the seat beside him, "you're in charge of her."

Carl got behind the wheel and backed out. Billy and Wayne followed in the Pennsylvania car. The two cars pulled around the mobile home, out the driveway, and onto the country road. They turned right and headed north.

In the Pennsylvania car, Billy looked back at the trailer as if in a daze. Jesus Christ, he thought almost drunkenly, we 251 stopped here to steal a few dollars for gas and food, and we're leaving five dead people behind.

Five dead people!

What in the hell had happened?

Behind them, the neat green-and-white house trailer looked serene and undisturbed. The little front lawn, the petunias, the blackeyed susans, were all intact, alive, blooming. The cornfield beyond was alive, blooming. The woods around the fields were alive, blooming.

Death was only inside the trailer.

Everywhere inside the trailer.

Ned.

Aubrey.

Jerry.

Shugie.

Jimmy.

All victims of sudden, senseless death.

28

Carl looked in the rearview mirror at the blindfolded, gagged Mary Alday. "Take them handkerchiefs off her face, George," he said.

Dungee untied the handkerchiefs. Mary took a deep breath and rubbed her eyes with both hands. Carl kept glancing in the rearview mirror at her. He waited until she was through rubbing her eyes before speaking to her. Then he caught her glance in the mirror

"You ain't never run up on nobody like us before, have you, babe?" he asked.

Mary grimaced at being called "babe" by someone like Carl. She shook her head. "No."

Carl nodded. "You know we left five dead people back yonder in that trailer, don't you?"

"Five?" Mary did not understand. She had only seen three.

"That's right, five. Five people deader'n hell." He locked eyes with her for a second. "You only got one way to save your life. You know what that way is?"

Mary shook her head. "N-no—"

"I'll tell you then," Carl said easily. "If you do exactly what I tell you to; do everything I tell you to and don't complain about nothing; well, I think I can persuade the others to let you live. You understand that?"

Mary nodded, sobbing. "Y-yes—"

"Okay," Carl said. "Stop that bawling now and just keep quiet."

Carl did not know exactly why he had told her that he might be able to save her life. It was a dumb promise to make. She knew about the killings in the trailer; she could identify them; it was obvious she would have to die. Carl supposed he had said what he did just to keep her quiet, keep her from causing any 253 trouble while they had her. He did not even know why they had brought her with them. Glancing up, he looked at her in the rearview mirror again; looked at her face, her lips. Yes, he did, he thought. He knew why they had brought her. Because they were not through with her yet.

Sighing quietly, Carl dismissed Mary from his mind for the time being and started looking for a place to get rid of the Pennsylvania car. It was dumb, he decided, to have two cars. They would just keep Mary's car; it was newer, ran better, and had Georgia plates. He scrutinized the terrain on both sides of the road, looking for some woods close enough to drive the cars into where they could not be seen. After driving about six miles, he saw a rutted dirt road that suited him, and pulled off into it. Wayne and Billy followed. The dirt road led back into a stand of trees and then curved slightly to the right, out of sight of the main road. Perfect, Carl thought.

He stopped the car and got out. As he did, the Pennsylvania car stopped behind him and Wayne came running up to him, excited.

"I lost my wallet," he said anxiously. "It must have dropped out of my pants while I was fucking that cunt."

Carl stared at him incredulously. "Jesus Christ," he said quietly. What a fucking asshole, he thought. What a dumb fucking asshole. "What's in it?" he asked, controlling his voice.

"ID," Wayne said. "My fucking name, my prison number, everything."

Carl looked down at the ground. His ID. Great. Might as well have left a signed fucking confession.

"Me and Billy'll go back for it," Wayne said.

"We'll *all* go back for it," Carl told him. "It's safer if we all stay together. Get in the car and back out."

They got the cars backed out onto the main road and turned around. Then they drove the six miles back to the trailer. Pulling up behind it again, they left both engines running and Carl and Wayne hurried into the trailer. The wallet was the first thing they saw when they rushed through the door—lying right where it had fallen. Wayne snatched it up and sighed a deep sigh of relief. He shoved it into his front trousers pocket.

"All right," said Carl, "we'll go back to the same place we just left. I want to dump that car you and Billy are in."

"I want another shot at that bitch too," Wayne said sullenly, "for making me lose my wallet."

Carl studied his half brother for a moment, then shook his head almost in contempt. He left the trailer—for what he sincerely hoped would be the last goddamned time.

The two cars proceeded back to the rutted dirt road and drove into the woods again. Carl led them farther in this time, to a small clearing that dropped gradually to a shallow depression in the ground. He got out and walked back to the other car.

"Pull it on around and get it in there as far back as you can," he told Wayne. "Billy, come over here to the other car, there's some rags in the trunk; I want you to wipe down that car before we leave it. No prints, babe, dig?"

While Wayne and Billy were down in the trees taking care of the Pennsylvania car, Carl went over and leaned against the front fender of Mary Alday's car. Mary was cowering as far back as she could get in one corner of the back seat, her head bent over on her left shoulder, eyes tightly closed. Both hands, still in fists, were pressed to her mouth and chin. She was the most absolutely wretched, miserable-looking person Carl had ever seen.

Like I'll be, he thought glumly, when the sons-of-bitches catch me. When they send me back to prison.

And they *would* catch him, he thought. Hell, hadn't they *always* caught him? For every fucking thing? Carl grunted softly. How in hell could they *not* catch him? Jesus, look at the crew he was running with. A half brother who was so fucking dumb he leaves his wallet at the scene of five killings. A nigger fuck-boy who don't do anything but sit around with an asshole grin on his face. And a fifteen-year-old kid brother who right now was on the verge of coming apart at the seams. Oh yeah, Carl shook his head, Billy was going to begin cracking, any time now.

So, he thought, how could he *not* figure on getting caught? It was—what was that word that a counselor had once said about Carl ending up in reform school?—oh yeah, "inevitable." That was the word. It was inevitable that he would be caught.

My whole life is inevitable, he thought morosely. Inevitable shit.

He looked in the back seat of the car again. Dungee was slumped down with his head resting against the window, eyes closed, looking like he was dozing. He was as far away from Mary Alday as he could get, just as she was as far away from   255 him as she could get. Looking at Dungee made Carl think about the niggers in prison again; how they had caught him in his cell during the riot, what they had done to him. His expression hardened. The motherfuckers.

He sighed heavily, from deep inside himself. Well, at least it'll never be like that again, he assured himself. Not after what he did today. Not after personally killing three people and helping Wayne kill a fourth. Next time he went inside, it would not be in a general population prison where the goddamned niggers could get at him. No, it would be in a special section, a high-security section, a death row section. Because he would surely be sentenced to death for killing those men.

But what if he wasn't? he wondered. Carl frowned a deep, worried frown. There was always a fucking catch, wasn't there? Always a "what if?" What if he *didn't* get the death sentence?

Was it at all possible, he wondered, that he *wouldn't?* After the blood he and Wayne had spilled back in that trailer? Was it possible that some asshole lawyer would be able to get up in court and convince some asshole judge or some asshole jury that poor Carl, because of his age, his background, his immaturity, was not responsible for what he did in that trailer? Could that happen?

Shit, yes! Sure it could happen, he convinced himself. The lawyers, the judges, the juries, and the courts were so thoroughly fucked up, *anything* could happen. Chances were good, *damned* good, that he could end up with three or four life sentences instead of the death penalty.

Which meant being sent to a regular prison.

Being put in the general prison population.

With the niggers.

Carl suddenly had a flashback of the time he had been raped. He closed his eyes, just as Mary Alday was doing, to shut out the scenes of his memory. But he could not do it. The picture in his mind was vivid: six throbbing, erect black pricks getting ready to penetrate his frail white body—

"No!" Carl said aloud.

In the car, George sat bolt upright. "Wha's matter, man?"

Carl looked into the car. Even Mary Alday had lifted her head and opened her eyes at his sudden outburst.

"Nothing's the matter," he said with an edge. "Go on back to sleep, man." Then he locked eyes with Mary. "Get out of the car."

256

She shook her head and started to cry. "No—please—no—"

"Get out of the fucking car!" he stormed.

He would not go back to the niggers, no matter what. He would make sure he got a death sentence.

Carl opened the car door and dragged Mary out by the arm. Slamming the door shut, he pushed her up against the car. "Strip," he ordered. "Every stitch. I want you buck-assed naked. Do it!"

Trembling, sobbing, the terrified young woman undressed. It took her only a moment: she only had on her two-piece pant-suit, bra, and shoes; the other articles she had been wearing were back at the trailer.

When Mary was nude, Carl put his hands on her shoulders and forced her to her knees. He unzipped his trousers.

"Suck it," he commanded.

Mary shook her head wildly. "No! No, I won't—"

Carl slapped her. "Do it!"

"I won't! No!"

He grabbed her by the shoulders and jerked her to her feet. "You said in the car you'd do whatever I told you to."

"I won't do that. You can kill me, I don't care."

George Dungee had gotten out of the car now and was watching them. Wayne and Billy walked back into the clearing just then.

"You guys want to fuck her?" Carl asked.

Billy looked away, embarrassed. Wayne shook his head. "I don't want the bitch no more," he said, apparently having forgotten that, in his mind, she was responsible for making him leave his wallet in the trailer. George Dungee looked at Wayne with an expression that Carl thought was disgust. Carl sensed that the black man was sore at Wayne for poking the woman back in the trailer. Maybe this is my chance to break them up, he thought.

"Last chance for anybody to fuck her," he said, looking directly at George.

"What about me?" George asked.

Carl smiled. "Why, sure, George. You want a little white meat, babe?" Carl glanced at Wayne and saw that he was frowning, looking at George with narrowed eyes.

Wayne stalked over to Mary. "Let's have a little fun with her first," he said. He took her by the arm and pushed her a few feet away from him. "Go on, honey, run naked through the woods for us and we'll chase after you."

"No, none of that shit," Carl said. "She's for fucking. Stay here, babe," he told Mary.

"No, go on and run," Wayne said. He stepped over and pushed her again.

Mary, crying, terrified, frantic, started to run. Carl sprang to her side and spun her around. "I told you not to," he said, and punched her in the face with his fist. Mary fell to the ground, dazed. "I'm gonna fuck her again," Carl told the others, "then George can have her."

Carl took off his trousers and underwear. He pulled the groggy Mary Alday to a sitting position.

"Suck it," he told her again.

Weak, nauseated, her head reeling slightly, Mary still refused. "No-no—"

"All right, babe," Carl said coldly, "if you won't give me a blow-job, then you'll have to give me some peanut butter."

He pushed her back down, turned her face down in the dirt, and raped her anally. While he was doing it, Mary screamed in pain and clawed at the dirt with her fingernails and pounded her head against the ground as if trying to knock herself unconscious.

When Carl was finished, he got up and walked away, leaving her there. While he was cleaning himself with a tissue from the car, Mary sat up, sobbing hysterically, wiping dirt off her face and breasts. "C-can—I—p-please—get dressed—now?" she stammered.

"No!" Carl snapped. "We ain't through with you yet."

Billy, who had been leaning against the car looking at the ground, suddenly said, "Come on, Carl, ain't we wasted enough time? Let's get the fuck out of here."

"I think he's right," Wayne said, glancing furtively at George. "Let's make tracks." Striding over to Mary, he grabbed her by the arm and started walking her toward the trees. "I'll take care of her—"

"Wait a minute," Carl said. "I promised her to Georgie."

Wayne stopped and glared at him. Carl just shrugged. Muttering a curse under his breath, Wayne flung Mary's arm down. "Let's just make it quick so's we can get the fuck out of here," he said sullenly.

Carl walked over to George Dungee and handed him the .22 pistol from the holster on his hip. "If you can fuck her, you can kill her," he said flatly. Then he went to the trunk of the car 258 and took out a shotgun. Holding it loosely in both hands, he smiled at George. "Go on," he said, "take her into the woods."

George, pistol in hand, walked over to Mary and gently pushed her ahead of him into the woods.

A quietness fell over the clearing for several moments. Carl went over to Wayne and said, "If he don't do it, Wayne, I'm gonna blow him away."

Wayne stared at his younger half brother but did not argue the point. Carl could see that Wayne was not at all happy about George taking the woman into the woods.

From where he stood by the car, Billy could see George and the woman just inside the stand of trees. George had made her lie down on the ground and he kept looking back at the clearing where Carl and Wayne stood. He seemed to be very nervous. At one point, when Carl glanced over at where he was, George got down on top of Mary Alday, almost as if pretending to rape her. Whatever he was doing, he kept glancing apprehensively back at Carl and Wayne.

Finally Carl and Wayne walked over to the trees. "Finished, George?" Carl asked.

"Yeah, I'm finished," the black man said. George's clothes did not look as if they had been disarranged at all; his belt was buckled, trousers zipped. Carl looked at him suspiciously for a moment, then shrugged. It made no difference to him whether Dungee had fucked her or not—as long as he killed her.

"Let's do it then, Georgie," Carl said evenly.

George, standing over the prone, naked woman, looked at Carl, at the coldness of his eyes, the steadiness of his hands, the shotgun he held seemingly so loosely yet so ready to fire. He pursed his lips, glanced at Wayne, glanced at Billy, then at Carl and the shotgun again.

Pointing the .22 pistol at Mary, George fired once, carelessly, without really aiming. The bullet hit the woman in the back, fifteen inches below her head. She made a hollow, almost gushing sound, then lay very still.

George looked over at the three white brothers again. They were still standing there together, still looking at him. Carl's expression and Wayne's expression cold, pitiless; Billy looking a little sick. But Carl and Wayne did not seem to be bothered at all; their stares were fixed and unyielding.

Swallowing dryly, George raised the pistol and fired again, aiming this time, trying to finish it for good. The second bullet was higher, entering the base of the woman's skull.

259

"Okay, let's go," Carl said, lowering the shotgun and walking away. Wayne and George followed him.

"Carl," Billy said, nodding back toward the still woman, "she's laying on an anthill."

"Who gives a shit," Carl said. He kept walking.

Billy stood there for a moment, indecisively. Then he hurried after his brothers.

The four of them piled into the woman's car and drove away, leaving the clearing absolutely still. It stayed that way for about an hour.

Then the ants started working.

5

AFTERMATH TO MURDER

29

Bud Alday, younger brother of Ned and Aubrey, had been on his way home from the paper mill where he worked. Up ahead on the road, he saw a familiar figure on a green John Deere tractor.

"There's ol' Jimmy coming in out of the field," Bud said.

Bud's passenger, Andy Alday, was the son of another of his brothers, Paul. "Looks like he's been discing," Andy said.

Bud's pickup reached the tractor just as it was about to turn into the drive leading to Jerry and Mary Alday's mobile home. Bud pulled over next to the tractor.

"Hey, boy," he greeted Jimmy.

Jimmy threw Bud a grin from the tractor seat. "Hey, Uncle Bud." He liked his Uncle Bud, who was the youngest of his daddy's brothers, just as Jimmy himself was the youngest of his string of brothers.

"You and your daddy going fishing with me and Sybil this evening?" Bud asked.

"I don't know about Daddy, but I sure am," Jimmy said.

Bud smiled at his nephew. That was Jimmy, all right. Any excuse to get out in those woods. Bud had never seen a young man who loved the outdoors so much.

"Well, me and Sybil will be going down right after supper. You know the spot. You and Ned come on down whenever you're ready, hear?"

"We'll do it, Uncle Bud."

Bud and Andy drove on away and Jimmy turned the tractor into the driveway and headed toward the mobile home.

The stolen Pennsylvania car was already parked behind the trailer.

Ned and Jerry were already dead inside.

Jimmy was then living the last ten minutes of his life.

263

Thirty minutes later, Barbara Alday, on her way home from work, remembered Mary's telephone call asking her to stop by the trailer and help her cut back some zinnias and marigolds. Barbara pulled into the drive and guided her car around back. There she saw Ned's jeep, Shugie's pickup, the tractor that Jimmy had been working on that day, Mary's car, and an unfamiliar car with a Pennsylvania license. Everyone, it seemed, was at the trailer. Even a visitor. It was no time to bother Mary about thinning out her flowerbeds.

Without even stopping, Barbara turned her car around and drove away. She went on home to her own trailer, a quarter of a mile down the road, in Ned's front yard.

Bud and Sybil went fishing after supper. They caught a dozen good-sized catfish. Ned and Jimmy never showed up.

"Wonder what in the world happened to them?" Sybil said as she and Bud took their catch and headed home.

"Ned's got some sows that are pretty near ready to drop," Bud said. "I'll bet they're out there tending to them."

Bud and Sybil went on home to their neat little house that set on a country road a mile or so from the big lake. Bud's brother Paul lived across the road in one direction, his brother Aubrey in the other direction. And there were other Aldays up and down every road around there. Seminole County was Alday country.

When Bud and Sybil got home, they cleaned and dressed their catfish and put them in the freezer. Then they watched a little television and went to bed.

Barbara waited a couple of hours after she got home, and when Shugie did not arrive, she tried to call Mary to see where everybody was. There was no answer at the trailer. Barb hung up and crossed the yard to Ned's house. Ernestine and her last remaining daughter, Faye, were watching TV, waiting for Ned and Jimmy to come home to supper.

"Have y'all heard from the men?" Barb asked.

Ernestine shook her head. "They're probably planting corn by tractor light," she said. The men had been working long days of late, to catch up on spring planting that had been delayed by an unusually rainy April.

"Jimmy said he was going fishing tonight with Uncle Bud," Faye mentioned.

"Not when there's planting to be done, he won't," Ernestine said matter-of-factly. "They'll be along in a little bit, I reckon."

Barb sat down and talked with Faye about her upcoming high school graduation, just two weeks away.

After a while, Barb went back out to her trailer.

At ten o'clock, Inez, Aubrey's wife, who lived across the road in one direction from Bud and Sybil, began to wonder just how late Aubrey intended to work.

"Come on, Curt," she said to her thirteen-year-old son, "let's take a drive and see if we can find your daddy."

They drove out along the field where Jerry had been planting corn that day but saw no one. Along the field where Jimmy had been discing, there was also no one around. They drove to several more places where night planting might be going on, but there was no sign of tractor lights anywhere.

Where in the world could those men be? she wondered.

On the seat next to her, Curt stifled a yawn. He's sleepy, she thought, and tomorrow's a school day. Best get him home to bed. Aubrey, she knew, would come home when the day's work was done—as he always did.

Driving back home, Inez and Curt passed the darkened green-and-white trailer with the flowers around it.

Barbara continued trying to telephone Mary throughout the evening. After she had tried a dozen times without getting an answer, she finally went back over to Ned's house and said to Faye, "I just can't imagine where those men are. Will you go down to the trailer with me to see if anything's the matter?"

"All right," said Faye.

The two women took Barb's car and drove the quarter mile down the road to Jerry and Mary's trailer. The driveway and clearing were dark, no light at all coming from the inside. Barb pulled around back and threw her headlight beams to bright. They lighted up the jeep, pickup, and tractor.

"Mary's car is gone," Barb said. "So is that other car that was here earlier, the one with the funny license."

"What in the world do you suppose has happened?" Faye asked nervously.

"I don't know. Do you think we should go in?"

"We better not. It's too dark. Anyhow, there can't be any- 265 body in there; there aren't any lights burning." She touched Barbara's arm. "Let's go back home."

"All right," said Barbara. She turned the car around and left the trailer once again in darkness.

Back at Ned's house, Barbara said, "I don't mean to worry nobody but I'm going to call the hospitals, just to see."

She telephoned the two Donalsonville hospitals, the one in Bainbridge, which was the next closest, and then two in Dothan, Alabama, just over the line. None of them had any record of an Alday being admitted or treated.

By then it was midnight.

At two o'clock in the morning, Ernestine was too worried to continue sitting around speculating; she decided it was time to take some definite action. She telephoned Bud Alday.

"Bud," she asked the sleepy voice at the other end of the line, "do you know where Ned and the boys are? It's two o'clock and they haven't come home yet."

Bud sat up in bed, no longer sleepy. Next to him, Sybil now came wide-awake too.

"You haven't heard from them at all?" Bud asked.

"No, not a word."

"I'll be right over there," Bud said.

Bud got up and went to the other bedroom where his daughter Becky and her husband Roy Barber were sleeping. Roy was the fourth young man who had come forward to be baptized with the three Alday brothers four years earlier. He was a ranger for nearby Seminole State Park.

"Roy, wake up and get dressed," Bud said urgently. "There's trouble over to Ned's place." As an afterthought he added, "Bring your gun."

Bud, Roy, and Andy, Paul's son who lived across the road and whom Bud had telephoned, got to Ned's house half an hour later. They found three now very upset and anxious women.

"I just can't for the life of me imagine where those men are," Ernestine said.

"Faye and me went down to the trailer, Uncle Bud," Barbara said, "but it was dark and we didn't try to go in." Barbara liked her Uncle-by-marriage Bud; now that he was there, she somehow felt safer.

266   "Well, let's just go back down there," Bud said.

Barb and Faye went in Barb's car again, and Bud, Roy, and Andy went in Bud's truck. The women got there first, pulled in with their headlights shining on the back door, and got out. The pickup truck was coming in after them. Bolstered both by the presence of the men and an urge to put an end to the mystery, the two women hurried up the steps and tried the door. It was unlocked. They opened it and peered inside, where a small nightlight in the kitchen threw off a hint of a luminous glow. Faye reached in and turned on the kitchen light. It threw a shadowy illumination into one of the bedrooms and the living room. Barbara looked in the bedroom and saw a tangle of feet: legs, boots, twisted limbs. She drew in a great gasp of air, tried to turn away, and her eyes caught sight of another form on the living room couch, a form with one foot and one hand draped ominously down to the floor. Barbara threw a hand up to her mouth and let out a choked scream. It frightened Faye and she jumped, and her hand turned the lights back off.

Faye urged Barb out of the doorway, came out herself, and pulled the door closed behind her. Bud, Roy, and Andy came hurrying out of the truck then. The two women moved quickly down the steps to the protection of the men's presence.

Bud Alday motioned for Roy and Andy to stay where they were. He ascended the steps and opened the door. Switching on the light, his eyes swept the kitchen. He saw Mary's purse dumped upside down on the table; Mary's panties thrown under the table; a beer can on the counter.

Something was bad wrong here.

Bud's jaw clenched. It was the beer can that did it. None of the Alday men were drinkers, beer or otherwise. Bud turned off the light and backed out, closing the door.

"Get your guns out," he told Roy and Andy. "One of you stay here in back, one of you go around front. Shoot anybody that comes out of that trailer if you don't know them."

Roy and Andy exchanged looks. Both were frightened, but both were also determined; if something bad had touched their family, they were prepared to do whatever they were called upon to do—scared or not.

Bud took the two women and drove them back up to Ned's house. He immediately telephoned Dan White, the Seminole County sheriff, and told him what he had found. The sheriff promised to come right away. Next, Bud thought for a moment about who Ned's nearest neighbors were. He decided they would be Hurby Johnson, a young cousin who farmed   267 nearby, and Eddie Chance, another farmer, in his midfifties, who lived about a quarter of a mile away. Bud telephoned both men with the same terse message.

"Get your gun and come to Ned's house. Something's happened down here."

Hurby and Chance arrived at Ned's house at the same time. Together with Bud they all drove down to the trailer, where Roy Barber and Andy Alday were standing guard. As they turned into the drive, they met Sheriff Dan White, who was also just arriving.

"Everything quiet?" Bud asked Roy Barber.

"Not a sound in there," Roy replied.

The men congregated behind the trailer. "Chance, you come inside with me," said Dan White, who had been sheriff of Seminole County for twenty-four years. "Rest of y'all stay out here and be ready for whatever happens."

Dan White led the way through the back door. Turning on the lights, he walked purposefully through each room.

He found Ned and Shugie first.

Then Jimmy.

Then Aubrey and Jerry.

It was the most terrible moment in his long law-enforcement career.

Back outside, he solemnly reported to Bud and the others, "They're all dead in there. All five of them. They've been murdered."

It fell to Bud Alday to do the notifying. He sat down at the telephone in Ned's house and began to call people. As stunned and numbed as he was by the grisly discovery in the trailer, he knew that it was up to him to take over. He and Paul were the only two brothers left, and Paul, although older than Bud, was not in the best of health. When Bud called the Paul Alday home, he spoke to Louise, Paul's wife, and asked her if she would go down the road to Aubrey's house and break the news to Inez. Louise, although herself shaken by the horrible news, said she would.

It was nearly four in the morning when Louise woke Inez Alday. Inez knew something was terribly wrong the moment she came to the door; people in Seminole County don't wake up other people at that time of night unless there is bad news.

268   "Inez, honey," Louise said, "I've come to get you and Curt to

take you over to be with Ernestine. They've found Ned and Aubrey and the boys. They've all been murdered."

Inez felt as if the life had suddenly been snatched from her body. Her first thought was of Curt, sleeping in the other room. Only thirteen years old and his father, whom he idolized, had been taken from him. The boy was going to be inconsolable. As terrible as she felt, Inez steeled herself for the hours ahead. Curt was going to need her. Ernestine was going to need her. This was a time for strength.

At Ned's house, Bud continued to make calls. Slowly, as the news spread, Aldays from all over Seminole began to arrive at Ned's house. In time of tragedy, time of need, the clan gathered quickly. The women closed in around Ernestine like a protective cloak. She was shocked beyond comprehension. Could this dreadful news actually be true? Her husband and all three of her sons: had they really been taken from her with such sudden swiftness? *All* of them? The other aggrieved were consoled for their losses according to whom they had lost: Inez her husband, young Curt his daddy, Bud two older brothers, Barbara her husband; but it was Ernestine whom the family felt had suffered down to her very soul. The enormity of her loss was overwhelming. Husband. Son. Son. Son.

Others besides the family and close friends also soon began to arrive—not at the house but down the road at the trailer. Grim-faced lawmen, shocked by coming face-to-face with a crime the dimensions of which they had previously only read about. Every lawman in Seminole County was on the job, as were the officers in adjacent jurisdictions not only in Georgia but next door in Alabama and Florida. Bulletins went out over the wires, and surrounding communities were alerted to the fact that a vicious killer or killers might now be in their town, on their streets. Seminole County itself took up arms and locked doors that had not been secured in years. Women and children were warned in the strongest terms to be extremely cautious, travel in groups, stay indoors if possible, and to report seeing any stranger or anything suspicious. It was generally assumed that outsiders had committed the ghastly crime. The victims were too well liked locally to have been harmed by anyone who knew them. They had been good men, all five of them, their individual and collective reputations as solid as the earth they tended. It had to have been outsiders, no doubt about it.

The magnitude of the crime called for immediate outside   269 help. Dan White was fifty-five years old and had been sheriff of Seminole County for two dozen years. He was a good country lawman, but he was not equipped to handle multiple murders. One of the first things he did was notify the Georgia Bureau of Investigation. Within three hours they had a team of experienced investigators at the scene, including people from the state crime lab. The forces of justice were beginning to function.

By midmorning, a sizable crowd of Seminole County residents had gathered in the fields and along the road immediately around the death trailer. Most of them were friends and neighbors of the Aldays, people who lived and worked around them, had grown up with one generation or another of the big family. They were there partly out of curiosity, but mostly to be available if any help was needed; they lived in and were part of a populace where neighbor stood ready to help neighbor in time of need. Many of them took time out from their own lives, their own work, to stand by in case they were needed. "We'll be around all day if you need us," they told Bud Alday in groups of three, four, more. "Anything needs doing, just let us know. Anything at all: work, going and fetching, taking folks places, bringing folks here—just anything."

One of the men in the crowd that morning was Jerry Godby, a thirty-one-year-old native of the county who had been back in Seminole four years after a hitch in the Army and a couple of years living up in Atlanta. Godby was a tall, muscular young man with direct eyes under lightly tinted glasses he habitually wore. He and his wife Linda lived nearby and Jerry rented land on which he grew peanuts. In 1964, at the age of twenty-two, he had gone to Atlanta to work, thinking he might like big-city life. He had not. Just about the time he was getting ready to settle down back in Seminole, when he was twenty-four, Vietnam came along and he was drafted. At Fort Carson, Colorado, he became a 106-millimeter recoilless rifle gunner, and later was sent to the Army's leadership school. When his military service was over, he returned to Seminole and started raising peanuts. Jerry Godby was not a great deal unlike many of the other young farmers in Seminole, except for one thing—during the time he lived in Atlanta, he had been a city policeman.

270   At some point during the terrible morning after the killings,

Jerry Godby got a chance to speak with Bud Alday, to whom he was a nephew by marriage.

"Uncle Bud, if there's anything needs doing, I'm here," he said, as so many others had that morning.

"I appreciate that, Jerry," said Bud. He looked tired and drawn, his face a grim mask of fatigue and grief.

"A little sleep would probably do you a lot of good," Jerry observed.

"Lord, Jerry," the older man said, "I don't know if I'll *ever* sleep again. God knows, I won't until we find out what's happened to poor Mary."

"Mary Alday?"

Bud nodded. "She's missing. Her car's gone too. They think whoever done this carried her off."

Jerry Godby's keen young mind began to put pieces together. All the things he had learned as an Atlanta policeman and in the Army leadership school meshed into action.

"What kind of car did she have, Uncle Bud?"

"A Chevy Impala. Blue and white. 1970."

Jerry nodded. Take it slow now, he told himself. Don't get everybody all excited.

"Listen, Uncle Bud, don't forget me now if you need anything done," he said. Then he left Bud Alday to other matters.

Jerry went to his pickup truck and drove away from the trailer. His mind was recreating the previous day, when he had been working in one of the peanut fields he rented. He had been spraying dinitro, a chemical that kills grass and weeds but does not harm the peanut crop. Jerry's peanuts had been planted ten days earlier; they had just broken ground and he was laying the first coat of dinitro over them. He had been working at the spraying most of the afternoon, to the point where the fumes had begun to give him a stomach ache. Pausing in his work for a moment, he had glanced over toward the road and seen two cars, driving fairly close together, make a turn and go off down an intersecting road. Not giving the incident much thought, Jerry had gone back to work. About an hour later, he had noticed one of the cars come back his way and head north, toward the main highway that led over to Alabama.

As he thought about it now, Jerry was certain that one of the two cars he had seen, and the one that later headed north, was a '70 Chevy, blue and white.

Jerry drove out to where he had seen the two cars turn. Following that road, he drove slowly, not even sure what he was looking for. Presently he came to a narrow dirt road, badly rutted, that led back into a thick stand of pine trees. Jerry stopped and from his truck studied the rutted dirt. There were definitely fresh tire tracks leading back into the trees. Godby's police-trained mind told him that the tracks might be valuable evidence and probably should be preserved. But his practical mind remembered that a young woman was missing and could possibly be tied up and still alive somewhere back in those woods. Ignoring the tracks, he drove over them and headed for the trees.

When he got close to the trees, Jerry noticed that some bark had been freshly rubbed off two of them next to the road. Someone had driven in there in a big hurry, he thought. He stopped his truck. Slow down, he told himself. There's five dead people back there in that trailer. No guarantee that whoever done it wasn't still in these woods, hiding out or waiting for someone to come after them. Better play it smart, he decided. It wouldn't do Mary Alday any good for him to go in there alone and maybe get killed. Backup, he needed backup—that's what they had taught him at the Atlanta police academy.

Jerry turned around and drove back to the road. He sped toward the trailer. When he got there, he studied the crowd of men and carefully made his selection. Men he knew he could rely on. Rudolph Spooner. Espy Gray. Wayne Easom. Max Trawick. One by one he singled them out, quietly, inconspicuously. The whispered message was the same for all of them.

"Get a gun and meet me at my place."

Less than an hour later, Jerry Godby was back on the rutted dirt road with his backup. Armed, stalking like hunters, the men spread out and entered the woods. They did not have to go far before they saw up ahead of them, where the ground sloped downward, the top of a car.

"Let's do it nice and easy now," Jerry said quietly. "Come up on it from both sides. Be careful; we don't know who might be in it."

They checked the car. There was no one in it. For a brief moment they felt relieved; they had half expected to find Mary Alday's body.

Their relief was all too brief, however.

272   "Oh, my god—" Espy Gray said. He had moved off to one

side about two hundred feet. The others went to him when they heard his voice. They did not have to ask what he had found.

Naked, lying face down, her body swarming with tiny, relentless red fire ants, was the last of the Alday victims.

Mary had been found.

30

So read the headlines of the *Donalsonville News*. In his weekly column "Out on a Limb . . ." Bo McLeod, the editor, wrote:

This week has brought grief and concern to our community because of the horrible murders committed Monday, in which six citizens of our county were cruelly and methodically shot by some kind of animal or animals. You couldn't call whoever did it human. As this is written, officers are doing all they can to find the guilty party or parties and bring them to justice. The usual rumors and wild reports have flown around us again, and this makes the task difficult, but we join with our neighbors in wishing swift success to the lawmen.

The Alday family is an important part of the life of this community. They have always been law-abiding, peaceful, friendly, hard-working folks, the kind that enjoys living and working together.

I can't remember having seen Aubrey or Ned many times when they were not laughing and joking about something.

Ned's sons were outstanding young men, hard-working and honest, like their parents. I remember their activities in FFA in high school, and I made their pictures many times.

In summary, every remark made about them has been a favorable remark. This was true before the tragedy, making it more impressive and pleasing.

The Aldays worked hard, helped one another and

274

their neighbors. They had many, many friends. We join in mourning for them, and we use this method to speak for the community in assuring the others of the family that we continue in prayer for them.

The rumors that Bo McLeod wrote of came from many quarters. A Mrs. Charles E. North, twenty-three, and her four-year-old son Charles, Jr., were injured late in the afternoon of the murders when the Norths' car ran off the road and over-turned. Even before a statement had been taken from Mrs. North, there was speculation that she had been deliberately forced off the road by the killers. Other stories had Mary Alday being followed home from the Family Services office; Mary being spotted by the men who were parked on the lot of the market where she stopped to shop, and followed home from there; and several persons were even sure they saw a car pass Mary's and then make a sudden U-turn and go speeding after her.

And, of course, after Mary's body was found as it was, nude in the woods, there was much shadowy talk about what had been done to her. Some of the stories that circulated about Mary's ordeal were grotesque: she had been hung by her heels; spread-eagled between four trees; mutilated, disemboweled; her breasts cut off and taken away.

After Mary's body had been removed, lawmen searched the surrounding wooded areas and found other evidence that the killers had been there. Jerry's wallet was found alongside the rutted dirt road. A dental appointment card for Shugie was found in the woods. Shugie's and Barb's hunting/fishing licenses were found, along with a plastic photo sleeve containing a selection of Alday family snapshots, which could have belonged to any of them. Personal items. Thrown away like so much trash by killers to whom they meant nothing. Just as, to them, the people to whom they had belonged meant nothing.

The only persons who actually knew what was going on in those first hours and days following the discovery of the bodies were the law-enforcement personnel on the scene. In addition to Sheriff Dan White and his deputies, GBI agent Ron Angel, head of the major case squad, was also there, along with T.R. Bentley, GBI agent from nearby Thomasville, and agents Billy Turner and Larry Funderburke. Kelly Fite headed up the crime lab contingent. These were the men, among others, who *knew* the accurate details of the crime as they unfolded. They 275 knew, for instance, that Mary's clothing had been found exactly 104 feet from her body. That a green tissue containing traces of feces and semen was found halfway between the two points. And other details more gruesome, such as what the fire ants had done to her body.

Dr. Larry Howard, director of the state crime laboratory, had performed autopsies on all the victims late Tuesday night in the embalming room of the Evans Funeral Home in Donalsonville. For the most part they were fairly routine, since all the bodies were intact.

Ned had been shot seven times in the back of the head and right side of the face. All but one bullet had been fired at very close range. Three .32-caliber slugs and three .22-caliber slugs were removed from his head. The seventh bullet could not be found.

Aubrey had been killed with a single .38-caliber slug in the back of his head. It was recovered.

Jerry had been shot four times in the back of the head. One bullet had exited the right side of his face next to his nose. Three others were recovered from his head. All were .22-caliber.

Shugie had been shot once with a .38-caliber bullet that entered his right ear and exited in front and above his left ear. The slug was recovered from a towel next to his face.

Jimmy had been killed by two .22-caliber bullets, one of which entered the back of his head and the other which had deflected off his skull and gone into the soft tissues of his neck. Both were recovered.

Mary Alday had three wounds that had been caused by two bullets. One had entered the left side of her back fifteen inches below the top of her head, severing her spinal cord and probably causing instantaneous unconsciousness and subsequent death. The other had entered eight inches below the top of her head, ricocheted back out, and reentered at the base of the skull. Both were .22-caliber slugs.

During Mary's autopsy, Dr. Howard also took vaginal washings. The swabs used in those washings showed the definite presence of spermatozoid matter.

By the second day after the killings, dozens of reporters and cameramen from all the news media had converged on Donalsonville and the rest of Seminole County. The story of the killings sent shock waves throughout the rural South. Even in the early 1970s, even after stories of madmen like Manson and Speck, there were still communities in America where people rarely locked their doors. These were quiet, out-of-the-way little hamlets where most families had lived for generations; where people were born and grew up together, lived as adults together, grew old together, and died together, usually in bed, of natural causes or old age. Everyone knew everyone else; strangers were rare—but when they did turn up, they were treated with courtesy and hospitality. If a stranger came upon a screen door that was latched, chances were it was because there was a toddler in the house—and the occupant *unlatching* it would invariably apologize for it. In some communities, a locked door was an insult to one's neighbors. People who lived in such places simply never imagined that ruthless, conscienceless men from other places, from urban netherworlds where life meant little, would ever show up to shatter the tranquility of their peaceful existence.

Their shock when it happened was compounded many times over.

The funeral of the murder victims was held on Thursday May 17. Mayor D. F. Wurst of Donalsonville closed all businesses by proclamation that afternoon.

The funeral was the largest ever conducted in Georgia. It was so large that the services had to be held in a huge, open field to accommodate the more than five thousand people who attended. More than seven hundred automobiles lined the country roads leading to Spring Creek Baptist Church. Two hundred of those in attendance were blood relatives of the deceased; another five hundred were indirectly related. One of the mourners was Mrs. Lillian Carter, mother of Governor Jimmy Carter. At the gravesite, there were more than one thousand square feet of flowers blanketing the ground.

Four ministers conducted the services. Reverend Fred Hill, who had brought Jerry, Shugie, and Jimmy to God, had tears in his eyes throughout most of the services. Reverend George Johnson, also of Spring Creek Baptist Church, assisted him. Reverend Luther Hastey, from nearby Iron City, also assisted, and Mary's family pastor, Reverend Jesse Holley, was there at the request of her family.

The six victims, in identical steel-gray metal coffins, were 277 buried in an eight-grave plot, side by side, with two plots remaining for the widows Ernestine and Inez.

One person who could not attend the funeral was Mary Alday's mother, Mrs. Idus Campbell. Prostrate with grief since learning of her only daughter's kidnapping, rape, and murder, Mrs. Campbell lay staring at the ceiling of her bedroom, too limp to move, until shortly before the funeral on Thursday. Then her condition worsened and she was rushed to the hospital. At three o'clock in the morning, just eleven hours after Mary was buried, her mother turned her face to the wall and died also.

Her cause of death was determined to be extreme grief over her daughter's horrible murder.

When the funeral was all over, after he had shaken hands with everybody who had passed by the coffins, after the many mourners had left and the family had dispersed to several homes, after he had made a final inspection of the burial site to see that everything was proper, Bud Alday, the youngest brother of Ned and Aubrey, who had been the family's rock for the past three days, who had shouldered the seemingly endless burden of things that had to be done, got into his pickup truck and drove alone deep into the backwoods. He drove on random dirt roads until they finally stopped in forest so thick they could go no further.

Then he got out and sat on the ground with his back to a pine tree and cried aloud, releasing all the tears he had been holding back since he found the bodies. There in the sanctuary of the forest, in the quiet, this strong man sobbed like a hurt child.

6

GEORGIA JUSTICE

31

Monday, May 21, 1973.

One week to the day after the murders were committed.

The killers had been captured. Their names and pictures had been on the front page of the *Donalsonville News*.

Now they were being brought back to Seminole County.

On Sunday evening, Bud Alday had a visitor. They talked in private.

"Mr. Alday," the man said respectfully, "I've come to get your feelings on a matter. As you know from reading the paper, they're bringing them dirty little sons-of-bitches back to Donalsonville for arraignment tomorrow. Now, I can have thirty armed men uptown when they get here. We can take those killers away from the troopers without firing a shot. If you'll just say the word, we'll take all four of 'em right out there behind Jerry's trailer and give 'em what they've got coming. We'll get justice for your family, Mr. Alday."

Bud shook his head, emphatically. "That trash is not fit to die where my people died," he said.

"All right then, sir, we'll take 'em out in the thicket somewheres and lynch 'em. We'll still get justice."

Bud thought about it for several moments, his brow furled in a frown. He studied the man in front of him, whom he knew to be an unofficial power in south Georgia, and on whom he knew he could rely. But finally he shook his head.

"No, I don't think so. There's been enough bloodshed in Seminole County. This is where I live, where all my people live. Nearly every friend I've got in the world lives right here in this county. I don't want to be responsible for any more violence here. We'll let the courts take care of them."

"I think you're making a bad mistake, Mr. Alday," the man said. "The courts in this country today are for the criminal, 281

not the victim. Let me tell you what'll happen if you leave it
up to the courts. First, a jury will find them dirty yellow little
bastards guilty and they'll be sentenced to the electric chair.
Then they won't be sent to the chair. They'll spend ten or
twelve years on Death Row, then they'll be commuted to life
imprisonment. But they won't serve that neither. Nobody ever
does; hell, nobody dies in prison no more: ever'body gets
turned loose sooner or later. These bastards will too. Mark my
words, Mr. Alday, they'll be free men someday."

Bud thought it over some more. But he could not bring himself to change his mind. The man who had come to him sighed
quietly and shook his head.

"I think you'll regret your decision someday," he said.

The decision Bud made that night was later reflected in another editorial by *Donalsonville News* editor Bo McLeod. He
wrote, in part:

> There are a few screwballs among us who get a thrill
> out of talking dumb and sounding off about what all
> they'd like to do to the four men. But they're in the
> extreme minority, and they are pretty well known for
> their lack of sense. Bud Alday spoke the sentiments
> of his family when he said they didn't want to see
> anybody else get hurt in this terrible tragedy that
> came our way. "Enough people have been hurt al-
> ready," he said. The Aldays know how painful such
> suffering is, and they're wise enough, and concerned
> enough, to not want to see more violence and sorrow.
> And there's no room for error here. The only thing
> that any kind of mob action, or inciting troublesome
> thoughts, can bring is more sorrow. Think about this
> often as the long, drawn-out trial days go slowly
> along. It's a hard fact of life, and there's no profit in
> forgetting it. The law must be obeyed.

Bud Alday and Bo McLeod spoke for most of the good people of Seminole County.

The Georgia-owned DC-3 landed at Donalsonville airport at
nine-thirty in the morning. A Bureau of Investigation van was
waiting at the end of the runway, along with a contingent of
state troopers assigned to guard the prisoners. When the
plane's propellers cut off, the four chained prisoners were led

off the aircraft and taken aboard the van. Two lawmen, either from the state police or the Department of Investigation, were assigned to each prisoner, and walked on either side of him to protect him from any attack.

The van drove the short distance to uptown Donalsonville and parked outside the large, old courthouse. Several hundred townspeople had gathered to get a look at the accused killers. They remained orderly and quiet, not even calling the prisoners names, which was the least it was felt they might do. Without incident, Carl, Wayne, Billy, and George Dungee were hurried inside and taken up to the second floor. From a holding room, they were then led one by one into the courtroom of Justice of the Peace J.B. Bowen to be formally charged with their crimes.

Billy was the first one to be taken in. For some reason, that made Carl suspicious. When he got the chance, he looked pointedly at Wayne and frowned. Wayne, with an even duller expression than usual on his face, merely shrugged. Sure, Carl thought. You don't give a shit, you retarded asshole. But cursing Wayne did not alleviate the sudden, cold fear that had sprung up in Carl's chest. *Was Billy going to talk?* The question had been nagging him ever since the GBI man had told him that his younger brother was "cooperating." Carl did not like dwelling on the possibility that his own brother would turn against him, but the thought just kept chipping away at his confidence. What a rotten blow it would be if Billy *did* take sides against him. Hell, even as low an opinion as he had of Wayne, and as much contempt as he had for George Dungee, Carl would never consider turning state's evidence against them. That was something that a person just did not do: take sides against his own kind.

But Billy was such a kid; maybe he had not had time to learn that. So the thought of betrayal continued to plague Carl. Just as the thought of what he and the others had done a week earlier also plagued him. What in hell had come over him? he asked himself a hundred times. Why hadn't he backed off when Wayne had said, "Let's blow 'em away"? What in the name of God had possessed him to stand up with Wayne like he did; to take one of those farmers into that bedroom; then, when he heard a shot from the other bedroom, to pull that trigger? Why hadn't he just grabbed hold of himself and said, "Hey, man, wait just a fucking minute! This here ain't car theft or burglary or escape; this here is fucking murder, babe." Why hadn't he *stopped*—before he started?

Carl sighed a deep, weary sigh as he waited for his turn to go into the courtroom. He hadn't stopped because he hadn't wanted to look like a chicken-liver, a punk, in front of Wayne. And Billy. Even in front of that nigger fuck-boy George. Carl knew that he himself, if anyone, had been the leader of the bunch. To have backed down in front of them had been totally repugnant to him, totally unthinkable. His status among them was all he had; he could not force himself to sacrifice it.

What a joke, he silently chastised himself. By *doing* what he had done, he succeeded only in reducing himself to Wayne's level; only by backing off would he have actually remained the same. Now he was just another asshole—like Wayne.

After the first killing, of course, he had no choice. He voided all his options the first time he pulled the trigger. He *had* to do that second farmer, and that third one. To leave live witnesses after killing the first one would have been ridiculous. You don't get no more volts in the electric chair for killing six than you do for one. And as for the woman, well—

Carl had promised himself he would not think about her. He did not want to relive that scene or think about the decision he had made in those woods. Mary Alday had been his guarantee that he would never again be put in a general prison population with niggers who could rape him. As far as he was concerned, it had been a good decision. If a dozen Mary Aldays had to suffer the way he had made her suffer, and die the way he had made her die, he did not care—as long as he did not have to be raped again by the dirty fucking niggers.

When Billy was brought back into the holding room from court, Carl fixed him with a long stare, but Billy refused to look at him, keeping his head lowered. That made Carl all the more suspicious, but he did not have the opportunity to do anything about it, because then it was his turn to be taken in for arraignment. His two escort guards led him into the high-ceilinged courtroom and he stood in front of the bench while a warrant was read charging him with the murder of Ned, Aubrey, Jerry, Chester, Jimmy, and Mary Alday. The murder warrants, signed by agent Ron Angel of the Bureau of Investigation, indicated the time of the crimes as between 4:00 and 8:00 P.M. on May 14. Carl remained silent until asked by the court if he understood the charges against him. Then he simply said, "Yes," very quietly.

In a section of the courtroom reserved for the Alday family, 284 Bud and other relatives sat in silence throughout the proceedings, as if to assure themselves that everything would be done right.

When the individual arraignments were over, the prisoners were returned to the state van. The size of the crowd around the courthouse had increased by that time, and there seemed to be some stirring and restlessness. The state troopers sensed this and literally trotted the chained prisoners through a cordon of officers and on board the van. Moments later, the van, with a heavily armed escort, sped north out of Donalsonville, headed toward an undisclosed jail where the accused killers would be held until the next hearing.

As the crowd around the old courthouse slowly dispersed, most of the talk was about what would happen next. Several of the more knowledgeable people began to spread the word, accurately, that the court would now appoint attorneys to defend each accused, and that in the near future they would have a committal hearing, which, in Georgia, was the same procedure as a preliminary hearing in other states. Simply put, it was a procedure to determine whether there was adequate evidence on which to bring an accused to trial. If there was, then a trial date and place would be set.

Talk of the eventual trial of the four accused killers ultimately turned to talk of the death penalty. In Georgia, as in other states, the death penalty as it had once stood had been abolished by his U.S. Supreme Court in its sweeping denunciation of that punishment across the land. Georgia, like many other states whose citizens demanded it, had moved rapidly to restore it to law, within the guidelines set down by the nation's high court. It was put back into law by an act of the Georgia General Assembly and signed by Governor Jimmy Carter on March 28, 1973—just forty-seven days before the Alday murders.

The death penalty could now be imposed in Georgia for the crimes of treason; aircraft hijacking; murder of a peace officer or corrections officer while engaged in the performance of his duty; murder committed by an escaped prisoner; murder or rape committed during the commission of a burglary or armed robbery; or murder committed in an outrageously or wantonly vile, horrible, or inhuman murder.

Most of the crowd leaving the Seminole County courthouse that day were certain that the Alday murders easily qualified under the latter two conditions.

32

Carl was the first one to be tried.

His lawyer, Bobby Hill, a black attorney from Savannah, and an elected state representative as well, had petitioned the court that Carl be tried separately from the other defendants. The motion had been granted.

In an unusual move, and because the impending trial had attracted so much notoriety, Judge Walter Geer had ruled that January 1, 1974, New Year's Day, would not be a court holiday, and that jury selection, which had commenced the previous day, would continue that day. He also barred spectators from the courtroom during jury selection, except for relatives of the victims who wanted to be there. Several members of the family did choose to watch the jury selection, among them Ernestine Alday and her eldest and sole surviving son, Norman, home on emergency leave from his U.S. Army post in West Germany.

Georgia state troopers were strategically placed not only in the courtroom itself, but at assigned guard posts at all courthouse entrances and on roving patrol around the building's perimeter. When Carl himself was brought into the courtroom, he was surrounded by a circle of lawmen. Pale after seven months in jail waiting for his trial to begin, Carl also had lost weight from worrying about his situation. He had let his hair grow down to his shoulders and attempted to grow a mustache and goatee, which turned out thin and wispy, and made him look that much more like a skinny little boy trying to be grown up.

Carl's jury was completed the afternoon of New Year's Day. It consisted of three white men and three black men, and two white women and four black women.

The trial got underway Wednesday, January 2, and the thing that Carl most dreaded, happened.

Billy was called as a witness against him.

Billy had accepted a deal offered him by the state of Georgia. He had only been fifteen years old at the time of the crimes, was only sixteen now, and the state did not want to ask for a death penalty in his case. So Billy was offered the opportunity to plead guilty to charges of burglary and armed robbery, have the murder and kidnapping charges against him dropped, and receive two twenty-year sentences to be served consecutively.

In exchange, Billy had to agree to be the state's star witness against Carl, Wayne, and George Dungee, who were scheduled to be tried in three separate proceedings.

Billy agreed.

When his younger brother took the witness stand against him, Carl fixed his eyes on him unrelentingly and kept them there during the entire two hours that Billy was on the stand. Billy would not play Carl's game, however; he refused to look at him and only once during his testimony did he even glance at Carl: that was when he had to officially identify him for the court.

Billy's testimony was devastating. Prompted by a carefully arranged sequence of questions from the prosecutor, Billy described in minute detail everything that had transpired in the trailer and later in the woods. He depicted with chilling clarity every shot that was fired, and by whom; every rape that was committed, and by whom. Mostly, of course, it was Carl. Carl shooting Jerry Alday four times. Carl shooting Ned Alday six times. Carl shooting Jimmy Alday. Carl shooting Shugie Alday. Carl raping Mary in the trailer, in the woods, after slapping her, punching her, cursing her, throwing her naked to the harsh ground. Through the voice of his younger brother, Carl was pictured as a vicious, merciless taker of human life, a young killer who dealt death without hesitation, without remorse. Although Carl sat glaring at Billy with contempt and open hatred, inside he felt as if an unseen hand were twisting his innards into pulp. He knew that his brother was killing him. He only hoped he could keep from being sick to his stomach until he got back to his cell.

The adversary portion of the trial ended Thursday after-noon. The state had called twenty-one witnesses to make its case, including a fingerprint expert to testify to the prints on the beer can that Carl had stupidly left on the counter in his eagerness to rape Mary. The defense called no one, and Carl did not testify in his own behalf. During their closing argu-ments, Carl's lawyer made an impassioned plea for the young accused killer's life. "It will only cheapen human life" to ex-ecute Carl, he said. There was obviously something wrong with Carl mentally, he contended, and proposed that the defendant be sent to prison for life so that he could be "studied." Carl silently resented the pleas. It was just his luck, he thought, to draw a fucking nigger for a lawyer. And what the fuck did he mean there was something "wrong" with him? That he ought to be "studied." Bobby Hill, Carl decided early on, was a shithead. And a black one, to boot.

The prosecution's closing argument was less impassioned than the defense's, but more to the point. "Feed Carl Issacs from the same spoon he fed the Aldays," the special prosecutor said.

The jury did just that. After deliberating only one hour and eight minutes, it returned with a verdict of guilty of murder in the first degree.

The panel then retired to conduct the penalty phase of the proceedings. That took them even less time: thirty-eight min-utes to unanimously say that Carl Issacs should go to the elec-tric chair.

Judge Geer sentenced Carl to die in six weeks, on February 15, 1974.

Carl's last confrontation with Billy came when Carl was being taken from the Seminole County jail to be transferred to Death Row at the state prison. Billy was remaining in the jail; he had two more trials at which to testify.

Heavily shackled, Carl was being led past a row of cells when he saw Billy standing up close to the bars in one of them. Carl stopped and stared at his younger brother. The escort deputies, curious, did not immediately prod him forward. For a long, tense moment, the two brothers stood with eyes locked in cold contempt. Finally, Billy broke the silence.

"I don't know what you're looking so pissed about, Junior," he said. "I'm the one ought to be pissed, the way you fucked up my life."

Carl grunted derisively. "You fucked up your own life, Billy. Nobody ever *made* you do nothing."

The deputies urged Carl forward then, and the brief, final meeting of the brothers was over. Billy, watching Carl go, had a sad, confused expression on his face.

You fucked up your own life.

Outside, there was the usual crowd of curious onlookers, waiting for a look at the condemned man on his way to the death house. Carl paused again at the top of the exterior courthouse steps.

"Say, how about a smoke?" he asked one of his escort deputies.

The deputy fished a cigarette out of the pack in Carl's shirt pocket, stuck it between Carl's lips, and lighted it for him.

"Thanks," Carl said, sucking in on the cigarette and exhaling through his nostrils. He looked around at the people who had come to watch him. Jesus, he thought, shaking his head briefly. All him and the others had done that day was stop to rob a fucking trailer. To get gas money. A few minutes earlier or later and none of it would have happened. But everybody happened to be right there at the right time and everything got all fucked up. A simple burglary had turned into a murder rap. Six people dead. Jesus.

Carl sighed and let the cigarette dangle from the corner of his mouth. "Okay," he said to the deputies, "let's go."

Down the steps and across the courthouse yard to the waiting cars, Carl remembered to swagger for the people watching. A slight smile curled his lips. It was easy to remember to swagger.

That was all he had left now.

33

The pattern set at Carl's trial would continue throughout the other two proceedings. Billy would be the star witness and would repeat his tale of horror twice more.

The second to be tried was George Dungee. His participation in the crimes was just as easy to prove: he still had Mary Alday's Timex watch in his pocket when he was captured by the posse in West Virginia. Billy testified too that he had seen George first rape and then shoot Mary to death. Unlike Carl, Billy had no doubts that George *had* raped the woman; after all, George had taken her naked into the woods, laid down on top of her, *appeared* to be raping her. Only Carl had suspected that George was only *pretending* to commit the rape—perhaps to show Wayne that two could play his game.

Not that it made any difference at this point. The murder of Mary was enough. The best George's defense counsel could do was ask the jury if it was going to "accept the testimony of a confessed felon?" Meaning Billy, of course, who had already pled guilty to his participation in the crimes and, three weeks earlier, four days before Christmas, formally received his consecutive twenty-year sentences.

The prosecution, never doubting for a moment that the jury would, indeed, believe Billy, concerned itself with the punishment of Dungee. "He *must* be removed from society," the prosecutor stated emphatically. There was no doubt in anyone's mind that the word "removed" did not mean merely incarceration; in this instance, it meant permanent removal.

George's jury took less than an hour to find him guilty: only fifty-eight minutes.

It then took two hours to decide to send him to the electric chair.

George looked bored and sleepy throughout.

290

Wayne's trial was last.

It began on Monday, January 14, eight months to the day after the murders. Jury selection of eight men and four women lasted until noon Tuesday. The presentation of evidence began that afternoon. Wayne was charged, among other things, with killing Shugie and participating in the murder of Ned.

Apparently it did not bother Wayne to have Billy testify against him. He had never trusted the little son-of-a-bitch anyway, so he was not surprised. During Billy's testimony, Wayne idly played with a book of matches, drummed his fingers silently on the counsel table, or read the September 1973 issue of *Front Page Detective* magazine, which had a story about him and the others entitled "Too Evil to Be Called Animals."

The case went to the jury late Thursday afternoon. Wayne's attorney, in his final plea, pointed out that at one time Wayne had told Bureau of Investigation agents that he had committed all the murders himself, in the trailer and in the woods. "There was compassion on the part of the defendant when he tried to take the rap for all of them. Isn't that enough humanity for his life to be spared?"

The prosecutor thought not. "This person has demonstrated his unfitness to live. Suppose he escaped? Would you want him back in Seminole County? Would you want him *anywhere* in America with a gun in his hand?

The jury also thought not. In fifty minutes it found Wayne guilty of murder in the first degree. When Wayne heard the verdict, he rolled his eyes toward the ceiling as if terribly bored.

Because it was so late in the day, court was recessed and the sentencing phase of the trial put off until Friday morning.

It took the jury an hour and a half to recommend the death penalty for Wayne. There was some speculation that the delay was because of the defense counsel's plea that his defendant be sentenced to prison for the term of his natural life in order that he could serve as a guinea pig for psychiatric research. That, however, was not true. The jury simply had difficulty framing its verdict the proper way to include the necessary aggravated circumstances to support a death penalty. There was never any question in its collective mind that Wayne deserved to die.

And so it was over.

The crimes had been committed, the criminals captured and tried, the verdicts rendered, the sentences pronounced. The people of the state of Georgia had spoken. All that remained now was for the sentences to be carried out. For justice to be done.

The people waited.

And waited.

And kept waiting.

Afterword:

THE ALDAY FAMILY

In Seminole County, life resumed for the living.

A slab of solid black East Indian marble, imported from South Africa, was placed across the eight-grave plot in which the six victims were buried. The slab, with beautifully detailed white inlays and hand-chiseled engravings, cost twenty thousand dollars. It is one of the most striking family monuments imaginable.

Engraved on the stone of each of the three brothers are the words, "They steer'd their course to the same quiet shore, not parted long, and now to part no more."

Above Mary's grave it reads, "Love can hope where reason would despair."

At the death trailer, the yard had turned brown. The fields around it, once alive with bright green stalks of corn, were now full of weeds growing over dead, beaten-down stalks. A white clothesline with an empty plastic jug on it was strung across the driveway to keep out the curious.

In December an auction was held at the Ned Alday home. Sold were two John Deere tractors, one so new that its warranty was still in force; a combine, a plow, a mower; a hay-baler, sprayer, stock trailer; a land leveler, post hole digger, rakes, shapers, planters, pickers.

All the tools a man needed to work the land.

The mobile home itself was eventually sold also, to some Alday third cousins who lived up north in Decatur County. But they did not have it for long.

A year after the murders, the trailer caught fire and burned to the ground.

At the site of the Spring Creek Baptist Church, where all the murder victims had attended services, and next to which they were buried, the old original church and schoolhouse, still situated on the land donated by Math Alday, was taken up off its foundations after a century of service, and moved to a nearby field to become a relic of the past. Where it had once stood, ground was broken for a new church, the money for which had begun coming in as part of an Alday memorial fund. The fund, contributed to by proceeds from such events as an all-night sing-along at the Donalsonville High School football field, provided more than twenty thousand dollars to get the new church appropriation going.

Once again, this time through senseless tragedy, the Alday family had been instrumental in providing a church to their community.

After he had been in prison three years, Billy Issacs, overcome with remorse for the part he had played in the tragedy in Seminole County, wrote a letter to Bud Alday. In it he said he realized that nothing in the world would bring back Bud's dead brothers, nephews, and niece, but he wanted Bud to know that he was sorry and that his conscience bothered him constantly.

Bud Alday dismissed the letter with quiet but deep contempt. "He's no different from the others," Bud said. "They all four deserve to die in the chair. The only reason he's not going to the chair is because he turned against the others and testified against them."

But the fact of the matter was, no one was going to the chair. Five more years passed. The death sentences were bogged down in a network of appeals. Every time Bud Alday read in the newspaper about another delay, he remembered the visit of the man the night before Carl and the others had been brought back to Seminole County for arraignment. The man's words were etched in his mind: "Thirty men . . . uptown . . . take those killers away from the troopers . . . take them out in the woods . . . get justice for the Alday family . . ."

Bud, who had never particularly supported the Ku Klux Klan, was beginning to think he had made a bad mistake when he said no that night.

Approaching the spring of 1983, it has been nearly ten years since the six Aldays were murdered.

Carl Issacs, Wayne Coleman, and George Dungee remain on Death Row.

Billy Issacs is in the general population at another prison

across the state. He is in his late twenties now, a tall, handsome young man with thick hair and straight shoulders. And hard, convict eyes.

"I know I've lost everything good in life," he says today. "I've lost my teen years, lost my twenties, and I'll lose my thirties, probably even my forties too. I've grown up in prison; I don't know any other life."

When he talks about it, his face turns very sad.

"I had one last chance, with Kelly, and I blew it. I pissed it away because Carl showed up. I listened to Carl, went with Carl." He grunts softly. "For being that stupid, I deserve whatever I get."

Billy faces the long prison years ahead of him with daily revulsion. He is certain he will lose his mind in prison.

Bud Alday and the rest of the populous Alday clan continue to live their once again peaceful if permanently tainted lives in the country around the big lake where Math Alday settled five generations ago. With every day that passes, Bud recalls the visit by the man who offered lynch justice to the Alday family, and whom Bud turned down in favor of justice through the courts.

"It was the worst mistake I ever made in my life," he says today.

Ernestine and Inez speak daily of their dear departed. They speak in soft, gentle voices full of love, but hinting of heartache. Neither of them understands the why of what happened, but they have faith that God had a reason for it. They believe that somewhere there is a hereafter in which Ned is spinning a tall tale, and Aubrey is watching a cowboy movie.

In which Jerry is arranging things just so, and Shugie is teasing him about it.

In which Mary is raising zinnias and marigolds.

And in which a young man named Jimmy has found some woods in which to cook himself a wild breakfast on the bank of a river, very early on one of God's new mornings.